NOTES OF A
NON-CONSPIRATOR

Efim Etkind

NOTES OF A
NON-CONSPIRATOR

Translated by
PETER FRANCE

*All will be here: what I have lived through
And what I shall live by in time to come*

BORIS PASTERNAK: *Waves*

Oxford   London   New York
OXFORD UNIVERSITY PRESS
1978

Oxford University Press, Walton Street, Oxford OX2 6DP

OXFORD LONDON GLASGOW
NEW YORK TORONTO MELBOURNE WELLINGTON
IBADAN NAIROBI DAR ES SALAAM LUSAKA CAPE TOWN
KUALA LUMPUR SINGAPORE JAKARTA HONG KONG TOKYO
DELHI BOMBAY CALCUTTA MADRAS KARACHI

British Library Cataloguing in Publication Data
Etkind, Efim
  Notes of a non-conspirator
  1. Russia—Intellectual life
  I. Title   II. France, Peter
  947.085′092′4   DK276   77–30159
  ISBN 0-19-211739-4

Printed in Great Britain by
William Clowes and Sons Limited

To
EKATERINA ZVORYKINA
who has shared my fate

Contents

Translator's Preface

Intelligentnost is the Russian abstract noun formed from *intelligent*, an intellectual. After translating *Notes of a Non-Conspirator* I found myself discussing with Efim Etkind the difficulty of rendering this word in English. 'Intellectual integrity' sounds too heroic, what is involved is rather a combination of education, decency, taste, love of ideas and language, sense of duty towards moral and cultural values, something which is represented for many Russians by the figure of Chekhov—indeed Chekhov is quoted by Etkind as saying: 'One must be intellectually clear, morally clean and physically tidy.' Opposed to *intelligentnost* is an equally untranslatable word, *khamstvo;* dictionaries will give you something impossible like 'caddishness', but really it is more like a sort of aggressive philistinism.

As we talked about these words I could see that a central point of Efim Etkind's book is the continuing struggle between *intelligentnost* and *khamstvo*. Indeed much of the value of the book to a British public must lie in the image it gives of a type of intellectual life and a set of values which will probably seem rather foreign to many of us—not for nothing is the word 'intellectual' so difficult to use in Britain without arrogance or mockery. It is not easy for people in our society to express the whole-hearted devotion to cultural values which is so evident in the 'lyrical digression' on the Mayakovsky Writers' House.

Efim Etkind's life has been primarily devoted to poetry and the culture of the word. He is an expert on such questions as the structure of verse, the nature of poetic language, and the problems of translation. What is more, he has always worked to make poetry more alive and accessible to a wide public. A particularly important side to this activity has been his long involvement with Western European literature and his refusal to be silenced by the chauvinism that has sometimes disfigured Soviet cultural life. Now that he lives in France, he concerns himself also with the translation of Russian poetry into French.

Naturally, then, in writing about his recent and not-so-recent experiences, he has given his book a distinctly literary form, with a deliberate disruption of chronology, a tendency to grotesque comedy, digressions that remind one of the eighteenth-century novel, and numerous quotations from Russian and European poetry. The poetry is not an adornment, it is at the heart of Etkind's subject. His book is rightly entitled *Notes of a Non-Conspirator*, but it is bound to raise in the reader's mind all sorts of questions about the politics of poetry. The immediate conclusions that it suggests about the future of Soviet culture are not cheerful ones, but I nevertheless believe that we can see in it not only a Kafkaesque black comedy, but also a non-conspiratorial contribution to the improvement of academic and literary life in the Soviet Union. In translating it I have felt that I was engaged in a task of professional and human solidarity.

One or two remarks about the English text. I have generally done what I could to translate poems and other literary quotations myself, though I have felt the usual despair at the impossibility of finding English equivalents for Pushkin or Akhmatova. I gratefully acknowledge the following debts to other translators:

For an extract from Mickiewicz in Chapter 1 to Jack Lindsay and the Sylvan Press, London.

For passages from two poems by Brodsky in Chapter 3 to *Selected Poems* translated by George L. Kline, Penguin Books and Harper & Row Inc., New York, 1974.

For a passage from Thomas Mann's *Genesis of a Novel* in Chapter 5 to R. and C. Winston, Secker and Warburg, and Alfred A. Knopf Inc.

For a passage from Tacitus' *Agricola* in Chapter 5 to H. Mattingly and Penguin Books.

For a passage from Kafka's *The Trial* in Chapter 6 to W. and E. Muir, Secker and Warburg, and Schoken Books Inc.

For Brecht's poem 'Concerning the label Emigrant', which closes the book, to Eyre Methuen Ltd., Suhrkamp Verlag, Frankfurt/Main, and *Poems: 1913–1956* by Bertolt Brecht, edited by John Willet and Ralph Manheim, translated by Stephen Spender.

Finally, I should explain that I have transliterated Russian proper names in accordance with a certain English non-academic usage, being consistent where possible and deliberately retaining such non-English Christian names as Aleksandr or Iosif. I have, however, chosen to be inconsistent where this enabled me to avoid unfortunate oddities (e.g. Babii Yar rather than Baby Yar) or to retain certain familiar spellings, particularly for surnames of German origin (e.g. Ehrenburg rather than Erenburg).

PETER FRANCE

Lewes, January 1977

Prologue

No, neither beneath an alien sky
Nor sheltering under alien wings
At that time I was with my people
Where my unhappy people lived

ANNA AKHMATOVA, 1961

In the West one quite often encounters a complete denial of all that the intelligentsia of the Soviet Union has lived by for nearly sixty years—all its literary and academic achievements and all those aspirations which are not clearly dissident in character. Some of the most radical émigré Russians close their eyes to the intellectual life of the Soviet Union, as if these six decades had never existed and throughout this whole period only one thing had happened: the oppression of the minds and souls of citizens by Party and state. This is an oversimplified and thus a distorted view of reality and it leads to false conclusions and logical blind alleys. Russian culture has made a road for itself, overcoming the obstacles set in its way by those whose aim was to muzzle thought, destroy poetry, and stifle theatre, music, and painting. I will go further: in its struggle for the right to live and breathe this culture has gained strength. And this is something which deserves study, that has hardly yet begun. Official history depicts our culture striding along a single triumphal road. If one reads a work such as the *History of Soviet Literature*, published in 1974 and edited by P. Z. Vykhodtsev, one might think that it was deliberately intended to provoke the indignation of well-informed readers. 'Socialism has increasingly become the life-breath of poetry and the organic quality of the spiritual world of the new humanity, whose spokesmen the new poets have recognized themselves to be.... Particularly through reminiscences of the past the intimate lyrical poetry of Anna Akhmatova has begun to show an excited awareness of the need to teach herself to live again, of the value of an art which is vital and active ("And the stone word fell . . .")' (pp. 306–7). In this account of the poetry of the thirties everything is seen moving 'onwards and upwards' and every word is a lie. The falsification is carried out in a typically crude and vulgar manner. The expression 'teach myself to live again' is taken from the cycle *Requiem*, which contains the poem beginning 'And the stone word fell'. It has nothing to do with 'the value of an art which is vital and active'; Anna Akhmatova is writing about the sentencing of her son Lev; this is the 'stone word' and the poem itself is entitled 'The Sentence'. It is she who has to 'teach herself to live again', without her son:

> And the stone word fell with a thud
> On my still living, beating heart.
> But never mind, I was prepared,
> Somehow I'll learn to cope with it.
>
> I'll have a busy day today.
> I'll have to turn my soul to stone,
> To finish stifling memory
> And teach myself to live again.
>
> And yet . . . the summer's rustling heat
> Is like a festive city crowd.
> Long, long ago I had foreseen
> This brilliant day and empty house.

I have quoted a very recent university textbook; you would think that the publishers might have realized, in 1974, that the days of impunity were over and that their lies would not go undetected.

That is one side of the coin. The Eastern side. There is a Western side too.

From this other side Soviet literature is seen in a diametrically opposed and equally misleading light. In Western writing about Akhmatova one sometimes reads that she lived at first as an internal émigrée in the Soviet Union, holding herself aloof from her surroundings and from other people, seeking solitude and separation from real life and society. This too is a falsehood: less glaring than the simple fraud of Vykhodtsev, but still a distortion of the truth.

Anna Akhmatova herself confessed in 1917, in the famous poem beginning 'When in the agony of suicide', that she heard a satanic but 'consoling' voice calling to her:

> Leave your benighted sinful land,
> Leave Russia for ever.
> I will wash the blood from your hands,
> I will take the black shame from your heart,
> I will clothe in a new name
> The pain of insult and defeat.

Why 'black shame'? Akhmatova bore no responsibility for the blood shed in revolutionary Russia; she was not a murderer. What we have here is in my opinion a noble stand, the only one possible for a poet who felt responsible for her native land, all its actions and all that happened within it. Forty-five years later Anna Akhmatova could proudly utter the words which stand at the head of my prologue.

That is not internal emigration, but sympathy and solidarity.

And the author of this book equally feels responsibility for all he witnessed and all he took part in. He cannot stand on one side and write with a spectator's *Schadenfreude* of the miseries and crimes of the country he has left behind. *Schadenfreude* is reserved for outsiders.

Shame, that 'black shame' which Akhmatova speaks of, is a feeling that presupposes involvement. I, like my contemporaries, knew this feeling from early on in an acute form. Before the war and for many years after we all lived in communal apartments where sullen housewives jostled round paraffin stoves and primuses in the kitchen—each had her own separate electricity meter, her own doorbell ('Romanov, three rings; Luryé, two long and three short'), her own seat in the lavatory. But it wasn't the kitchen that depressed me, it was the rule forbidding us to invite foreigners home; 'Take your guests to a restaurant,' I was advised at the Writers' Union, 'you can't invite them to a communal apartment.' But why not? The way we live is the way we live. What have we to fear? Who can condemn us? No, it's not allowed. Foreigners can't be allowed to see our everyday life. Every time I came up against this 'not allowed', I was seized by shame.

Does the reader know what is meant by *pokazukha*?[1] In the

---

[1] From the Russian word meaning 'to show'. [Tr.]

Soviet Union there are certain highways that foreigners are allowed to drive on. They are surfaced with smooth tarmac. On either side you can see pretty houses surrounded by fences and flowerbeds, or stalls with brightly coloured *matryoshka* dolls. Behind the bushes lies the old village road, deep in mud. No pretty stalls there, just the occasional village shop with bread and vodka. Foreigners don't see the village shop, they don't get stuck in the mud but drive on to their hotels with nothing to disturb their comfortable habits. In the Astoria everything is laid on to keep them away from reality at all costs; there's even a Beryozka shop, with a splendid selection of luxury goods to be bought with foreign currency. All round the hotel everything is pretty and the shops are very nice—foreigners don't go far and within their walking radius everything is planned. There is no meat in the butcher's shop two blocks away but here there are luxury shops with unwanted but impressive TV sets and old china.

This is *pokazukha*. It is everywhere. The Soviet Union shows itself off to foreigners by erecting cardboard cutouts and coating itself with makeup.

Every time I saw this *pokazukha* I felt the most bitter shame. It was I who was the deceiver, as if I were hiding from the woman I loved that I was wearing a wig and was really bald.

In the street where we lived in Leningrad there were some young lime trees—they made the rather plain dusty avenue charming and homely, transforming it into a shady little boulevard. One morning I saw a tipper lorry carrying off the last of our limes—away too went the digger which had rooted them out. I was dumbfounded—who on earth could have wanted these trees? Subsequently it appeared that Nixon was due to arrive in Leningrad two days later and it was necessary to beautify one of the streets he would drive through—so that was where they had taken our little trees. This happened in May and the trees soon withered and died. But for a brief moment the President's eyes had rested on green leaves rather than waste ground. And on other roads along his route the houses were cleaned and even painted, but only the ground floor; he wasn't going to get out of his car and from a car you only see the ground floor.

This was *pokazukha* too—people called it *Knixon*.[1] And it made me feel ashamed.

[1] The Russian word for a curtsy. [Tr.]

At the end of the war the Soviet armies marched into Europe and I marched with them through Romania, Hungary, Austria, and Bulgaria. How happy and proud we felt as officers of an army that had defeated fascism! How the women of Romania and Bulgaria loved us, and ran with flowers to greet our tank regiments. I was proud and happy because we had defeated the Nazis and liberated our friends. But when these liberators drank themselves silly on new wine, invaded a watch-maker's shop and stuffed their enormous bag so full of watches that the whole thing twitched and ticked as if it were alive, I felt agonizing shame. I could not look them in the face, the Romanians I had been embracing the day before. We were the liberators, we were the plunderers.

And when in 1968 the troops of the Warsaw Pact countries invaded Czechoslovakia I could understand why my friends in Prague and Brno stopped writing to me or answering my letters; they held me responsible for the occupation. I was deeply moved by the powerful lines of Aleksandr Tvardorsky which circulated clandestinely:

> What shall I do with you, my oath?
> Where shall I find words to relate
> How Prague received us in forty-five
> And how in sixty-eight?

Nor can I forget the moving lines of another Soviet poet, written after the Twentieth Congress and filled with the same tragic sense of complicity:

> We are all the winners of prizes
> To honour his name.
> We have marched unflinchingly
> Through a deadly time.
>
> We are all his fellow soldiers,
> All held our tongues
> When out of our silence grew
> Russia's undoing.
>
> Hiding from one another
> Not sleeping at nights
> When he took his hired killers
> From among our midst.

For statues we dug out tons
Of rock and stone,
Drowning with odes of praise
The people's groans.

With the noble, lofty, enlightened
Truths we proclaimed
We shed the blood and darkness
Of Lubyanka and jail.

Let posterity mark our names
With the brand of scorn,
All equal, all alike,
We confess our shame.

Yes, the evidence of these truths
Is clear indeed.
It is our blindness we hate,
Not the man now dead.

We and they ... can Westerners understand how hard, how impossible even, it sometimes is to distinguish between these two pronouns. In the Western democracies there are political parties, and members of one can refer to the others as 'they'. The left wing of a party can call the right wing 'they'. And it is the same between young and old, between Christians and atheists. Everything is clear and distinct. My colleague N. is a member of a socialist party because he is a convinced socialist, and not because he was forced to join; the party is not a source of personal advantage or inconvenience to him. He remains himself; if he should become disillusioned with his socialist ideals he can leave the party and perhaps join a different one. Everyone has his own newspaper, his own circle, his own club. With us it is quite different, and Westerners find this hard to understand. Take a man carrying the card of the Communist Party of the Soviet Union. Who is he, one of 'them', or one of 'us' (independently of the meaning given to the pronouns in a given context)?

Is he a Leninist of the old guard, who still believes with naïve certainty in the ideals of 1917? Or a soldier of the war against fascism who joined the Party at the time of Stalingrad when everyone was united by a single aspiration, a single faith in a new future? Or a careerist on the lookout for a quick way to the top? Or a weak and unprincipled victim of intimidation? Or a political idealist, convinced that honest people must join the Party *en masse* so as to give it new life and dignity? Or a simple-minded conformist who takes everything he hears on the radio or reads in *Pravda* at face value? Or perhaps a sceptic, long rid of his erstwhile illusions but now condemned to carry his Party card either to his dying day or until the time when his heretical views come to light and he is expelled? The problem is that you cannot leave the Party; to do so would be like committing civic suicide or applying to emigrate. And naturally every member of the CPSU bears responsibility for everything that the Party does, and even for everything that is written in its newspapers. He is responsible even when he takes no part in what is done and knows nothing about it. And this is not only because he carries the red booklet in his pocket; as a member of the Party he is obliged to submit to the law of 'democratic centralism': he must defend the majority decision whether he voted for or against, and with no regard to the pressures which may have influenced the decision. Every writers' meeting is preceded by a Party meeting; here it is still possible timidly to put forward a personal opinion, but subsequently, at the general meeting attended by Party members and non-Party members alike, every communist is obliged (on pain of expulsion) to defend the Party line worked out at the previous meeting. He is no longer a human being, but a mere cog in a machine. Thus he may be one of 'us', but he is transformed willy-nilly into one of 'them'. Party members very rarely revolt. One may condemn their docility and even be indignant about it, but millions and millions of similar acts of docility make up a reality which cannot be ignored and which is at one and the same time a tragedy and a crime. The Party is an all-powerful church—were heretics ever very common?

Non-Party members in the Soviet Union likewise inevitably become involved in this diabolical quid pro quo, assuming that they want to get on with their work and not remain idle bystanders. Are they to be blamed for this? Doctors treat patients, composers compose music, journalists write articles, teachers teach children, and engineers carry out the Plan. They are conscientious people trying to do their job as honestly as possible; it is they who create the culture of their country, often stifling in an airless space in the process, or trembling with indignation and recoiling in horror at the hypocrisy imposed on society and at the awareness of their own immoral behaviour. Very few join the ranks of open opposition, a handful in a nation of 280 million people. And why should they?—what good would it do? Not many people believe that the feeble attempts of the isolated few can change the overall shape of things. Not many people see any sense in emigration, which seems a purely individual act, separating your own fate from the fate of your own country and society. There are not many heroes willing to pay for a truthful word or a courageous act with years of hard labour.

'We' and 'they'. . . . How much easier it is to live with such clear distinctions! And how hard to live in an undifferentiated and unclear society where there are so many of 'them' among 'us' and so many of 'us' among 'them'.

This book was written in the West, when I was already 'beneath an alien sky' and even 'sheltering under alien wings'. I could allow myself to tell of much that I have witnessed, often as a victim. But even so, I look at what happens in the Soviet Union not from outside, but from within, and I do not write all this in order to accuse my country. It is my country, and I have no other.

lord. But then they in their turn were the masters of their own vassals and similarly made up for their powerlessness by tyrannical rudeness.

Alas, we do not know our own society; sociologists have no opportunity of studying it, or writers of representing it in their novels, or historians and philosophers of deducing the laws that govern it. They are all compelled to take as their starting point not reality—which is unknown to them—but some model which has been set up in advance. Until we study society we are in no position to make proposals about it; starting with a model—and it makes no difference whether it is rosy or black—we can only put forward attractive or not so attractive, but in any case equally utopian, solutions. In the nineteenth century the study of the new bourgeois society that had arisen in France during the Restoration period began from physiological sketches; the master of this genre was Balzac, who wrote a *Physiology of Toilet*, a *Physiology of Coiffure*, and a *Physiology of Gait*. Collections of monographs were published describing the types of contemporary society as tribes and peoples are described in anthropology textbooks. Not only novelists but also politicians learned a lot from books such as the four-volume *Les Français*, containing literary portraits of the cook and the *modiste*, the gendarme and the innkeeper, the tightrope-walker and the general, the prostitute and the professor, the *clochard*, the miner, and the minister. We by contrast know nothing about ourselves. The writer of any sort of narrative inevitably gets sidetracked into doing these physiological sketches. It is not only foreign readers who do not know Russia, even Soviet citizens have no conception—except perhaps intuitively—of the world they live in. If they do happen to know something, it is only at the level of ordinary observation. And unfortunately it is rare for even the most outstanding minds of our time to go beyond this ordinary commonplace knowledge. You cannot study contemporary society on your own, but collective research is out of the question.

I am far from claiming to carry out this programme here. I would not wish the reader to take Rector B. as the most typical kind of Soviet manager. However, the characteristics outlined above are not his alone; they are those of the social group to which he belongs. Fear of higher authority and despotism towards subordinates—this combination grows up in every modern baron, even if nature created him magnanimous and noble, honest and kind. After all, the barons of old were of different kinds too; they were brought up to believe in honour and there were plenty of Cornelian heroes who were prepared to wash away an insult in their own blood. B., the modern baron, is endowed with the notion of honour and even the more recent category of conscience. Not that either of them stops him being a baron.

So I gave 'this' lecture, realizing that it was my last. My audience seemed to realize it too; the emotion and unusual solemnity in my voice probably communicated themselves to my listeners. My subject was an episode in French literature; I was discussing the poetry of Théophile Gautier. I hope the reader will forgive this apparently random detail, since for me it is not only important, but symbolic. I noticed for the first time an interesting coincidence: Gautier's collection *Émaux et camées* first appeared in 1853, the same year as *Les Châtiments* of the exiled Victor Hugo. Gautier was composing for posterity, he wrote of art and love, immortality and fame. Hugo's poems were what we should now call ephemeral; their political topicality has long vanished into the past. Even so, the 'imperishable' *Émaux et camées*, for all their artistic perfection, have faded and the 'ephemerality' of Hugo's furious invectives has stood the test of time; his fierce criticism of the pseudo-Napoleon and all his gang are as alive today as they were a hundred and twenty years ago:

Since the just man is beaten down,
Since crime is deemed fit to wear the crown,
Since every right has been betrayed,
Since the most stalwart are unmanned,
Since the dishonour of the land
Is posted in every street . . .

Since every soul is weak with fear,
Since people crawl, since they forget
The true, the pure, the fair, the good,
And history's indignant stare,
And honour, glory, rights and law,
And those who sleep among the dead;

Then welcome exile, welcome pain!
Let sadness be my diadem!
I love you, noble poverty!
I love my weather-beaten door,
I love the statue of solemn grief
Who comes to share my home with me.

(*Les Châtiments*, II.5)

These lines were soon to become relevant to my own situation—
all too soon! But at the time of my lecture it was only two months
since Solzhenitsyn had been flown into exile and my audience did
not need me to interpret for them the figure of the exile standing up
against the tyranny he loathed:

Let the degraded people bow their heads
To honour this vile, cheating renegade;
Let England and America reject
The exile, saying: 'Go, we are afraid.'

Let us be as dead leaves, or turned away
By those who seek Caesar's favour, let us be poor
Outcasts who have been torn like rags on nails
By fellow-men, and chased from door to door;

Let even the desert, God's reproach to man,
Banish the banished, drive away the driven;
Or let the grave, like human kind, base, mean,
Cast out the dead, deny their hope of heaven;

I will not flinch. With uncomplaining voice,
In calm contempt, with heart in mourning clad,
I will embrace you in this savage place,
My altar, France, and liberty, my flag! . . .

Under the ash and sack-cloth I shall be
The voice saying 'Misery', the mouth saying 'No',
And while your lackeys, Caesar, magnify
Your palaces, your hovels I will show.

I'll fold my arms, indignant but serene,
Watching the traitors bow their heads and kneel.
Sombre fidelity to fallen things,
Be thou my strength, my joy, my staff of steel . . .

Harsh exile I accept, no end in sight . . .

('Ultima Verba', *Les Châtiments*, VII.16)

As I said, my listeners never needed commentaries. In order for them to understand the modern relevance of Hugo's *Châtiments* there was no need for the mutual humiliation of ambiguous allusions and ironical hints. For it was not a question of allusions, but of the constancy of historical situations. Karl Marx, rephrasing Hegel, once said that all history repeats itself, first as tragedy, then as farce. Our experience is different: the repetition is a second and even more terrible tragedy. And listening to the white-hot invectives of Hugo, our contemporaries understand them in their own way. Similarly they have their own way of reading the bitter and ironical reflections of Pushkin, which he disguised as the work of the Italian Pindemonte:

> Little I prize those rights so loudly praised
> That turn the heads of people nowadays.
> I'll not complain if Heaven deny the subject
> The precious freedom to debate the budget,
> Or to compel their kings to live in peace;
> And little grieve I if the press is free
> To fool the blockhead reader, or the censor
> Can subtly clip the mad wings of the writer.
> All that, dear reader, is just words, words, words.
> But other, better rights are dear to me,
> I need another, better kind of freedom:
> Dependence on the Tsar or on the people,
> What does it matter? Let it pass?
>   To give
> A reckoning to no one, and to serve
> And please yourself alone, and not to bow
> Your conscience, thought or neck to rank and power . . .

('From Pindemonte', 1836)

Pushkin had his own reading of Hamlet's 'words, words, words' and we have our reading of Pushkin. This is normal and inevitable. Understanding Soviet people means among other things learning to read the great literature of the past through their eyes. And there is nothing surprising in the fact that not long ago the Polish authorities prohibited the staging of Mickiewicz's *Dziady*; a poem written

a century and a half ago had too much of a topical ring about it and
the Poles read (and *a fortiori* listened to) the lines of their national
poet as a contemporary denunciation of the continuing coloniza-
tion, enslavement, and pillaging of Poland:

> Others, maybe, bear heavier loads by far.
> One, branded with the honours of the state,
> Has sold his freeborn spirit to the Tsar
> And cringes on the doorsteps of the great.
>
> With salaried tongue he praises every yoke
> And grins in triumph when a comrade bleeds.
> Smeared with my blood, he now betrays my folk
> And brags in pious terms of vilest deeds.

('To my Russian Friends', 1832, tr. Jack Lindsay)

It is undignified and in any case unnecessary to play games with
readers, thrusting one's allusions on them, or to wink knowingly to
students, inviting them to make political connections. Soviet
people know how to read and they know how to listen.

And so I crossed the threshold of the Rector's immense oak-
panelled office. He got up to greet me, closed the door, sat me down
beside him and said: 'The day after tomorrow there will be a meeting of the Academic Council of the Institute to discuss your case.
You are charged with . . . [I omit the list of charges, all the details
are in a later chapter]. This time we shall not be able to help you;
six years ago we managed to save you because there was a different
line [I interpret: last time it was the Party, this time the KGB]. It's
beyond our power. You will lose your job, but possibly [possibly!]
we shall be able to save your degrees and titles. It all depends on
your behaviour. You should come to the Council meeting and
behave sensibly.'

He spoke in an official dry manner, but it was as if he were wash-
ing his hands of what was to follow; the civic execution had to be
carried out under his chairmanship and indeed by him, and he found
this repugnant; he did not really know the nature of the charges
against me. I gathered from his vague hints that he had been summoned to the Big House[1] and had been shown my 'case' or at least

[1] The Big House is the Leningraders' name for the KGB building at
6 Liteiny Prospect. [Author's note.]

some sort of summary of it, but the 'case' itself had made less impression on him than the categorical judgements of his hosts. Now he had the hardest job of all: setting up the show known as an Academic Council meeting whose function was to reach a totally free and independent decision.

Digression concerning Stage-Management

> Humanity has entered a new phase in which its concepts and relationships are being transformed.
>
> V. MEIERHOLD, 1920

The writing of the script and the rules of production have long been familiar. Even I, who had never been more than a mere participant in such gatherings, knew the order of the day off by heart. And the Rector, who had organized dozens of them, knew how to run them with impeccable tact and the necessary show of conviction. The procedure usually went as follows. The Rector would be summoned to the Provincial Committee of the Party and given to understand that there must be a creative discussion of the Academic Council which would lead to a free resolution of censure against, let us say, L., a professor of genetics and a partisan of pseudo-science serving the interests of neo-fascism. Returning to the Institute, the Rector, together with the secretary of the Party organization, would choose the leading actors, and would then invite each of them in turn to see him for a long and confidential chat. The difficulty lies not so much in the abstract principles of genetics (although an honest academic will not want to lie about them either), but in the fate of Professor L., a gifted and conscientious researcher, a popular lecturer and a decent man, who is going to have to be called a charlatan, a parasite, and an obscurantist. He has to be compromised somehow—he has too great an influence on students and carries too much weight with his colleagues. But it's no good giving this dirty work to the secretary of the Party Committee—who would take a word he says seriously? Speeches are needed from white-haired professors and accusations from former pupils who are now scientific leaders in their own right. Otherwise the Provincial Committee will express their dissatisfaction at shoddy work. And so the poor Rector invites the white-haired elders one after another and sets up the meeting.

There are well-tried tactics and techniques of persuasion, whose success depends largely on the Rector's own skill, charm, cunning, and urbanity.

First comes an old professor of zoology with a great reputation and numerous publications. What does the old fellow want? In the first place, it's high time he was an academician, or at least a corresponding member; the Institute where he has worked for forty years can put his name forward to the Academy of Science (but it can also not put his name forward). Secondly, he wouldn't object to being a member or at least a corresponding member of the Academy of Pedagogical Science (Acapedy, rudely and for short) and this depends entirely on the Institute, i.e. the Rector. And thirdly, he is long past retirement age and has been kept on in the Institute out of respect for his services to science: this could change any day and the next morning the professor of zoology would wake up no longer a head of department and member of several academic councils and editorial boards, but a poor obscure old pensioner. And it all depends on the Rector.

'You really ought to express your opinion, Ivan Stepanovich', the experienced diplomat tempts the professor of zoology. 'Your contribution will enable the Council to keep within the limits of genuine scientific debate. You know what our colleagues are like; they can easily descend to gossip, squabbling, and vulgar abuse. But with you . . . and then think how helpful and flattering your participation will be to Professor L. After all, you're not a Morganist, are you? And you don't agree with the principles of bourgeois genetics? Why not declare yourself then? Why not remind everyone that an eminent zoologist such as you considers this scientific line to be, well, mistaken? [And a month from now there will be the elections to the Academy of Science and a month later to the Acapedy, and if you don't speak, you've only yourself to blame. The professor of zoology understands this only too well and he also has in mind the stories about Yougo: Yougo is what they call the grandfather of the family who is told: 'You go for the milk. . . . You go and take your granddaughter for a walk in the park. . . . You go and buy a newspaper. . . .' Better dead than Yougo, thinks the professor.] Meanwhile the Rector is saying: 'I want to keep this cool too. They're out for blood in the Provincial Committee, they want us to drum him out of the Institute. But we can defend him. It will mean speaking out very firmly against him and not being afraid to be brutal if necessary, but then reaching a fairly gentle conclusion—we'll say that he's a capable man who admits his mistakes and that we can re-educate him. But to make things go this way we need your authority.' And the professor of zoology is gradually persuaded to speak: he'll save a man in danger (oh yes, not drown him but save him!) and he won't be shoved into retirement—that's Yougo avoided for another year or two—and he may even make the Academy. . . . And once you're in the Academy, how useful you can be, you can stick up for the persecuted and you don't have to fear anyone or anything. And what's more, you get a *dacha* and a luxurious Academy apartment, and a special funeral. . . . 'Well, I'll think about it', says the professor of zoology. 'But you know me, I think for myself and I say what I think. I have no intention of taking part in a witch hunt, but if it's a scientific discussion, why not?' (And he is indeed sure that he is a decent man and later he will be the first to wonder what came over him? How did it happen that colleagues refuse to shake hands with him?)

But the Rector is already busy with the next customer, and this next customer is a well-established academician with an Academy *dacha*, an Academy apartment and the certainty that after his death there will be a four-volume or even a six-volume edition of his works and a first-rate funeral for him. He is an academician, he needs nothing and he has nothing to fear. A different approach is needed.

'Have you really never been to Japan, Stepan Ivanovich? I was in Tokyo recently and they think highly of you there. It's very interesting, quite unlike all we know in Europe. . . . You should apply for a visit, there oughtn't to be any problem. The Party Committee is sure to support you. After all, you will support the Party Committee, won't you, Stepan Ivanovich? Oh, and by the way, about your daughter: I gather she didn't get into the Conservatoire [indeed she was rejected twice because of her Jewish name, and even with all his contacts he could do nothing about it]. Let me see if I can do something, I'll have a word with the Provincial Committee or even the Central Committee if necessary; it's a scandal, refusing such a talented pianist . . . [Oh yes, the academician needs nothing and has nothing to fear, but it has been his life's dream to visit Japan, and now it turns out that his daughter's fate is in his hands as well. He is old and sick and hasn't much longer to live, but that's no reason for being selfish and not looking after your children's interests; his daughter will never forgive him if he misses this exceptional opportunity.] 'All right,' says the academician, 'but don't expect any speeches from me, I'll say a few words and that's all; I am only speaking because I don't agree with Professor L.'s scientific position and I want to protect the younger people against his wrong ideas. I like L., but truth is more important.'

And now into the oak-panelled office comes a young woman who has recently taken her doctor's degree and has always been known for her outspoken honesty. It will be harder still with her; she owes everything to Professor L., she studied under him and attended his lectures enthusiastically, he gave her the subject for her candidate's[1] dissertation and suggested one for the doctorate—in short, he has been a spiritual father to her.

'Oh, we have no intention of starting a witch-hunt against your teacher, or getting him dismissed, heaven forbid! The Academic Council is going to examine his publications and discuss his ideas, his lectures, and his seminars. You're no longer a little girl, you've got ideas of your own, haven't you? Unfortunately people are saying that none of your work has been done independently, that you're only L.'s assistant. Most of your articles are jointly signed by you and him. Why's that? Either you really are just a technical assistant [and in that case why were you given a doctorate?] or else he is exploiting you, using your research for his own career. No? You work in collaboration? But who's going to believe that? Who is to know that you are an independent-minded scientist? Prove it to the Academic Council, show them how your ideas differ from those of your professor. They don't differ? So you're not really a Doctor of Science but merely his lab. assistant? Look here, you're putting yourself in an awkward position, your doctorate hasn't been confirmed by the VAK[2] yet, there will be a representative from the Ministry there and you'll hardly get support from him.

---

[1] The degree of 'candidate' is the first post-graduate degree, preceding the doctorate. [Tr.]

[2] *Vysshy Attestatsionny Komitet*—Higher Degree-Awarding Committee. [Tr.]

What, you don't want to betray your teacher? But who's talking about betrayal? Do you think we are still living in the Middle Ages? I am inviting you to take part in a scientific debate. Your professor belongs to another generation, he hasn't kept up with contemporary developments, it's only natural. You have gone on ahead of him, you use mathematical methods, but he doesn't know any mathematics and rejects its application to biology. That's right, isn't it? Surely you can speak about that? And let's be frank, Professor L. doesn't know any Marxism either, and you are a Marxist. You'd rather not speak about politics? But that's quite unnecessary, that's not what I want at all, you can keep strictly to academic problems and scientific debate. [If her doctorate is not confirmed and she is regarded as L.'s assistant without an idea of her own, she can fear the worst. The number of posts is being reduced every year, she will be dismissed, and where will she find a job then with a black mark like that against her? Professor L. is protected by his books and his world reputation, he is rich and has nothing to fear, however much he is persecuted. But she is defenceless and terribly vulnerable. What good will it do him if his pupil is ruined? But once she has her doctorate she will be able to help him. . . . And then she has a baby, she is an unmarried mother with old parents to support. And she wants to continue her experiments; without the Institute how will she be able to get hold of the mice and frogs she needs? Or the technicians? Or the apparatus?] 'All right then, I'll speak, but only on specific questions, not a word about politics. Don't expect anything more from me.'

But no one expected anything more from her. There will be plenty of volunteers for the political speeches from the departments of Party history, political economy, and philosophy. They will pick up what Ivan Stepanovich and Stepan Ivanovich say, and what she, the devoted pupil, has to say about her professor's backwardness in relation to contemporary scientific method, and will put it all in a correct political light, dotting the i's and crossing the t's. They will declare (you can foresee it all) that Professor L. is not a Marxist, that his biology is idealistic in character, that his ideas were refuted long ago in Lenin's work of genius *Materialism and Empiriocriticism*, that his lectures are suspect—he is always referring to reactionary Western authors, thus revealing his undervaluing of Soviet science and consequently his anti-patriotism; the analysis of students' lecture notes shows that Professor L. despises his audience and peppers his lectures with obscure pseudo-scientific terms of foreign origin, instead of explaining to the students the materialistic foundations of Michurin's biology. And finally there have been several thefts in the student hostel and a week ago a fireman was found one morning in the room of girl student Z. Where was Professor L.? Was he doing his job, visiting the hostel and having educational talks? No, no visits, no talks. Can such a professor (if that is the right word) be trusted with the education and upbringing of Soviet youth?

And then will come the concluding speech from the secretary of the Party committee, who will read out isolated sentences from the works of 'pseudo-Professor' L. so that everyone will be persuaded that the author is at best a militant non-Party man, that Marxism-Leninism is quite foreign to him, that he takes the liberty of quoting from Werner Heisenberg ('who collaborated with the Nazis and has in recent years been living on American monopoly capital') and from Niels Bohr ('who in 1943 was brought from Denmark to Sweden by the British Intelligence Service and then sent to America where he played a part in the making of the atom bomb'), and that finally he is a geneticist and genetics is 'biological superstition', 'the obscurantists who dominate bourgeois genetics are closely connected with the obscurantists who run Western atomic physics'. And by way of conclusion: 'The stinking corpse of Machism has been galvanized into life and dragged back into contemporary natural science.'[1] Such discussions always proceed by escalation; each successive speaker goes one step further, and in the end one is dealing not with a professor but with a pseudo or ersatz professor, not with a biologist whose ideas are being discussed among colleagues but with a running-dog of fascism who must be expelled from his department or for greater security placed under arrest.

So the Rector had the job of setting up more or less this sort of meeting in two days' time. It was 1974, and not easy to return to the ill-famed 50s, but the Rector had plenty of experience and

[1] All these quotations come from an article by V. Lvov published in the journal *Zvezda*, 1949 No. 1, pp. 149–50. [Author's Note.]

knew that with good organization things always go smoothly. I knew as much too. There was no point in arguing or being indignant. I thanked him for his kindness in informing me and left.

I had not yet had time to go home when I was rung up from the Writers' Union. 'You are required to attend a meeting of the Secretariat at 3 p.m. on April 25th', said an official voice. I understood that the play was going to be in two acts. At nine in the morning there would be the Academic Council meeting, which would dismiss me from the Institute and strip me of my degrees and titles. At three in the afternoon the Secretariat would meet to expel me from the Writers' Union. By evening the operation would be concluded and I would be 'a poor bare forked animal'. And then what would they do with me? Arrest me? Send me to Siberia? Throw me into exile, as they had done with Solzhenitsyn two and a half months ago? Or leave me to moulder, without work and without the right to teach or publish? One thing was clear: I could not grace their show with my presence. I had only to be there and they would shower me with provocative questions, which I could not answer because to lie was repugnant and to tell the truth would ruin me. Not that I minded saying what I thought in the Institute or the Writers' Union, but then they could concentrate on my answers and thus be on surer ground. But if I didn't turn up, what would they be able to talk about in their speeches? Rumours? The odd sentence or two in private letters? Suspect allusions and ambiguities discovered in my articles? Or my lectures, which didn't seem to have been attended by any informers? And I didn't have to pretend: my heart was giving me trouble and it was open to me to ignore it or to treat it as the first signs of a heart attack.

I called the doctor the next day; he diagnosed alarming symptoms and ordered me to bed for three days. This finally decided me. I was itching for a fight, I was full of curiosity—it's rather interesting to attend your own funeral—but I realized that there was no point in falling for provocation. They needed my presence, and kept insisting on it over the telephone, but the more my enemy tried to tempt me out, the less I felt inclined to meet him half-way. In the middle of the day I had a telephone call from the First Secretary of the Writers' Union, G. K. Kholopov, who demanded that I should speak to him personally, however ill I was.

'You must come', he said in a threatening voice. 'There are times when you can't refuse.'

'But I'm not refusing, I'm ill. Can't you put off your meeting for a few days?' [That seems natural enough, to put it off until the man is better. . . . But I knew that they wouldn't agree—the Big House had told them to finish the operation in one day.]

'It can't be postponed. It's the end of April, everyone will be going away and it will be impossible to get hold of them. No, you must attend. . . .'

'Would you like it if I dropped dead in your office, Georgy Konstantinovich?'

'We don't want you dying, but you must come', was all Kholopov could find to say to me. This answer meant: 'I've been ordered— by hook or by crook—to hold the meeting without delay, and in any case we have people from the Provincial Committee, the City Committee, and the District Committee coming at three o'clock tomorrow, and you don't expect me to put them off, do you? Do you think they will believe that the victim is ill? And everyone's already been summoned, we must avoid wastage.' Of course to discuss a member of the Writers' Union in his absence, and even more so to expel him from the Union in his absence, would be im- proper and unprecedented, and indeed impossible. But it was equally impossible to postpone the meeting because of the illness of the subject of discussion—there would be hell to pay. Kholopov had the choice between a scandalously undemocratic course of action and another course which would bring down the wrath of the authorities on him. Which was the stronger, shame or fear? Which was the stronger, conscience or self-preservation?

I later learned that it would indeed have been difficult to post- pone it. The organizers of the meeting had taken exceptional steps to ensure that all the Secretaries would be there (many of them were away from Leningrad)—and these steps did not originate from the Writers' Union. One of the members of the Secretariat, Professor V. G. Bazanov, was in Moscow for a meeting of the Lenin Prize Committee; he was telephoned in his hotel and told in the name of the KGB to leave immediately for Leningrad, where there was an urgent meeting. It was in vain that Bazanov tried to get out of it on the pretext that the Committee was on the point of meeting and even voting; he was forced to comply. Another of them, the poet Mikhail Dudin, was on holiday in the Crimea; he was contacted in his writers' rest home, and obediently flew north. They say that when he got the telegram he went straight to bed and stayed there all day [What did he think about? Did he realize that he was going to have to act the part of executioner? Did he feel that his honour was at stake? Most probably he did, but fear won the day], and then went off to the airport without saying goodbye to anybody. Yet another, the poet Anatoly Chepurov, was with Daniil Granin in Tbilisi at some writers' congress; the telegram ordered them both to return, but Granin refused outright (he had a speech to give the following day on the working class in Soviet literature). Granin turned out to be more clearsighted, more honest, and above all braver than his colleagues; Chepurov, however, went off pale and trembling to cover himself with shame in Leningrad. And yet another of the Secretaries was off in some distant nature reserve; they sent a helicopter, but luckily for him they couldn't find him. Thus they had assembled a quorum; in such circumstances could one really expect them to take any notice of such a trivial detail as the illness of the accused? And in any case did it matter what he said in his defence, or indeed whether he said anything at all? The decision had been taken in advance and the Union Secretariat had merely to rubber-stamp it and give it the appearance of legality.

All this I discovered later. But already on 23 and 24 April one thing was clear to me: the fifty-odd professors on the Academic Council and the dozen or so writers who made up the Secretariat were merely extras. The Party and police authorities were sure of themselves and their tactics, they were well acquainted with the people they had been manipulating all these years. There was no danger of resistance.

2

Drama in Four Acts:
The Civic Execution (25 April 1974)

ACT ONE

On 25 April 1974, the day when my fate as a citizen was being decided, I sat at home all day. The telephone stood silent. From time to time there was a brief ring on the doorbell, friends coming to shake hands, to tell me about the rumours that had leaked out, and to sit in silence (the room was bugged, but this way they might get by unobserved). There were also visits from shocked pupils; these twenty-year-olds did not have the experience that my contemporaries had gathered over the decades, they had not known the Stalin period, had grown up after the Twentieth Congress, and had at most only heard tales of civic executions from their elders. 'What does it mean?' they all asked in astonishment. 'How can it have happened? How can they summon a professor from the lecture room and without warning declare him a criminal? Why didn't they explain what he had done wrong? Why? . . . why? . . .' They were not so much indignant as upset. For most of them my sudden expulsion was a catastrophe, a moral catastrophe because over the years they had got to know their teacher fairly well and it had never crossed their minds that he was a conspirator, and a material catastrophe because their dissertations, class papers, examination work, and translations were suddenly all rendered absolutely worthless. That day I was due to continue my series of lectures; the class was told that they could go home and that their professor was no longer on the staff of the Institute. They asked for explanations, but were told nothing. They went *en masse* to the Dean, A. I. Domashnev; he, taken unawares, could only mumble something vague—he hadn't yet been told how much he was allowed to disclose. The students insisted; the Dean, exasperated by their tactlessness and his own powerlessness, swore at them and sent them packing. Yes,

this discreet and suave gentleman, with his diplomatic training, un-
failingly smart, correct, courteous, never raising his voice, respectable and affable, allowed himself to shout at them and even apparently to stamp his feet. The students looked at him in amazement
and left. What did he do, when he was left on his own? Did he
remember all the flattering things he had said about the books and
articles that the saboteur had invariably presented to him with cor-
dial dedications? Did he accuse the Party bosses who had condemned him to this pathetic role of powerless executive? Was he
furious with his subordinate who had gone about for years under
the disguise of a professor of philology and had now dealt a crushing blow to his career? Did he telephone the Big House to report the
students who had shown solidarity with the criminal? Or did he
remember the last Academic Council where as Dean he had insulted
a man who could not answer back, hoping perhaps that his shameful speech would not go beyond the walls of the meeting hall? If
that is the case then Domashnev was wrong: before two weeks had
gone by his speech was published in the Western newspapers—
above all the *Washington Post* with its circulation of millions—and
had been broadcast—in Russian!—by the foreign radio stations.

Digression concerning Publicity

> ... Everything takes place in the most terrible secrecy, the weak are
> exposed with impunity to the vengeance of the powerful, and the
> proceedings, which are kept from the public or falsified so as to
> deceive it, remain hidden, like the error or iniquity of the judges, in
> eternal silence, unless some extraordinary chance brings them to
> light.
>
> ROUSSEAU, *Rousseau the Judge of Jean-Jacques*, Dialogue I

The time is past when it was possible to stifle people in the
dark, to murder with impunity and to make your way over
corpses amidst universal silence. The world has changed. In
our day everything that was secret is coming into the open. It is
not so long since the Domashnevs had an easier time of it: they
did their hatchet work, more often with repulsion than with
enjoyment, but understanding that a brilliant career is worth a
little dirty dealing. And where's the harm in dirty dealing if no
one knows about it except for a few collaborators? This is how
it was in the early fifties—who had heard of the denunciations

hidden in the depths of the Big House? Who knew about the murderous speeches made at the 'criticism' sessions when pupils denounced the aestheticism or cosmopolitanism or anti-patriotism of their teachers? Or about the actions of administrations which hounded out of the universities and academies, conservatoires and theatres, Jewish scholars, Jewish artists, and Jewish teachers? Happy days! This was the time when a Georgy Berdnikov, Dean of the Faculty of Philology in the University of Leningrad, who had already contributed by his denunciations to the arrest of his beloved professor Grigory Gukovsky (who died during interrogation in prison in 1949 at the age of 48), when Berdnikov could in the presence of a thousand students in the great hall of the University thunder against Viktor Zhirmunsky, the greatest and most wide-ranging philologist of our age: 'Have you written one single line which was necessary to the Soviet people?'

This was in 1950, when Zhirmunsky was expelled from the University—where for more than three decades he had been in charge of the Department of Western European Literatures—for cosmopolitanism (i.e. Jewishness), for subscribing to the theories of the great comparativist Aleksandr Veselovsky, for having in his youth belonged to the circle of Russian Formalists, for the books he had written, and for not having written other books in praise of his persecutors. Berdnikov meanwhile, in recognition of his outstanding services, was raised to the rank of Deputy Minister of Culture and then rose higher still to hold some sort of secret post from which he controlled Soviet literature and laid down literary policy.... (Not long ago, in 1974, he published a biography of Chekhov. Why on earth do these double-dyed villains feel the urge to write about Chekhov? Chekhov said: 'One must be intellectually clear, morally clean, and physically tidy.' Do they remember these words? Of course they do, but there is obviously an as yet unstudied type of intellectual masochism.) So we have a Berdnikov quite unknown in the West; in the years when he was climbing the ladder of corpses there was still no Samizdat, nor even a Tamizdat,[1] nor the all-pervading radio broadcasts which now proclaim the names of scoundrels to the whole world. Dean

[1] i.e. Western publication of Russian works, from the Russian word *tam*, meaning 'there'. [Tr.]

Domashnev was less lucky than his predecessor Dean Berdnikov; hardly had he done the deed than everyone knew about it,
even in all likelihood his own son who, having heard the speech
of Domashnev senior on 'Voice of America' or the BBC, would
see his father in a different light. Domashnev was a specialist in
Austrian German and was in the habit of visiting Vienna,
where he was surrounded with respect and gratitude. What can he
do now, where can he go? Of course Western scholars have short
memories for Russian surnames, but there is a fair chance they
will remember Domashnev. And what if they start spitting on
his name? It makes you wonder whether a mediocre career is
worth a lot of dirty dealing.

In this connection it is instructive to recall three trials that
took place in Leningrad in the twenty-five years between 1949
and 1974.

1949. *The case of Ilya Serman.* A historian of Russian literature of the eighteenth century and a pupil of Gukovsky, he was
accused of anti-Soviet tendencies. There were two trials: at the
first one he was given ten years in the labour camps, but this
seemed too lenient and he was 'retried'. At the second session
one of the witnesses for the prosecution was his (indeed our
mutual) university friend Evgeny Brandis, who affirmed repeatedly that Serman had expressed Jewish nationalist opinions,
allegedly saying that Jews didn't get taken on to do graduate
work although they were naturally more gifted for academic
work than Russians. Even the Public Prosecutor was in some
doubt and asked Brandis if these were Serman's actual words.
Did the witness stick to his allegation that the accused talked in
general about such matters? After all, there were no other witnesses to confirm these statements. Brandis stuck to his line.
And this time Serman got 25 (twenty-five!) years in the camps.
Brandis's testimony alone had added another fifteen years. If
the sentence had been carried out in full, Serman would only
now be returning; fortunately he and his wife (who was also
condemned) were set free soon after the death of Stalin.

The social-psychological phenomenon represented by Brandis had long been of interest to me. Evgeny Pavlovich Brandis is
a man of some literary ability, a well-educated Germanist, a
genuine lover of poetry who himself once used to write verse,
and a gifted translator; subsequently he worked on the history

and theory of science fiction, wrote a book about Jules Verne, edited and translated his works and was in charge of the science fiction section of the Leningrad Writers' Union. In all probability he was not a police spy or an informer, but was simply scared stiff by being summoned to the Big House. It was already known that our friend Brandis was not distinguished by his bravery, the war had shown that clearly enough, but after the war. . . . After the war Brandis acted treacherously out of cowardice. Besides cowardice there was another factor: the knowledge of impunity. The legal proceedings were secret, the statements made within those four walls would remain there, Serman was sentenced to twenty-five years in the camps and over such an immense period any crime can be forgotten. But the main thing was that neither Serman's case nor Brandis's part in it would become publicly known. Not in the press, nor on the radio, never a word to anybody. And indeed a quarter of a century has gone by and I, cast up by fortune in the West, am naming Brandis for the first time in print. Or to be more accurate, his name has already appeared more than once, in books, on title pages and in notes, as a literary scholar and as a writer. Whereas he should be known if not as an *agent provocateur* then at least as an active collaborator with the police. But it was 1949, we were cut off and Samizdat did not yet exist. They could eliminate us in the dark and in silence.

1963. *The case of Iosif Brodsky.* At this trial, when the poet was accused of social parasitism (we shall return to it later), the chief prosecution witness was Evgeny Voevodin, a young prose writer. This time it was an open trial, a few outsiders were allowed into the court-room (which had been previously packed with building workers brought in on lorries), and Voevodin knew he was making his career in public, not only in front of the building workers, but also of a dozen or so writers. But he was not prepared for the world-wide publicity. Very soon the world press published a full account of the trial and even in the Soviet Union this account, a brilliant piece of reporting by Frida Vigdorova, was passed from hand to hand and became widely known.[1] The name of Evgeny Voevodin became a symbol of turpitude, and since his father, also a writer and also a Voevodin (Vsevolod), had not been renowned for his decency either,

[1] See Appendix 1.

someone composed a splendid epigram pillorying the pair of them:

> Is your body itching,
> Homeland of the true?
> It's just the Voevodins
> Crawling over you.

Evgeny Voevodin miscalculated: he was thinking in terms of the silence of former days, but times had changed. Naturally he was not to know that the affair he was involved in would bring Samizdat into being—even the word did not exist then, it was just coming into existence, at first in a slightly different form, 'Samoizdat'. And were the then leaders of the Leningrad Writers' Union to know that they would go down in history thanks to the case of Brodsky? Particularly the poet Aleksandr Prokofiev, to whom I shall return.

1974. *The case of Mikhail Heifets.* Here we have a young historian and writer accused of writing a preface to the Samizdat edition of Brodsky's collected verse (edited by V. Maramzin), and also of having in his possession typewritten copies of articles which have been declared anti-Soviet for one reason or another (e.g. those of A. Amalrik). The prosecution has called a large number of witnesses, at least a dozen of them. Among them for instance is the prose writer Valery Voskoboinikov; it was he who informed on Heifets. But what happens? Even Voskoboinikov, when he speaks in court, weighs every word and attempts to 'retain a noble bearing in his baseness'. It's hard to say which he fears the most, the KGB or international public opinion. Of course the security organization has complete power over him, it controls his contracts, his publications, his income and his privileges; but to get into the broadcasts of the BBC or the 'Chronicle of Current Events',[1] or *Le Monde* and thence into the newspapers of many lands as a police stooge, for a writer (even a minor provincial third-rate writer—and no author sees himself this way) this is the worst fate of all.

Let us imagine in place of Brandis, Voevodin, and Voskoboinikov a single individual; after all they are all literary men, they all 'helped with inquiries', they all agreed to appear for the

---

[1] A Samizdat journal published at irregular intervals by human rights workers in the USSR.

prosecution, and none of them was afraid to slander a fellow-author. In 1949 our average witness X was only afraid of the KGB and he was not mistaken in this. In 1963 he was still only afraid of the KGB, but this time he was mistaken, he should by now have been afraid of world opinion. And in 1974 he was afraid of the KGB, of Samizdat, of the radio, and of the Western press; over twenty-five years witness X had quietened down and learned cunning and the art of covering his tracks. Fear of public opinion had not yet overcome fear of the State Security organization, but the essential thing was that where there had been one fear, there were now two—two mutually contradictory fears. Times have changed. The position of the witness has become an unenviable one.

Remember this, you who have not yet had to face the test, you who will be urged in oak-panelled offices to make speeches of denunciation and who will be promised in return an apart-ment, delayed retirement, the publication of a book or even, in exceptional cases, of your complete works, remember:

You will not be able to hide in the dark. The time of publicity has come. Your treachery will be exposed to the general gaze, your denunciations will be brought out of the safes and archives, your name will be made an object of shame. To a man of letters what matters more than his name? Perhaps only truth.

And if he has spat on truth and covered his name with shame, what is left to him? To hang himself.

But let us return to 25 April. While my silent friends and tearful students were visiting me, the meeting of the General Academic Council of the Institute was taking place in the large hall of the Institute, under the huge portraits of Marx and Lenin. The members, who had received notices telling them to attend at 10 a.m. but not containing any precise information, saw in the room a number of quiet young men sitting at various small tables; eventually they realized that these were agents who had been sent to keep an eye on them and watch the secret ballot at the end of the ceremony. All this I know from what people told me, but now I must step aside and make way for a document, a transcript of the meeting made by one of those present. The records of meetings given in this chapter contain a good deal of repetitive material that may confuse the reader, as it confused those who were present. In the following chapters I shall clear up this confusion as best I can; meanwhile I must ask my readers to be patient while I allow them to taste the full flavour of official life in the Soviet Union.

Record of the meeting of the Academic Council of the Herzen Pedagogical Institute in Leningrad, April 25th, 1974.
On the agenda: the case of E. G. Etkind, Professor of the Institute.

Present: the members of the Academic Council, numerous members of the public, press correspondents, the secretary of the City Committee of the Party, B. S. Andreev. Professor Etkind himself is not present at the meeting, having forwarded to the Rectorate an official medical certificate to the effect that he is suffering from an attack of stenocardia and is confined to bed. Notwithstanding Professor Etkind's illness, the meeting took place.

The meeting is opened by the Rector of the Institute. This is not the first time, he says, that the Academic Council has discussed Professor Etkind. In 1968 it had to examine the political error committed by him in the introduction to the 2-volume *Masters of Russian Verse Translation* in which, as we know, he says: 'Deprived of the possibility of expressing themselves to the full in original writing, Russian poets—especially between the 19th and 20th Party Congresses, used the language of Goethe, Shakespeare, Orbeliani or Hugo to talk to the reader.' The Academic Council took a serious view of this and gave Professor Etkind a warning. But Professor Etkind did not alter his views in the slightest: he maintained close links with Solzhenitsyn and composed an appeal to young Jews about to emigrate to Israel.

The Rector proposes that the Council should discuss the removal of Etkind from his post as professor in the Institute and puts this proposal to the vote. It is carried unanimously. The Rector informs the meeting:

'Etkind is absent from the Council meeting. I had a conversation with him on April 23rd. The following day his wife came to see me and handed me an envelope containing a letter to members of the Council. The letter will be read out to the meeting.'

The Rector proceeds to give an account of Professor Etkind's activity and reads a report from the KGB.

KGB Report (shortened version)

'Etkind came to the notice of the KGB in 1969. He has been acquainted with Solzhenitsyn for more than 10 years, has met him, aided and abetted him, and kept in his apartment libellous writings, the typescript of *The Gulag Archipelago*. Through Solzhenitsyn he knew Voronyanskaya,[1] his typist, and was on good terms with her. When interrogated

---

[1] Elizaveta Voronyanskaya (1905–73): after being held for several days by the KGB in August 1973, she returned home and hanged herself.

Voronyanskaya declared: "Solzhenitsyn visited Leningrad in 1971; he handed over two copies of the G.A. manuscript to Etkind and subsequently Etkind personally brought two copies to my apartment." This is confirmed by former Vlasovite[1] Samutin: "Several times in 1971–2 Voronyanskaya mentioned letters which she sent or received by way of Etkind or his wife on their visits to Moscow. In the summer of 1970 Voronyanskaya was living at Etkind's *dacha*."

'Further facts concerning Etkind's activities. At the beginning of April this year the State Security administration brought a criminal case concerning the dissemination of libellous anti-Soviet documents. Searches took place at the apartments of Maramzin and Heifets, members of the Literary Fund union group,[2] who were responsible for the 5-volume Samizdat edition of the poems of Iosif Brodsky; in Heifets' apartment was found a preface to this edition in which the author slanders the foreign policy of the CPSU ("After the occupation of Czechoslovakia the Soviet state has become a semi-colonial power . . . etc."). Also seized was a review of this preface by Etkind containing a favourable account of its political content. When interrogated, Etkind admitted to being the author of this review and stated that he had never made a secret of his attitude to the events in Czechoslovakia. Heifets stated that Etkind had close relations with Brodsky and was openly well disposed towards him. Etkind attempted to inculcate in young writers his opinion concerning the right of talented people to choose their own way of life.

'In March 1964 Etkind's conduct at the trial of Brodsky was discussed at a meeting of the Writers' Union, but there also Etkind refused to recognize the harmful nature of his views.

'A further proof of Etkind's harmful activity is his "Letter to Young Jews wishing to emigrate"; this contains appeals to Jews not to go abroad but to fight for their freedom and civic rights here.

'It has also been established that Etkind uses his position in society in order to drag into his works ideas opposed to the Soviet system. This was the case with the introduction to the 2-volume edition of translations published in the "Poet's Library" collection in 1968 and justly condemned by public opinion. However, Etkind has continued to publish harmful books. Here are opinions on them from leading Soviet scholars:

'Doctor of Philology Professor P. S. Vykhodtsev: "Etkind's views on

---

[1] i.e. a member of General Vlasov's army, which fought on the German side in World War 2. [Tr.]

[2] This group includes young writers who are not yet members of the Writers' Union. The Literary Fund is an organization giving financial help to writers, its funds being drawn from a percentage levied on sales of all literary works published in the Soviet Union. [Tr.]

poetry are completely foreign to me and are irreconcilable with the principles of Marxism-Leninsim."

'Candidate of Philology and writer E. Serebrovskaya (on the book *Talking about Poetry*): "There is no class consciousness in Etkind, no words like 'fatherland' and 'patriotism', no ideological evaluation of poetry."

'The writer A. N. Chepurov speaks of the political danger of such works of Etkind as his article "Paul Wins, translator of Soviet poetry" in the publication entitled *The Art of Translation* and his book on Brecht. The incorrect positions of the book on Brecht were also criticized by A. Dymshits in a review in *Literary Russia*.

'In 1949 Etkind was dismissed from the Leningrad Institute of Foreign Languages because of methodological errors in his candidate's dissertation, after which he joined the Tula Pedagogical Institute. In 1968 he made political errors in the introduction to his *Masters of Russian Verse Translation*.

'In 1973–4 various measures were taken in connection with Solzhenitsyn and his circle. But Etkind failed to draw the appropriate conclusions. Over a long period he has been deliberately engaging in ideologically harmful and hostile actitivies. He has acted like a political double-dealer.'

Voices in the hall: 'Read Etkind's letter.' It is read out:

'*To the Academic Council of the Herzen Pedagogical Institute:*
'Dear Council Members,

'Unfortunately a heart complaint has prevented me from attending the meeting of the Council at which my case will be discussed. I would ask those present to take note of the following declaration, which I would have made in person had I been able to speak.

' 1. I have been a teacher in the Herzen Institute for the last 23 years. In other words, I have spent virtually my whole professional life within these walls; I work here with colleagues of long standing and pupils who have become fellow-workers. The Herzen Institute has become a second home to me. I want to express my deep gratitude and say that if I have achieved anything in the world of learning I owe it in large part to the Herzen Institute.

'2. There is a lot I could say in my defence. But in the present declaration I think it is only necessary to point out that in my quarter of a century at the Institute I have done all in my power to inspire in my pupils love for the poetic word, interest in the humanities, and respect for true cultural values. In the lecture course on the theory and history of translation which I have given for many years I have invariably insisted on the importance of the interpenetration and cross-fertilization of cultures and on the role of translation as a practical contribution to internationalism in literature and science. You will hardly find one of my colleagues, research students, or pupils who will accuse me of carrying out my duties in a casual or indifferent way over these 23 years, or of teaching what I was not supposed to teach. The consciousness of duty accomplished allows me to feel some small measure of satisfaction.

'Naturally this satisfaction is clouded by the recent events which have given rise to the present discussion. All I can do is submit to the decisions of this meeting of the Academic Council, decisions which, if I may anticipate, will involve my departure from the Institute. Please remember, however, that the guiding line of my actions is not to be determined by two or three unfortunate sentences taken from *private* letters on private matters—the statements being held against me are taken precisely from documents of this kind. Last October I was elected a member of the PEN Club ("for outstanding services in the field of poetic translation from German literature and for work in German studies") but I refused this honour in an official letter and a telegram, declaring that I considered it immoral to take responsibility for decisions and declarations made in my absence and without my agreement. I could act in no other way, because my fate is here.

April 24, 1974'

A voice: 'A Jesuitical letter!'

Speeches by members of the Council:
    Galina Ivanovna Shchukina (Professor and Head of the Department of Education):
'I am sorry that Etkind is not here to answer some questions: Has he done his duty conscientiously, or has he done all he could to undermine our preparation of specialists, educators, and teachers? What is his status in Soviet society? What philosophy does he profess? What ideology does he stand for? Why does he have active links with people who have broken with our society? The material that has been read out to us speaks for itself. Etkind is a double-dealer, or worse still. [A voice: "He is anti-Soviet."] Quite right. He has not conscientiously fulfilled any duty to scholarship. It's all quite clear now. Here's a man trying to undermine our system and at the same time trying to tell us that he is conscientiously fulfilling his duty. He has been fighting on behalf of anti-socialist, anti-Soviet assertions concerning morality [?]. He has been leading our young people astray, calling on them to fight, and against what system? Against the system which has fed him and reared him [etc., etc.]. There can be no doubt that Etkind has no place, not only in the ranks of the teachers of our Institute, but among our educators in general.'

B. D. Parygin (Professor, Doctor of Philosophy, Head of the Department of Philosophy):
'Obviously Etkind wasn't born like this, but his evolution follows a
regular pattern. From his present position it's only one step to ideological subversion. This is incompatible with his continuing presence in
our Institute.'

Anatoly Ivanovich Domashnev (Dean of the Faculty of Foreign Languages, Professor, Head of the Department of German Philology):
'Etkind worked in the Faculty of Foreign Languages. I deliberately use
the past tense. Nevertheless, I think he is an anti-Soviet renegade, a
double-dealer. He never declared his anti-Soviet views openly. He did
not emigrate to Israel, but worked in a more subtle way. These tactics of
concealment enabled him to remain for a long time in our midst. Pre-
serving a front of respectability, he was able to pursue this line of his
over a long period. What we want now is not a long discussion but a
decision. There is no place for people like Etkind in a Soviet collective
of teachers. He must be expelled from the Institute and stripped of the
academic degree and title that he received in our Institute.'

Andrey Ivanovich Zotov (?):
'The documents which have been presented to us are sufficient proof of
Etkind's hostile activities. In his letter he shows that his activities are
still continuing; here too he takes refuge in lies. He not only was, but
still is, hostile to our ideology and our system. There is no place for him
among Soviet scholars, he is unworthy not only of being a Doctor of
Science, but even of being a professor of the Soviet Union [?!].'

A. Merzon (Lecturer in Philosophy):
'This case should be a lesson to us that one must not act like a two-faced
Janus, sitting on the fence. Today every moment of our active lives calls
for particular vigilance. We know how Lenin criticized nationalism:
what we have heard today is an expression of inverted Jewish nationalism [!]. Even if ideological deviations are not very great at the beginning
they lead to disaster in the end.'

Pavel Lvovich Ivanov (Professor in the Department of Philosophy):
'I have no questions to put to Etkind. The documents show that he
worked as an ideological saboteur in our midst, an internal Solzhenitsyn.
He's not of the same calibre, but they are alike in the role they play in
international reactionary politics. Etkind doesn't sit on the fence, he's
firmly on one side of it, like Solzhenitsyn. We must get rid of him and
hand him his papers today.'

Professor Kulba (Head of the Department of Inorganic Chemistry):
' "Birds of a feather" . . . It's not a question of errors, but of deliberate
well-organized subversive activity in the midst of the Soviet people.
Etkind should be advised to follow Solzhenitsyn—he can write and do
what he likes there.'

Isaak Stanislavovich Eventov (Professor in the Department of Soviet Literature):
'I have had very little contact with Etkind. It is obvious from his letter that he doesn't understand what a Soviet teacher is. [Noise in the hall: "He understands well enough."] He failed to take into account that a teacher is a moral educator. He became a spiritual father to ne'er-do-wells, young anti-Soviets, distributors of Samizdat. These saboteurs, who were energetic but still young—Heifets, Maramzin—looked to Etkind for inspiration. They needed the blessing of someone who occupied a position in society. To a certain degree he was a figurehead for a certain group of young people whom Comrade Brezhnev in his speech to the 17th Congress of the Communist Youth League called garbage. Someone like Etkind has no place among Soviet teachers.'
A voice from the hall: 'What about his work in the Writers' Union?'
I. S. Eventov: 'We belong to different sections. I only know his works and I agree with what has been said about them.'
Raimond Genrikhovich Piotrovsky (Professor, Head of the Department of French Language):
'I think the main point is quite clear. On behalf of those members of the Department who have seen the documents I consider [!] that there is no place among us for the ideological saboteur Etkind. If necessary this will be discussed by the Department. There are complicated organizational questions: Etkind gave courses on French literature. Unfortunately these were not given under the control of the Department of Foreign Literature. Together with that department we must analyse Etkind's works in detail and correct them—for the future. [Confusion in the hall.] In any case we must discuss the organization of this course.'
Aleksandr Izrailevich Raikh (?):
'It is certain that we all bear responsibility for all that has happened. It is certain that this conduct is repeated in Etkind's request that his letter should be read out at the end of the meeting. I give my full support . . . [etc., etc.].'
L. Manizer (Head of the Department of Biology):
'As a Soviet citizen and a member of the Party I wish to give my judgement on Etkind's conduct. I owe all my work to the Herzen Institute, the atmosphere here is not and must not be conducive to the development of duplicity.'
Yury Vyacheslavovich Kozhukhov (Professor of Soviet History, Corresponding Member of the Academy of Pedagogical Science, Academic Pro-Rector):
'I would have no questions to put to Etkind either. There is no duplicity here; his are the tactics of an enemy. He has held the same position consistently over many years, from 1949 to the 1970s, when history inevitably brought him into contact with dregs such as Solzhenitsyn, Heifets,

Brodsky, and others. Our Institute took certain preventive measures: in this very hall in 1968 the Academic Council condemned Etkind's conduct, but to no effect.

'It is our misfortune and our responsibility that in all Eventovs' 23 years here [laughter], sorry, Etkind's, we never found him out.

'In his letter he writes that he spoke to his students of love for the poetic word, of the humanities, and that he tried to inspire in them "respect for true cultural values", but he says nothing about developing their communist convictions. But how did we let this happen? We made life a bed of roses for him. He directed research students, travelled all over the place, examined theses, published and edited academic works, and was entrusted with important lectures. This means that our teaching programme is badly organized and that we don't know our teachers properly. I agree with both proposals: we must not allow Etkind within gunshot range of our students. And on the basis of the new directives from the VAK we have the right to strip him of the academic title of professor. [He reads a paragraph concerning the submission of requests to the VAK.] We can take away his title as of today. As for his degree, that question must be decided by the academic council that awarded it.'

A speaker from the presidium (presumably the secretary of the Party Committee):

'It is a day of shame for us: there is a stain on the name "Herzenite", which always meant "educator in civic and political maturity". Etkind has pursued his negative line brilliantly in his 23 years in the Institute. His basic weapon has been his own conviction as a teacher; students accept their teacher's position. How could the Faculty describe Etkind's lectures as brilliant? It was precisely in his work here that he advanced his hostile position.

'Let us cast our eyes on ourselves. We must consider not the volume of learned work people produce but their political and civic maturity. Our literary public did not know his works at all well.

'Two hours ago there was a joint meeting of the Party Committee and the Local Committee. They decided to ask the Academic Council to take away Etkind's title and dismiss him from the Institute.'

The Rector:

'There are many more people wanting to speak, but the question is clear by now. Etkind's activity has been correctly assessed and the necessary points have been made.'

Tellers are elected: Ivanov (chairman), Domashnev, Volkova. There are two motions: (1) to dismiss Etkind; (2) to request the VAK to strip him of his title of professor. Both motions are carried unanimously (57 in favour, 0 against).

Such then is the document, which allows the reader to sit in on this extraordinary meeting. I originally wanted to comment on it as I went along, but I changed my mind; the document in its entirety gives a true picture and my comments would only have destroyed its unity. It has been published both in Russian and in translation; it is not surprising that in France and Germany, notwithstanding all their respect for the printed word, people don't believe it. On more than one occasion I have heard of quite categorical judgements by university teachers and students saying that it was a fake. French communist circles were even more uncompromising, calling it a piece of anti-communist provocation, the latest in a line of unworthy attempts to set the Western intellectuals against the Soviet Union. And what a crude, unintelligent piece of provocation! Is it conceivable that fifty-seven professors should be unanimous in condemning and expelling a colleague who had worked in their midst for a quarter of a century, and this on the basis of vague unfounded accusations and without asking to hear what he had to say in self-defence? Is it conceivable that police and Party officials could invade the university, occupy the hall, and impose their will on the Academic Council by silently terrorizing its members? Is it conceivable that in 1974 a scholar could be accused among other things of 'ideological errors' committed in 1949, i.e. at the height of the long-condemned Stalinist dictatorship? Is it conceivable that the Communist Party of the Soviet Union should accept responsibility for what was done twenty-five years ago, in 1949, and that such an areopagus of scholars, such a synod of elders, as the Academic Council of the Pedagogical Institute, should agree to share this responsibility? It is all too incredible. It did not happen, because it could never have happened. It is 'irrational, therefore unreal'.

Yes, my dear Western colleagues, irrational it may be, but it is none the less real for that. And it happened not in China at the time of the Cultural Revolution, but in Europe, not far from you, in the European city of Leningrad, where Voltaire's library is preserved, where one can see the finest canvases of Matisse, where in the twenties there lived the Russian Formalists, the Serapion Brothers,[1] the Oberiu circle, where Pushkin, Tyutchev, and Blok wrote,

[1] A literary grouping set up in Petrograd in 1921 and including V. Ivanov, M. Zoshchenko, M. Kazakov, M. Slonimsky, N. Nikitin, L. Lunts, K. Fedin, V. Kaverin, E. Polonskaya, and N. Tikhonov.

where there was (once) one of the best universities in the world (long ago in ruins—it is not for nothing that it bears the name of Zhdanov).[1] Many readers of this transcript will be puzzled and want to ask me a number of questions, and this is not surprising— they are mainly foreigners, they are not in the know, and anyhow it's not so important for them, since they don't have to vote. The same questions crossed the minds of the members of the Academic Council—they too did not know or understand anything that was going on, and not one of them dared open his mouth to ask, merely to ask. No, Mr. Chairman, I do not raise my hand in order to object; would you perhaps be kind enough to explain to me (or rather to us, we are all equally in the dark):

—What is the political mistake mentioned in the KGB report as appearing in *Masters of Russian Verse Translation*? It is not at all clear from the passage quoted.

—How does the KGB know whether or not Etkind kept a manuscript of *The Gulag Archipelago* in his apartment? Was it found in a search? What else did they find?

—What is this appeal to young Jews? What does it appeal for?

—Who are Voronyanskaya and Samutin? Why were they interrogated? And why accept the testimony of a former Vlasovite?

—What is the Heifets and Maramzin affair? What connection has it with Etkind?

—What were Etkind's relations with Brodsky? What in fact happened at the Secretariat of the Writers' Union?

—The 'Report' mentions the opinions of Vykhodtsev, Serebrovskaya, and Chepurov. Who are these people? Where are their opinions published? What is meant by 'to drag into his works ideas opposed to the Soviet system'? Has he got his own publishing house, or is he not subject to the laws of Soviet censorship?

—What are these methodological errors of 1949? Why does the 'Report' mention things that happened a quarter of a century ago?

—In his letter Etkind speaks of a refusal to become a member of the PEN Club. What are the circumstances of this refusal? What are the reasons for it?

Of course the most important question—which has been put to me again and again, both orally and in writing—is the one already mentioned: how could the fifty-seven members of the Academic

---

[1] Andrei Zhdanov (1896–1948), ideological leader of the CPSU during the Stalinist period (1934–48).

Council, unanimously, in a *secret* ballot, when it is enough to cross out the word 'Yes' rather than the word 'No', all demand the expulsion of a professor with whom they had worked for nearly a quarter of a century? How could the same fifty-seven members vote for the absurd, not to say indecent, demand that their colleague should be stripped of the title of professor? How are we to explain this? Is it because they were all convinced that they were dealing with a political conspirator, an enemy of the Soviet regime? Or because they were all dedicated supporters of this regime, detesting anyone who disagreed with them?

At the Academic Council meeting not one of these quite natural questions was asked. There is one more unavoidable question:

—Why did no one ask a single question at the meeting?

I shall answer all the other questions in due course. But this last question I can answer straight away. It was out of soul-chilling, brain-numbing, silencing, familiar and unsurmountable, shameful and terrible—FEAR.

—What were your relations with all these people who spoke at the meeting? Who were they? Did you often meet them in all those years of working together? Were some of them perhaps motivated by rivalry, personal hostility, or envy?

Several people have asked me this, too, attempting—as is only natural—to replace enigmatic forces by ordinary human explanations. I must answer immediately, particularly since, as the reader will see, the question also concerns the subsequent part of my story.

Of the twelve speakers at the meeting, I only know four. The rest I have never set eyes on, or if I have met them, I would be hard put to recognize them. One can similarly assume that they did not know me; no, there were no reasons for personal hostility on the part of Shchukina, Parygin, Zotov, Ivanov, Kulba, and the rest. They were fulfilling (not always particularly cleverly or conscientiously) their Party task, staking their claim to be kept on after retirement, to get an apartment, or to go to Japan. They are sound enough in their respective fields, with one apparent exception, this character Zotov.

Let me say a few words about one who is an acquaintance, Isaak Eventov. Eventov is a critic who writes about Soviet literature; not long ago (and not unaided by me) he took his doctorate on Gorky's satirical journalism. When he says that he 'had very little contact with Etkind', he is lying; he had more than a little contact. He even used to visit me at home and give me copies of his publications with heartfelt dedications ('to show my deep respect and affection'); he was quite open with me and had no doubts about the decency of his host. Some two weeks after the meeting I allowed myself one harmless gesture: I returned to Eventov his book *Lyric Poetry and Satire*, which he had presented to me with an excessively friendly and respectful inscription, and accompanied it with a letter to the effect that I was sending back his esteemed gift in case it should be found in a search and cause him to be accused of double-dealing. 'I only know his works and I agree with what has been said about them', said Eventov to the Academic Council, and that is a lie too. Before the meeting, which was to be for him a test in honesty and courage, he had reacted pretty favourably to such books and articles of mine as he had read; he had come to my defence without feeling the need to say that he considered me an ideological saboteur. Hypocrisy? Certainly, but then Eventov could speak with impunity; I was not at the meeting and those who were present were reliable and, better still, intimidated; who could publicize his speech? In answer to the note I sent with *Lyric Poetry and Satire* he wrote me a cunning, evasive letter: there were all sorts of rumours going about, I shouldn't believe all the silly reports of his speech, I hadn't seen a transcript of it. . . . But in fact I had seen one. As I said earlier, times have changed and everything now becomes known and publicized. Eventov's behaviour is all too understandable: he is 65, and a Jew; by all the rules he should be made to retire. And undoubtedly he would have been if he hadn't made his speech saying that Etkind, whom he hardly knew, had become a spiritual father to ne'er-do-wells and young anti-Soviets. Not that this speech did him all that much good in the eyes of the authorities. Pro-Rector Kozhukhov, whose anti-Semitic views are well known, made a slip of the tongue, saying Eventov instead of Etkind, and this raised a laugh even in this mortally intimidated audience. Just a slip of the tongue, but like all such slips it had its reasons. For Kozhukhov Eventov was above all a Jew, his name beginning with an 'E'—how can you avoid confusing them? That was why they laughed, the one moment of jollity in the medieval blackness of the meeting hall.

The meeting finished with a secret ballot. Members of the Council received ballot papers and each of them was left alone with his conscience, as they say. 'Alone' is what they say, but each of them bending over the table to cross out 'Yes' or 'No' could imagine an informer hovering behind his back watching the movements of his pencil. You daren't look round, or you're too embarrassed—they might think you're afraid of something. And in any case criminology has come on a lot: *they* can tell who voted against by the sort of pencil, the way it is used, and the finger-prints. If only we could wear gloves. . . . This is not my fantasizing; it is what I have been told by witnesses. And what if the 'Yes' or 'No' meant the firing squad? Or hanging, drawing and quartering, breaking on a wheel or drowning? Would fear still really outweigh conscience? The experience of recent decades says yes. Fear conquers everything: honour, conscience, friendship, decency, and all that one might expect of an intellectual. These are all acquired cultural characteristics, but fear is a biological instinct, the animal need for physical self-preservation.

ACT TWO

The results of the ballot are announced. The members of the Council disperse, avoiding one another's eyes. But they are not all free to go home; at 1 p.m. there is a second Academic Council meeting, at Faculty level. This second meeting has nothing to decide, everything is already fixed, its sole task is to pillory a professor who has worked for many years in the Faculty. There is a considerable difference: on the 'Big Council' people hardly knew Etkind, here everyone met him almost daily. The second meeting is a riskier business both to run and to be involved in, though it does not have anything to decide by secret voting. Its members meet in the Dean's office and most of them don't know what it's all about, they have just heard ominous rumours. Once again I make way for a document; this time, however, I do not have a living record written down by a sympathetic witness, but the official minutes signed by the chairman and secretary and bearing a round official stamp.

MINUTES: No. 18

Meeting of the Council of the Faculty of Foreign Languages in the Herzen Pedagogical Institute, Leningrad, April 25th, 1974.

Agenda: 1. The form of aesthetic education of students in the Faculty.
       2. Other business.

Present: Members of the Council of the Faculty, members of the Party and Union Bureaus, Party and Union organizers, 35 people in all.

A motion was proposed by the Chairman to include on the agenda the question of Professor Etkind discussed by the Council of the Institute on April 25th, and to take this item first.
Motion carried.
The Dean of the Faculty, A. I. Domashnev, reported the decision of the Council of the Institute dated 25.4.74 that E. G. Etkind, Professor in the Department of French Language, be dismissed from his post and deprived of his academic title.

E. G. Etkind had for many years deliberately engaged in activities directed against the Party and the government, had maintained constant relations with Solzhenitsyn personally during the visits of the latter to Leningrad and also through a third party, and had kept in his apartment a Samizdat copy of Solzhenitsyn's book *The Gulag Archipelago*.

On being cautioned several years ago concerning the anti-Soviet nature of several of his articles, E. G. Etkind had admitted his errors and promised to correct them.

In spite of this E. G. Etkind had maintained his anti-Soviet and nationalistic positions. He had addressed an appeal to young Jews which contained a definite political platform permeated with anti-Sovietism, calling on young people not to leave the Soviet Union but to wage internal, subversive, anti-government propaganda, this being in his opinion more effective than anti-Soviet pronouncements made from abroad. In so doing Etkind had shown that he shared the position and political convictions of Solzhenitsyn.

For these reasons the Council of the Institute had resolved that Professor E. G. Etkind of the Department of French Language in the Faculty of Foreign Languages be dismissed from his post and deprived of his academic title and that a request be made to the VAK that E. G. Etkind be deprived of the academic title of Doctor of Philology.

M. M. Segal (Senior Lecturer in the Department of English Language):
'Did E. G. Etkind attempt to justify his actions, or does he admit his guilt before the people and the country?'

The Dean:
'Etkind did not admit his guilt and did not attempt to justify himself; he is unrepentant.'

K. K. Zhuchkova (Member of the Party Committee):
'This question was discussed today at a joint meeting of the Party Committee and the Local Committee, at which an entirely correct appraisal was given of the insufficiently careful work of the Dean's office, the Party Bureau, and the Union Bureau of the Faculty of Foreign

Languages. It was impossible to overlook the political blindness of E. G. Etkind, who "went astray" as early as 1949. Etkind's standing prevented his comrades from pointing out his mistakes to him and helping him to become aware of them.'

Z. Y. Turaeva (Head of the Department of English Language):
'The report on the activities of E. G. Etkind is an exceedingly heavy blow for the teachers of the Faculty, who are astounded at Etkind's duplicity. Much was given to him, he had every opportunity for fruitful academic work, and his conduct is thus all the more unforgivable. All the members of the Faculty Council unanimously support the decision of the Institute Council.'

M. M. Segal:
'Etkind had been moving away from a proletarian class position for many years. It is painful for us to discover that behind our backs he was acting as our class enemy. We are not always correct in our judgements of people. We must judge them not on external appearance, but on their inner heart, we cannot appraise personal qualities on the basis of academic activities. In this case our mistake was not to have given an overall appraisal of Etkind. The Institute Council has acted correctly in dismissing Etkind from his post and depriving him of his academic title.'

V. V. Kabakchi (Lecturer in English Language, Member of the Party Bureau):
'One of the preceding speeches contained a just reproach to the Party Bureau. The example of E. G. Etkind shows how the ideological struggle has invaded our lives. E. G. Etkind not only went astray, he tried to influence young people, and particularly the young Jews, of whom we have many in our faculty.'

A. L. Afanasieva (Head of the Inter-Faculty Department of French Language):
'We have known E. G. Etkind for many years and experienced the attractiveness of his personality in many ways. Unfortunately we did not know many of the negative sides of his personality. It is painful to realize that Etkind preferred the dissidents to us, small fry as they are. His individualism and lack of involvement with the collective are to blame for this. The Faculty is partly to blame too. Etkind was allowed to raise his ideological level independently; although he taught in the Herzen Institute for more than twenty years, he was not a member of the Faculty union organization, since his union membership was under the Writers' Union.

'The collective of the Inter-Faculty Department of French Language supports the decision of the Institute Council.'

B. A. Dianova (Secretary of the Faculty Party Bureau, Lecturer in German Language):
'Etkind's conduct is only worthy of blame. This conduct was caused by

his total political illiteracy. Etkind does not understand the essence of the class struggle. He repeatedly presented the events in Hungary and Czechoslovakia from hostile class positions. He forgot the truth that the class struggle is continuous. We must conclude from this case that Heads of Department should know their staff better.'

N. V. Bagramova (Lecturer, Chairman of the Union Bureau of the Faculty):

'As M. M. Segal correctly pointed out, we do not always employ all possible criteria in our appraisal of the personality of a teacher. In the present case the teachers of the Faculty were under the influence of Etkind's academic authority. His exceptional talent as a lecturer and his personal charm made Etkind an "idol" for the students and those who attended the advanced pedagogical courses. So much the greater was the damage he did to the Faculty, since in lecturing to this last group of students he was extending his influence to representatives of higher education establishments in other parts of the country.

'The Union Bureau of the Faculty supports the decision of the Institute Council.'

The Dean:

'Etkind had a hand in the publication of Samizdat literature. He wrote a review of a preface by Heifets in which he spoke not as a reviewer but as the mentor of an anti-Soviet group. In this document Etkind consciously expounds his position, going beyond the bounds of a review. It is a clear case. We have before us a mature personality who put his ideological position into practice. There can be no two opinions on this matter, and we must draw the necessary conclusions. Unfortunately our Faculty has seen many cases of betrayal or rejection of the Fatherland.

'Previous speakers have correctly observed the need for a clear appraisal of people's personalities. There was no ambiguity about Etkind. He wanted to remain in the Soviet Union so as to carry on his activities internally and do underground work in conflict with the interests of our Fatherland.

'We must draw the appropriate conclusions from all this and not flatter ourselves that everything is in order here from the point of view of ideological work. The Party Bureau must place ideological work on the right level and follow the correct principles in its dealings with each individual teacher.'

N. M. Aleksandrov (Professor in the Department of German Language):

'We must scrutinize our own activities and those of the comrades around us. We need to pay attention not only to the academic, but also to the political work of teachers.'

B. A. Dianova (question addressed to R. G. Piotrovsky):

'At the meeting of the Institute Council you said that literature lectures should be given not by members of the linguistic departments, but by teachers from the Department of Foreign Literature. Could you please explain this statement.'

R. G. *Piotrovsky* (Head of the Department of French Language):
'Handing over the literature lectures to the Department of Foreign Literature is one possibility. Another would be to organize a committee on foreign literature and area studies under the direction of the Department of Foreign Literature.

'When Etkind was lecturing on stylistics, he was in the public eye and appeared in colloquia at least two or three times a year.

'As far as Etkind's activities as a literary scholar are concerned, there were things which were regarded as mistakes or lapses. I went to several of his lectures on literature, but could not check on what he said, since there can sometimes be concealed meanings that only an expert can verify.'

The Dean:
'I agree with the opinion of R. G. Piotrovsky concerning the need to reorganize the literature lectures. Clearly we need to set up an inter-faculty organization to deal with literature. We must maintain inter-faculty links with the Department of Foreign Literature. We must increase our vigilance towards ourselves, and the staff we employ. But for the time being the faculty and the departments are fully responsible for the content of teaching programmes relating to literature.

'I should like to express my certainty that all the members of the Council, the Party Bureau and the Union Bureau who are present, being unanimous in their appraisal of Etkind's personality, will be able to answer correctly any questions that may be raised by those who are not present at this meeting.'

Chairman of the Council of the Faculty of Foreign Languages: Professor A. I. Domashnev.

Minutes kept by the Chairman of the Union Bureau: N. V. Bagramova.

Once again, as at the other meeting, not a single question. There at least there was the KGB report and a few scraps of information, inadequate, distorted, and falsified, but still information. But here? The document I have quoted speaks for itself, no further clarification seems to be needed. But at the risk of prolixity let me venture a few comments. Let me ask my reader (who perhaps teaches at the Sorbonne or Oxford, Göttingen or Amsterdam, Zurich or Geneva, Vienna or Aix-en-Provence) to make an effort of the imagination and put himself in the place of any one of the participants at this meeting—let us say Professor Aleksandrov.

Digression concerning an Old Professor

> Report of them the world permits not to exist;
> Mercy and Justice hold them in disdain:
> Let us not speak of them; but look and pass.

DANTE, Inferno, III. 49–51

Nikolai Mikhailovich Aleksandrov is an old man (not long ago he celebrated his seventieth birthday), a conscientious scholar specializing in German and Russian grammar, and an old acquaintance of mine, talkative and kind, distinguished by his exquisite old-world manners, his refined aristocratic pronunciation in all languages, and his military bearing. One day he comes along to a regular meeting of his Council, where, according to the agenda, there is going to be a discussion of a question of great interest to him as a highly cultured man: 'The form of aesthetic education of students in the faculty.' Making his way to the meeting he looks forward perhaps to seeing his colleague Etkind and chatting with him as usual about poetry or the theatre. Entering the Rector's well-lit office, where the members of the Council (and on this occasion a large number of guests) are sitting at the long table and around the walls, he senses that something is wrong and as he sits down at the table asks his neighbour: 'What has happened?' His neighbour says nothing. Everyone is silent. The Dean rises and the meeting begins. Far from being about the aesthetic education of students, it concerns E. G. Etkind, who 'for many years deliberately engaged in activities directed against the Party and the government'. Professor Aleksandrov does not know what it is all about yet, but he hears ominous expressions which take him back not only to 1949, but to 1937 and to the twenties; he is among those who can clearly remember the annihilation of the opposition and the death penalties demanded for Bukharin, Rykov, and Zinoviev, the crushing of Formalism and the Formalists, the eradication of idealism in linguistics, the stifling of Zoshchenko and Akhmatova, the suppression of the cosmopolitans, the exposing of the Marrites[1] and the Veselovskians,[2]

---

[1] Followers of the linguistic theories of N. Y. Marr (1864–1934), considered until 1950 as the only true Marxist linguist, but subsequently attacked by Stalin.

[2] Followers of the academician Aleksandr Veselovsky (1838–1906) who was mistakenly presented by Zhdanov as a founder of 'cosmopolitanism'.

the hounding out of Pasternak. . . . There are many young people around him who have not undergone the same schooling, but he does not look at them; he knows that at such meetings you can only look at the speaker or make doodles on the paper in front of you. Long-familiar words catch his failing hearing: 'against Party and government policy', 'through a third party', 'the anti-Soviet nature of his articles', 'admitted his errors', 'anti-Soviet and nationalistic positions', 'address an appeal', 'subversive anti-government propaganda', 'political blindness', 'proletarian class position'. All the well-tried phrases! As well as linguistic questions, Professor Aleksandrov has studied the use of specialist jargon—here's some good material for his theoretical analyses! It's true that among the tired old turns of phrase there are some new names and new lexical themes: 'relations with Solzhenitsyn', 'a Samizdat copy', 'young Jews', 'dismissed from his post and deprived of his academic title', 'the events in Hungary and Czechoslovakia' . . . What's it all about then? It's clear that Etkind is being given a thorough going-over and that he will most likely be arrested—otherwise why take away his degrees? But it's not quite clear what for. Professor Aleksandrov begins to listen more carefully and to take note of what is said: Etkind 'maintained constant relations with Solzhenitsyn personally during the visits of the latter to Leningrad'. It sounds menacing even if not entirely clear: what are these 'constant relations . . . during the visits of the latter to Leningrad'? Were there constant relations, or only when Solzhenitsyn was in Leningrad? And why shouldn't a writer 'maintain relations' with another? And how often did Solzhenitsyn come? 'Kept in his apartment a Samizdat copy of Solzhenitsyn's book *The Gulag Archipelago*.' Why did he keep it? Did he let other people read it? Who? Or did he just keep it, for posterity? There are plenty of us who keep things without showing them to anybody. In any case, how did they get to know what Etkind kept in his apartment? Did they search it and find the book? Or was there no search and did Etkind himself confess to the KGB that he was keeping it? But what's next? 'On being cautioned several years ago concerning the anti-Soviet nature of several of his articles, E. G. Etkind had admitted his errors and promised to correct them.' Professor Aleksandrov is over 70 and he has heard some silly things in his time, but this takes some beating. So

Etkind was cautioned about the anti-Soviet nature . . . Cautioned? In our country you are not cautioned about being anti-Soviet, you are put away, or at best thrown out. And he was 'cautioned' and 'admitted his errors' (anti-Soviet ones?) and they kept on publishing him and publishing him. Only two weeks ago he gave me his latest book, *Russian Poet-Translators from Trediakovsky to Pushkin*, published by the Academy of Science. Indeed in the last few years he has been publishing more than usual. What does this sentence mean? What are the 'several' anti-Soviet articles?

Then what? 'An appeal to young Jews'. . . . Now that's more serious. What has he been appealing to them to do? To emigrate to Israel? To fight the Arabs? No, it seems this is 'a definite political platform, permeated with anti-Sovietism' (platform . . . permeated? Hm . . .) and that Etkind calls on young people 'not to leave the Soviet Union'. Good for him, quite right, it's high time these young people were told that by emigrating to Israel they leave behind their country and their culture. . . . Ah, but this is it, he appealed to them to stay here so as to 'wage internal, subversive, anti-government propaganda, this being in his view more effective than anti-Soviet statements made from abroad'. He's right, of course, it is more effective from within than from without—but did he really write all that? Where? And how did he manage to address all the young Jews? In the press? On the radio? Strange. . . .

And Professor Aleksandrov, as he doodles, jots down on the same sheet of paper a few questions which need putting to the Dean; unless they are cleared up the charges can't be taken seriously. What sort of relations with Solzhenitsyn, constant or not? Did Etkind keep *The Gulag Archipelago* or distribute it? Who found this copy, and how? . . . There are a lot of questions, at least ten of them, and he would like to put some of them, not so much out of protest but as a simple matter of honesty. But as he listens to his colleagues, who know no more than he does, their voices grow increasingly harsh and menacing: 'guilt before the people and the country', 'acting behind our backs as our class enemy', 'the ideological struggle has invaded our lives', 'total political illiteracy', 'does not understand the essence of the class struggle', 'underground work', 'betrayal of the Fatherland'.

'Who else wishes to speak? Nikolai Mikhailovich?'

Professor Aleksandrov understands: the chairman has turned to him as a member of the older generation, a scholar of authority, whose voice will carry weight with the younger people. Yes, he would like to speak, he stands up slowly. Now he can ask his puzzled questions.

But he is over seventy; why don't the younger people ask questions and raise objections? They are not threatened by retirement or a stroke. He is old, his fate hangs by a thread. For some time now he has been kept on at the Institute out of charity; as he gets up to speak, he remembers an episode that took place twelve years before. I shall interrupt the narrative to tell the story myself, in my own words.

One day—probably in 1962—all the teachers of foreign languages were called into the office of the Rector, at that time A. I. Shcherbakov. He told us:

'We are here in connection with a most unfortunate incident which casts shame on the Institute. I will ask the representative of the State Security Committee (KGB) to put us in the picture.'

In the corner we saw a young man in a discreet brown jacket. He told us in a quiet voice that for some years the Supreme Soviet of the USSR had been receiving anonymous letters slandering the Soviet system and socialist reality. The KGB had searched in vain for the author; neither the handwriting, nor the post-marks, nor various other clues were any help. 'At last we have found out the anonymous author', drawled the young man. 'It is a teacher in this Institute, Senior Lecturer Nikolai Mikhailovich Aleksandrov. He is here among you, let us hear from him why and how he wrote these dirty slanders.'

White as a sheet, Aleksandrov begins to speak in a trembling voice. For many years he has been living in one room with his mentally ill wife and his own mind is not entirely in order. But each of these letters was written under the impact of some powerful experience. His last letter, for example. That day he had heard of a terrible disaster in Kiev: a dam had burst near Babii Yar and a thirty-foot wave of mud had hit the town, flooding houses, trams and cars and killing a large number of people. (Aleksandrov's voice grows firmer.) He went out into the street expecting to see the newspaper with a black edging

round it as a sign of national mourning, but found the bill-
boards covered with triumphant headlines: yet another space
conquest. The loudspeakers in the streets and squares were
announcing it exultantly. Shaken by the contrast between ex-
pectation and reality, Aleksandrov went into the post office and
there and then wrote with his left hand, to disguise his writing,
the next in his series of indignant letters.

The members of the Council felt uneasy. Who was this
Aleksandrov, a madman or a saint? The Rector asked in turn
for the opinions of those present, speeches began to hot up, the
law of escalation came into play. When it was the turn of the
shamelessly demagogical Galina Kachkina (Stukachkina,[1] as
she was lovingly called behind her back) and she began to trot
out all the familiar stuff about forgetting the class struggle,
grist to the mill of American imperialism and West German
revanchism, the impossibility of allowing such a cunning enemy
and such a double dealer within gunshot range of the students
etc., etc., suddenly the young man in the brown jacket got up
and, interrupting the unbridled flow of fanatical declamation,
said quietly:

'We are handing over this case to you in the Pedagogical
Institute so that you as teachers can take the appropriate steps.
We in the Committee do not consider it essential that Nikolai
Mikhailovich be dismissed. He teaches German grammar,
doesn't he? Well, let him teach it. Maybe he should be relieved
of administrative duties in the Department, but that's up to
you. If you dismiss him you deprive yourself and us of the
chance to educate him.'

Such was the mild KGB of 1962, in the golden days of
Khrushchev.

Aleksandrov not only remained a teacher, he even took his
doctorate and became a professor, and continued in the Institute to the respectable age of 70. But always he lived under this
sword of Damocles; at any time those anonymous letters could
be held against him.

And this is why Professor Aleksandrov, getting up with the
intention of asking a few questions, ends up against his will by
making a speech. He does not pillory Etkind, calling him a

[1] Familiar Russian *stukach* = an informer. [Tr.]

subversive or a terrorist, he keeps within the bounds of decency:
'We must scrutinize our own activities and those of our colleagues'; he chews over the same old cud as everyone else and
notices to his own satisfaction that he is talking utter gibberish.
'We need to pay attention not only to the academic, but also to
the political work of teachers.' The second sentence is no more
meaningful than the first and Aleksandrov can sit down with
the feeling of duty done and danger avoided. And indeed he
has not spoken against his conscience or said anything shameful;
he has not betrayed his comrade, but the authorities, too, seem
to be satisfied. They were not expecting a political speech from
him—others can do that—but simply that he should appear
among the speakers; he has played his part in the show. Everyone is happy.

Everyone is happy. And even I cannot hold it against Professor
Aleksandrov. Naturally I regret that he did not ask the questions
that were worrying him and demanding to be asked. But it is not this
that depresses me; it is that even an upright man who cares about
the truth can be transformed into a cautious self-centred individual.
And how can it be otherwise? One of the most frightening characteristics of the system is the way it distorts people and destroys
them as independent, self-directed personalities. And I am sad too
that not once in these meetings, neither in the morning nor in the
afternoon, was a human voice to be heard.

Perhaps in the evening?

ACT THREE

Here, however, I must break the unity of time and the chrono-
logical sequence of my story. In the one day of 25 April the Institute did not have time to do all it had been told to; the 'Big Council'
passed a resolution depriving Etkind of his title of professor, but it
did not have the right to strip him of his degree of Doctor of Philology. In law (and how we love the letter of the law!) a degree can
only be removed by the council which awarded it—in this case the
Council of the Philological Faculty (officially the Faculty of
Russian Language and Literature). This was where I had taken my
doctorate in October 1965, and taken it in unusual circumstances,

in the great Hall of the Institute, with a large audience, and two renowned academicians, V. M. Zhirmunsky and M. P. Alekseev, as examiners. In spite of the rather specialized nature of the subject—'Verse translation as a problem in comparative stylistics'—the public had reacted enthusiastically and it had all gone rather well.

The same Council, which ten years earlier had awarded the doctorate unanimously and with distinction, now had to remove it. The authorities had correctly concluded that this was a risky business: what if the Council jibbed at the thought of spitting in its own face? The more so as I had been a member, a very active member, for the last nine years. The Council contains professors of literature and linguistics who are far from easy to manipulate; many of them are independent, far-sighted people who value their sometimes international reputations. What was to be done? What if there was a hitch? It was too big a risk.

Someone—I do not know who—found a rather clever solution. A special Council was arranged, philological in a way, but not entirely—it would appear to be a meeting of academic specialists, although it stood higher in the administrative hierarchy than the Council it replaced. This was the Council of the Humanities. Naturally it would contain a few of the philologists, the most reliable, trusted, and docile ones. But there would also be other members, our own people—historians of the Communist Party and the Soviet Union, sociologists, philosophers, political economists, theorists of atheism. . . . On the 'Big Council' there were mathematicians, biologists, chemists (one of the chemists even spoke out for the prosecution), but here there would be nothing but arts people, and that simplified things. You can't be sure of physicists or geneticists, there's no knowing what they might blurt out, especially if you happen on a pupil of Academician Sakharov or a disciple of Academician Vavilov. Luckily everything went off all right, but the organizers felt a constant nagging worry. . . . But your professors of Party history or philosophy are right-thinking, submissive people, and what's more they are undoubtedly 'arts people' and therefore specialists. So everything was being done according to the rules—a beautiful job.

The meeting needed some preparation, the more so as the Council did not in fact exist and had to be specially created. This is why ten whole days (together with all the holidays, 1 May, 2 May, Saturdays, Sundays) went by between the removal of my title and the removal of my degree. At the beginning of May (I was in Moscow) my wife received the following very typical official message:

Efim Grigorievich,
You are invited to a meeting of the Institute Academic Council of the Humanities at 10 a.m. on May 8th 1974 in the Meeting Hall.
May 6th 1974   Academic Secretary of the Council
                                              (signature illegible)

My wife told me over the 'phone about this message and its unusual form of address (not even the basic 'Dear . . .'), and also about the telephone calls demanding my attendance at this Council. But I had every reason to fear arrest or at least provocations which would lead to my arrest, and I stayed in Moscow.

My wife went to the Council meeting; she arrived late, having had difficulty in finding the meeting hall. It appears, however, that only the very beginning of the meeting is missing from her transcript; in all probability the Rector, who is by now familiar to the reader, gave a brief account of the same old KGB report, and then the former Rector, arch-reactionary Aleksandr Ilich Shcherbakov, expounded the aim of the meeting, the removal of the academic degrees. The original idea had been simply to take away Etkind's doctorate, but then some fertile mind suggested that his candidate's degree could be removed too—even though it had not been awarded here but in the University in 1947. Perhaps this idea came from Shcherbakov himself, this is the sort of original thinking he is capable of. Then there was a speech from Pro-Rector Y. V. Kozhukhov (also familiar to the reader), and it was during this speech that my wife came in. Here is her transcript:

Transcript of the meeting of the Institute Council of the Humanities, May 8th 1974

Present: in the hall, 22 people; on the presidium, 4 people.

Yury Vyacheslavovich Kozhukhov (Professor of History, Corresponding Member of the Academy of Pedagogical Science, Academic Pro-Rector):
'. . . Heifets declared when questioned that Etkind liked his preface. Brodsky is the author of verse of a harmful and damaging nature; his verse has been used against the interests of the USSR. Etkind spoke at

Brodsky's trial, defending the "right of talented people to choose their own way of life". So in 1964 we have an ill-considered defence of the parasite Brodsky. Together with Heifets and Maramzin Etkind prepared an edition of Brodsky's verse. In his "Letter to Young Jews" Etkind drags in . . . etc. In 1968 a resolution of the Academic Council of the Institute declared: "Etkind's introduction to the two-volume *Masters of Russian Verse Translation* contains a politically harmful notion in the sentence about Russian poets who were deprived of the possibility of expressing themselves to the full in original writing. . . ."

'The analysis of a series of recent literary works by Etkind shows that he is continuing to publish his pernicious political ideas, skilfully introducing them into his books. In 1973–4 measures were taken in relation to Solzhenitsyn. But Etkind took no notice of this. He is doing considerable damage to the interests of our country. He is compromising his academic title.'

   Vitaly Ivanovich Kodukhov (Professor in the Department of Russian Literature):

'Etkind's activities are pernicious and the Academic Council was correct in its decision. We have been given a convincing picture of the subversive activities of a scholar. Etkind's ideology is clearly damaging. If he does not have firm Marxist convictions he is not in a position to carry on the struggle actively. Former Professor Etkind not only did not adopt a communist ideological position, but did not even attempt to adopt one. Communism is the road to the promised goal. It is not always a smooth road, and sometimes it is necessary to struggle. A Soviet scholar must be capable of carrying on this struggle. Not only did he not carry on the struggle with hostile ideologies, all his anti-Soviet activities showed that he is incapable of fruitful work. Because of his amoral and anti-patriotic acts, which are incompatible with the title of a Soviet scholar, Efim Grigorevich Etkind should be stripped of the degrees of Candidate and Doctor of Philology.'

   Aleksandr Ivanovich Khvatov (Professor, Head of the Department of Soviet Literature):

'Every day it is proved to us that there is no such thing as pure art or pure science. They are both fields in which the class struggle is carried on in an acute form. This struggle determines the laws of the contemporary world. If one considers the essence of the facts characterizing Etkind's activity as teacher and scholar, one sees clearly how great our responsibility is to the people when it is a question of ideological struggle. When one considers what started and impelled Etkind on the road that led him into the camp of our ideological enemies, one comes to the following conclusions:

'In the first place, social factors.

'In the second place, psychological factors.

Vanity, egoism, arrogance, unwillingness to listen to criticism, these were the attitudes accompanying his actions.

'One's intellectual position is inseparable from one's political level. There is a widespread delusion that it is possible to combine methodological unsoundness with a high professional standard. But Etkind's work can be characterized not only as methodologically unsound, but as professionally inadequate. What is the highest aim of research? The discovery of the truth. In his work of 1968 he distracted the reader from the discovery of historical truth and led him into disagreement with the historical process. He permitted himself the affirmation that Russian poets could not express themselves fully and therefore became translators. What, was Marshak hampered in the use of his talent? He is both a children's writer and a lyric poet. The evolution of Pasternak shows that in the last years of his work the specific weight of original work is much greater than that of translation . . . .'

A. D. Boborykin (correcting him): 'Marshak, you mean.'

Khvatov: 'Yes, of course, Marshak. Nikolai Zabolotsky wrote his best lyric poetry in the period which Etkind is writing about. And we can see the same thing in the creative destiny of other poets. Can we regard Etkind's research as scientific? No! Our knowledge of the material allows us to conclude that Etkind has indeed deprived himself of the right to the title of Soviet scholar. The professional level of many of his works and their contradictory character give us the right, nay the duty, to request that he be relieved of the degree of Doctor of Philology.'

Konstantin Markovich Levin (?):

'The great humanist Gorky taught us: "He who is not with us is against us." It has fallen to my lot to defend Soviet power with a gun in my hands. Our enemy's greatest weapon in the struggle has always been the ideological struggle. They needed people to carry this on, and they found them in the persons of Solzhenitsyn, Brodsky, and Etkind.

'I will confine myself to the letter to young Jews. In this letter Etkind calls on his reader to struggle against Soviet power with—or without— a gun in his hands. Can we tolerate such an enemy in our midst? How can we tolerate him when he calls for the overthrow of Soviet power? But Soviet power is extremely humane. Remember that Trotsky was exiled from the Soviet Union. We did the same to Solzhenitsyn. When you hear of these organic links with Solzhenitsyn you wonder how we have tolerated him so long.

'Etkind has acted as a traitor and an enemy. We must propose to the VAK that he be deprived of his Candidate's and Doctor's degrees.'

Anna Aleksandrovna Lyublinskaya (Professor, Head of the Department of Primary Education):

'I am not a literary specialist, but the facts have shocked me. This is real ideological subversion. And this subversion made its nest in our

Institute. I have worked here for fifty years. How we have fought to give young people a better education! How these young people have grown up before our eyes! And now we see people attempting to introduce discord, to introduce pernicious ideas. Etkind deliberately, obstinately, and arrogantly ignored the advice of his comrades. One can only be amazed at our patience. Etkind is not too stupid to understand, but he didn't want to understand. He cannot be allowed to represent Soviet scholarship.'

Furaev (Professor in the Department of the History of the CPSU): 'I too am not a literary specialist, but I have often had to do with hostile ideologies. Unfortunately certain comrades, especially the younger ones, were great followers of Etkind. There was a lot of talk about his brilliant lectures: had they seen the hidden meanings? Unfortunately no one can answer this. But we should. It is perhaps worth saying that in the opinion of some colleagues Etkind was politically illiterate. On the contrary, he had a political credo and he followed it unswervingly. He took an active part in the ideological struggle. But he was not on our side, he was on the other side of the barricade. I support the proposal of Aleksandr Ilich. We have no place for chameleons!'

Aleksandr Maksimovich Dokusov (Professor in the Department of Methodology, lecturing on Russian Literature):
'I shall try to be brief. We shall be unanimous in this matter. When it is a question of the psychological atmosphere in which such inveterate enemies as Etkind can work, then we must say that his works are unsound. In recent years we have become tolerant and complacent; in recent years we have grown lax and our vigilance has slackened. I call on everyone to reject tolerance and complacency and so to protect our students.'

Anatoly Ivanovich Domashnev (Professor, Head of the Department of German Philology, Dean of the Faculty of Foreign Language):
'On April 25th the Council of the Institute decided to dismiss Etkind and deprive him of the title of professor. After this there was a meeting of the Faculty of Foreign Languages. At this meeting the group discussed this question. The group decided unanimously that Etkind had soiled the title of professor. Various speakers observed that Etkind had lost his class consciousness. We needed to intensify our educational activity. The appropriate conclusions were drawn. As a scholar Etkind had not justified our hopes in him. As a member of the Party Committee I can declare that Etkind is unworthy of the title of professor and of his degrees, which he has not justified.

The Rector: 'There is one proposal: to remove from Efim Grigorievich Etkind the degrees of Candidate and Doctor of Philology and to take away from him the corresponding diplomas. Let us proceed to a secret ballot.'

Tellers are elected: A. I. Shcherbakov, Zinaida Ivanovna Vasilieva,

Sergei Ivanovich Ivanov (strangely enough, neither of the latter two is a member of the Council).

The count shows the motion to be carried unanimously.

This third Institute meeting had been better prepared than the others, both of which had inevitably left some room for improvisation. Here the parts had been distributed in advance. The linguist Kodukhov discusses general ideological problems ('If he does not have firm Marxist convictions'); the historian of Soviet literature Khvatov takes professional questions connected with Soviet literature and the work of Marshak (whom he gets mixed up with Pasternak, however. Obviously while he was composing his speech at home he realized the shakiness of his position, remembering the fate of Pasternak, and felt afraid of an unseen opponent who might cite the case of Pasternak against him. So Pasternak was hindering him, and at the meeting suddenly popped out unexpectedly— according to the same law which confused Eventov and Etkind) and the work of Zabolotsky ('Can we regard Etkind's research as scientific? No!'); the Jew Levin (whom no one on the staff of the Institute knows—he was obviously making a guest appearance) takes on the Jewish question ('In this letter Etkind calls on his reader to struggle against Soviet power with—or without—a gun in his hands'—what on earth does he mean, with or without?); the seventy-year-old specialist in primary education Lyubinskaya talks about the education of the younger generation ('How these young people have grown up before our eyes! And now we see people . . .'); Furaev, the historian of the Communist Party, deals with political literacy ('He had a political credo'—*had*! It's like a funeral); and then there is the literary methodologist Dokusov, an old hand at witch-hunting who earned the confidence of the KGB in days gone by—the only representative of the old generation of literary scholars and author of a book about Lermontov.

Digression concerning the Year 1949

> . . . Utterer of rubbish,
> Flabby, tèdious, heavy, rather stupid . . .
>
> PUSHKIN, Epigram.

The eighty-year-old Aleksandr Maksimivich Dokusov never showed the slightest sign of talent in his many years of teaching and research. Students tried to avoid his lectures and he himself in all probability realized how boring his books and articles were. So he made his career not so much by his scholarship as by the imitation of it known as 'the methodology of literary study', until the happy time of 1949 when the order went out 'to eliminate all bourgeois cosmopolitans and aesthetes', whose main aim was to 'disparage Soviet literature, hamper its further development, discourage talented writers who are capable of writing new works which are needed by the people. . . . Cosmopolitanism acts as a channel for reactionary bourgeois influences' (these are quotations from the speech of Anatoly Safronov at the Party Conference of the Writers' Union of the USSR, published in the journal *Znamya*, 1949, No. 2, pp. 168–76). This was a call for an anti-Semitic pogrom which turned into a crushing of the intelligentsia. Dokusov was in his element; at last he had the unexpected opportunity to avenge himself with impunity (or so it seemed at the time!) on all those towards whom he had until then felt hopeless and tormenting envy, the people he called flashy charlatans in public, while knowing all the time in his secret heart that the hateful Eikhenbaum, Zhirmunsky, Gukovsky, and Tomashevsky who took all his light were in fact brilliant minds bringing joy to the world around them. But around Dokusov everything was always grey, drab, and dreary. The articles he wrote in 1949 seethe with long-contained hatred which has suddenly come to the surface. But here's the rub—even hatred is incapable of lending a spark of talent to Dokusov's writing. Hate can illuminate the style of gifted people, giving it the sparkle of the unexpected and the appeal of spontaneity. But even in hate Dokusov was incapable of originality; his writing was still a patchwork of tedious clichés, and doubtless this only added to his fury. Thus in an article of 1949 with the highly original title 'Against the slander of great Russian writers' (*Zvezda*, 1949, No. 3), he attacks Tomashevsky and Eikhenbaum for their notes on the works of Pushkin and Lermontov; both critics had taken the liberty of indicating a number of foreign sources for these Russian classics. Quoting a passage from Tomashevsky to the effect that the motif of the hiring of a workman for three slaps in the face in Pushkin's 'Tale of a priest and his workman Balda' is related to one of the tales of the brothers Grimm, Dokusov writes:

One may perhaps pity the luckless interpreter of Pushkin, but one cannot pass over in silence such an interpretation of Russian literature. It has to be said loudly and clearly that the notes of B. Tomashevsky are a slander on the glorious name of Pushkin, a slander on the people who produced a poet whose name receives a tribute of devout respect from the best people in the world (p. 184).

And all this speechmaking in connection with Balda and his possible ancestry in the brothers Grimm! What a sense of proportion! But there's more to come:

Pushkin is Russian in every atom of his being; he lives the life of his people and his country. His work is rooted in the fundamental principles of the life of the people. . . . And to annotate Pushkin as has been done in the present volume means completely deforming Pushkin and disorientating the Soviet reader (p. 185).

Having finished with Pushkin and Tomashevsky, Dokusov moves on to Lermontov and Eikhenbaum. Like Tomashevsky, Eikhenbaum has hidden his pernicious ideas in his notes, but they come down to the assertion: 'Everything in Lermontov is foreign' (p. 185). But who is this Eikhenbaum? Listen: '. . . an inveterate formalist, aesthete and cosmopolitan', engaged in shameless self-advertisement; and later, in even more scathing terms: 'a "proudly" self-confessed cosmopolitan, a formalist and aesthete in the study of literature, who views our great Russian literature with deep contempt and even indifference' (p. 186). The exposure of Eikhenbaum finishes by virtually passing sentence on him:

Enough of this! The reader, like us, feels not only anger but repulsion at the slanderous brew of this 'learned' Lermontov scholar. . . . Is it not time to put an end to the work of these 'dry pedants' who 'interpret' our great popular writers? Is it not time to bring out into the open the pernicious meaning of their 'research' . . . ? (p. 189)

Do you know what these rhetorical flights of class hatred remind me of, this 'enough' and 'not only anger but repulsion' and 'is it not time to put an end to'? The prosecution speeches of Vyshinsky and Krylenko at the trials of the wreckers, the right-Trotskyite centre, and similar counter-revolutionaries. One is just waiting for Dokusov to exclaim in conclusion: 'Let the dogs die a dog's death!' But his orders did not extend to this.

Let us make an interim summing-up. Tomashevsky and Eikhenbaum are universally—and now not only in the decadent West but in the Soviet Union—recognized as classics of literary science, and even these same notes (not to speak of all their other writings) are reprinted from edition to edition. Meanwhile Dokusov, who defamed them, is living out his shameful life in obscurity, surrounded by general indifference and without even having acquired the dignity of old age: he keeps fussing about, putting his name forward, and until recently was ready to let the authorities walk all over him so long as they put up with him and did not push him into retirement. When he exclaimed on the 8th of May 1974: 'In recent years we have become tolerant and complacent; in recent years we have grown lax and our vigilance has slackened', he was giving vent to his nostalgia for 1949. As he proceeded in the old familiar way to unmask the enemy, Dokusov was showing himself and all of us that that year of glorious memory was still not forgotten or consigned to the scrap-heap of history.

And he was not wrong: if the KGB report accused me of methodological errors committed in 1949 and these errors were the very crimes of which Tomashevsky and Eikhenbaum had been found guilty, then one can conclude that it was not in vain that the Dokusovs had made their speeches. Their time had come round again. Once again they had been given the right to exclaim: 'Enough of this! . . . not only anger but repulsion at the slanderous brew . . .'

But even so. . . . Why did no one on the Academic Council, after listening to Dokusov's speech, get up and read out the criminal—yes, criminal—passages from his 1949 articles that I have quoted here? Why did no one say: 'Dokusov (and others of that ilk) committed a crime against humanity. He took part in a witch-hunt against our intelligentsia. He is an accomplice in murder. We are listening to him and tacitly giving him our approval. Dokusov has not changed, he is just as he was a quarter of a century ago, in 1949. Etkind, whom he is unmasking now, having previously unmasked Etkind's teachers, is not guilty of anything of the kind; he has not been involved in witch-hunts, murders, denunciations and pogroms.' But no one got up and said this. Everyone listened to Dokusov in silence, and silence meant agreement. And by agreeing with him in

1974, they were approving of his speeches and articles of 1949. They kept silent out of fear. They kept silent out of the habit of keeping silent. They kept silent out of lack of confidence in their power. I continue to think of this with a deep sorrow that borders on despair.

From a professional point of view, too, it is worth taking a look at this meeting of a 'special' Council called to establish the scientific unsoundness of a former professor's work. There are speeches from a psychologist, a historian of the Party, specialists in the Russian language, in primary education, in Soviet literature (Khvatov has written and continues to write about Sholokhov), in the methodology of Russian literature. But I got my candidate's and doctor's degrees not for Russian grammar or even the study of Sholokhov; I wrote about the novels of Zola and comparative stylistics, about the theory of poetic translation and the structure of verse. Not a word is said about science, only Professor Khvatov declares emotionally that 'the highest aim of research' is 'truth', whereas Etkind 'distracted his reader from the discovery of historical truth', and that 'the professional level of many [not all, however!] of his works and their contradictory character give us the right, nay the duty, to request that he be relieved of the degree of Doctor of Philology' (it seems he allowed me to remain a Candidate).

I was not too upset by this meeting; among the participants there was not a single scholar of any value, not a single person for whom I felt any respect or affection. Among the arts faculty of the Institute I have quite a lot of dear and trusted friends; a speech by any of them would have been a heavy blow to me—though I was prepared even for this. But fate preserved me from this additional pain. My friends stood firm. The consciousness of this integrity— albeit silent—is even now capable of comforting me. I am not particularly demanding.

(My wife, however, *was* upset. All the way home her mind was filled with bitter reflections: Heavens, how feeble! It's pathetic, in Leningrad, in a highly distinguished Institute bearing the name of Herzen, a lot of old men (most of them were indeed getting on) sitting in the semi-darkness, boring, bad-tempered people exciting one another, getting all worked up, feeling themselves protected by strangers who clearly belong to the authorities, realizing their total impunity and trotting out a load of malicious, boring rubbish. Even she, who had a personal interest in the case, found the clichés unbearably tedious. And not a word about the case itself; if they were set on a witch-hunt, they might at least have done their homework and gone over one of his lectures or articles. How feeble! How pathetic!)

For the first time in our university history, it seems, this meeting of the Council of the Humanities decided to take away the degree of doctor (and even of candidate) from a scholar who was neither a plagiarist nor a bribe-taker. The Ministry (the VAK) was surprised and taken aback, and for a long time did not confirm the decision. I wonder if the confirmation came in the end. I do not know; I had left by then.

ACT FOUR

It was 3 p.m. on 25 April; all the members of the Writers' Union Secretariat who could be scraped up from the four corners of the Soviet Union, had gathered at the Mayakovsky Writers' House; one had been brought from Georgia, another from the Crimea, a third from Moscow. They already knew why they were there and were glancing at one another, looking for the two people whose broad backs they were hoping to hide behind: Fyodor Abramov and Daniil Granin. Alas, neither of them was to be seen. What a pity—it would have been nice to share the responsibility with them. Poor show on their part, very uncomradely. In Moscow now, when they were expelling Lidia Chukovskaya, Valentin Kataev came specially to town to take part in the unpleasant process, old and ill as he was; naturally everyone else felt better for his presence, the rest of them were all small fry, not a single genuine writer among them, let alone anyone famous—Norovchatov, Agnia Barto, and so on. . . . Valentin Kataev displayed a sense of group responsibility, he's a man with a conscience. He understands that the Party and the Government didn't make him famous for nothing. He couldn't leave his comrades in the lurch, so he overcame his old age and his bad health and didn't even worry about the stupid things that the Western press was bound to say about him—after all, what does it matter if you're called an executioner or an assistant executioner once or twice, it doesn't stick and you'll have helped your side and not let them down at a difficult time. But what about these lords of creation? One of them is clinging to some Caucasian conference—just look at him, the specialist on the working class! A sly fox he is, and stuck up to boot. And the other one simply refused his invitation with disgust—work out your own salvation, I'm not going to take part in your filthy dealings. And now we've no support, no one to hide behind. You can't expect to hide behind Kholopov: he may be First Secretary of the Leningrad Union, our Kholopov, and even chief editor of *Zvezda*, but you can't pretend he's a writer, he's nothing like a Kataev. And we need a Kataev, we really do. At least the egghead intelligentsia is represented—we have Vladimir Orlov. He is known all over the world as the long-standing editor of the 'Poet's Library' and of the works of Blok—let's hope he will behave properly and follow the Party line (even though he's not a Party member). He has every reason to dislike Etkind, after all it was really Etkind who threw a bomb into the 'Poet's Library' and spoilt Orlov's career; he was relieved of his editorship because of a sentence of Etkind's, he hasn't forgiven him yet and he won't forgive him now. But you can never tell with these intellectuals. Maybe he will have been reading too much Blok and will suddenly up and say what he really thinks. And what he really thinks is this (it's not hard to guess, since they are all thinking the same): 'We've been grovelling long enough to big despots and little despots; we are still ashamed to remember the way in this very place thirty years ago we unanimously supported a brutal hatchet-man and drove out a great poet and a major prose-writer, Anna Akhmatova and Mikhail Zoshchenko, the way we listened in shame-faced silence to the stammerer Mikhalkov slandering Boris Pasternak and then voted for the exclusion of this great poet too, and the way we contributed to the hounding of Iosif Brodsky and failed to stand up for Grigory Gukovsky as we had earlier failed to stand up for Benedikt Livshits, David Vygodsky, Sergei Spassky, and many, many more who were our pride and joy and whom we allowed them to murder. And what is Etkind accused of? Knowing Solzhenitsyn? Supporting Brodsky? How stupid and ridiculous! Writers can't be expelled from a writers' organization for things like that. And all the rest is even more stupid and even more ridiculous, unproved and unsupported allegations; you don't come to a writer with that sort of amateurish stuff, it's like a provincial detective story.' That is what you might expect from Vladimir Orlov or he might even get really bold and start quoting his beloved Blok, something along these lines:

The philistine rabble, like all other human groups, only progresses very slowly. Thus, for instance, although over the last few centuries the human brain has swollen to the detriment of all our other organic functions, people have only had the wit to set apart in the state one organ—censorship—for the protection of their world as expressed in the forms of the state.

He may remember too that not long before his death Blok quoted with reverence the lines from Pushkin about freedom, both personal and political:

> . . . and not to bow
> Your conscience, thought or neck to rank and power . . .

Vladimir Orlov was gloomy and inscrutable. Together with the others, he went down to the restaurant before the meeting and took a swig of brandy to give himself courage.

Among the members of the Secretariat there is one other from whom there is an outside chance of hearing something unplanned: Mikhail Dudin. He is a romantic and a poet—can a poet be programmed? He is a soldier, and those who fought with him on the Hanko peninsula[1] remember his cheerful bravery. What if he should blurt out in his soldier's way something quite unpoetic? Translated into literary language it might read something like this: 'Get lost, the lot of you . . . I don't want anything to do with your schemes, my good name means more to me than all your promises. Commit murder if you like, but not with my hands.'

The secretary of the City Committee of the Party, Boris Andreev, glanced around rather uneasily at the writers' leaders sitting round the table. (He, Andreev, is hardly likely to remember Pushkin's words, 'not to bow . . .', but they all remember them.) There's the talkative Gleb Goryshin, a prose-writer of the new generation that is not yet paralysed and dumb with fear. Then there's the lyric poet Semyon Botvinnik; there was trouble with him before, we promoted him to the Secretariat, counting on his ambition and docility, but what if he, a Jew and not a Party member, should suddenly forget the anniversary edition that he has been promised and act against instructions? Etkind is not here, he

[1] The southernmost point of Finland, scene of fighting in 1942.

has pleaded illness; in one sense that is a good thing—with him here they might have shrunk from mauling and abusing their recent colleague, particularly since it is a closed meeting and everyone has sworn not to divulge the proceedings. In another way it is dangerous: might not these unreliable Orlovs, Goryshins, and Botvinniks demand a postponement until the victim is well enough to come and defend himself? Technically they would be in the right and it would be hard to answer them.

The meeting begins. First of all the chairman reads out a letter:

To the Secretariat of the Leningrad Writers' Organization.
Dear Comrades,
A heart ailment prevents me from attending today's meeting of the Secretariat, at which G. K. Kholopov tells me my case will be discussed. I hope that the Secretariat will postpone this discussion until I recover. I know of no case in the history of the Writers' Union at which the fate of a writer was decided in his absence.

Is it possible for an official hearing to consider accusations against a member of an artists' union without the participation of the accused? Is it possible for this member of the union not to be given the chance to defend himself? The right of defence is the most elementary right of any human being, no matter at what level he is being tried.

April 25th 1974   E. Etkind

There is a short pause.

'It is only with difficulty that we have gathered a sufficient number of Secretaries', says Kholopov. 'It is the end of April; in a week's time we should risk being inquorate. I think it would be undesirable to postpone the meeting.'

The secretary of the City Committee looks on approvingly. Likewise the discreet young men from the Big House (which is visible through the window). The writers sit staring at the table. Kholopov starts speaking again.

There follow the official minutes, which include the text of a KGB report; this is similar to the one given to the Academic Council, but differs from it in being more fully developed, with long quotations from interrogations and attempts at a more convincing argument—after all it is meant for writers!

Minutes of the Meeting of the Secretariat of the Leningrad Section of the Writers' Union of the RSFSR, 25 April 1974.
The meeting begins with a factual report from G. K. Kholopov, First Secretary of the Leningrad Section and chief editor of the journal

Zvezda. He states that he will begin with 'documents submitted by the Provincial Committee of the Party'. Then he reads out the official text.

REPORT

Etkind came to the notice of the KGB in 1969 for being in contact with Solzhenitsyn and aiding and abetting him in his hostile activities.

In the course of the verification of these facts it has been established that Etkind has indeed been acquainted with Solzhenitsyn for more than ten years, has had regular meetings with him, and has given him practical assistance in his anti-Soviet activities. He read all of Solzhenitsyn's anti-Soviet publications, which are not published in the USSR, and over a long period kept in his apartment two copies of *The Gulag Archipelago*. Through Solzhenitsyn Etkind was acquainted from 1963 with Elizaveta Denisovna Voronyanskaya, who over a period of ten years typed nearly all of Solzhenitsyn's writings, including *The Gulag Archipelago*.

Etkind was on good terms with Voronyanskaya, and received from her various works of Solzhenitsyn which are unpublished in the Soviet Union. In August 1973, Voronyanskaya, interrogated at the State Security Headquarters, declared:

'. . . when Solzhenitsyn came to Leningrad in 1971, I can't remember the exact date, he made arrangements to remove a number of pages from two copies of "Archip" [*The Gulag Archipelago*], and entrusted the task to me. It was then that I discovered that S. had given two copies to E. G. Etkind, living in Leningrad at the address: Flat 17, 6 Aleksandr Nevsky Street. Etkind brought me personally his two copies of "Archip", and I removed the pages indicated by the author. There were about 200 of them. I returned the two shortened versions to Etkind.'

The fact that Etkind had in his keeping *The Gulag Archipelago* is also confirmed in the declaration of L. A. Samutin, a former Vlasovite, previously tried for treasonable activities. . . . Samutin was on good terms with Voronyanskaya, and Solzhenitsyn knew about their collaboration in hostile activities. In his statement Samutin declares:

'. . . several times in the years 1970–1972 Voronyanskaya mentioned letters which she sent to Solzhenitsyn or received from him by way of Professor E. G. Etkind or his wife during their visits to Moscow. Samutin had heard from Voronyanskaya that Solzhenitsyn had several times stayed at Etkind's apartment during his visits to Leningrad. Voronyanskaya told me at the beginning of 1973 that Professor Etkind had read Solzhenitsyn's works including *The Gulag Archipelago*, one part of which she thought to have been at one time in Professor Etkind's keeping. . . . The closeness of Voronyanskaya's relations with Professor Etkind is shown by the fact that in the summer of 1970 Voronyanskaya was living at Etkind's *dacha*.'

There are other indications of Etkind's hostile activities. At the beginning of April in the current year, in connection with one of the criminal affairs concerning the copying and distribution of documents containing slander against the Soviet state and social system, the Committee for State Security carried out searches which resulted in the confiscation of many of the above-mentioned documents.

In particular there were searches at the apartments of Maramzin and Heifets [both born in 1934], members of the Union group[1] of the Leningrad section of the Writers' Union. During these searches there was confiscated from Maramzin the so-called 5-volume collection of Brodsky's verse [about 2,000 pages], ready for distribution, and from Heifets a preface to the said collection entitled 'Iosif Brodsky and our generation'. In this preface the author slanders the internal and external policies of the CPSU, alleging that the non-recognition of Brodsky's works in the USSR bears witness to the lack of creative freedom in our country.

In his preface Heifets writes: [I omit the quotations from the preface, as they are given in Chapter 6 below].

Apart from this preface there was also confiscated from Heifets a manuscript document of which Etkind is the author. This document is a review of the above-mentioned preface.

In his review Etkind, speaking favourably of the political direction of Heifets' preface, recommends him to take into account the 1956 events in Hungary, which in his view bear witness to the anti-democratic nature of the Soviet state and were a turning point in Brodsky's writing. . . . Etkind writes:

'Just think, there had been the 20th Congress, the truth had been told, everyone's eyes had been opened on their own past and even on the true nature of our victories, and then suddenly it was bombs and ropes on the other side and tanks and machine-guns on this. Budapest awakened a disgust for imperialism, but also a feeling of hopelessness. After the 20th Congress it came as an immense shock. Iosif Brodsky is right to refer to it. But 1968? Everything that had been said at the 20th and 22nd Congresses had already been forgotten, the fateful affair of Kirov[2] had already been consigned to the dustbin, and the good-hearted tyrant N.K. had long ago been put in his place. In a context like this you couldn't really be surprised by the tanks in Prague.'

On being questioned as a witness in the above-mentioned criminal affair, Etkind confirmed that he was the author of this review and that he

---

[1] See note, p. 33 above.
[2] Sergei Kirov, a popular leader of the CPSU, was murdered on 1 Dec. 1934; this was the signal for an immense wave of 'red terror'. It later transpired that this murder was set up by Stalin in order to get rid of his enemies.

understood that in his preface Heifets was expressing disagreement with various aspects of the policy of the CPSU and the Soviet Government. He further declared that he had never made a secret of his negative attitude to the entry of Warsaw Pact troops into Czechoslovakia in 1968.

Under questioning, Heifets stated that Etkind had liked the preface.

It is well known that E. was closely connected with Brodsky, who emigrated from the USSR to Israel in 1972 and now lives in the USA.

Brodsky is the author of verse of an ideologically pernicious and damaging nature, he was in constant touch with foreigners, passed on his verse to them, and slandered the Soviet Government and the social system. The said verse and statements of Brodsky were actively used by bourgeois propagandists to the detriment of the interests of the Soviet Union.

By openly declaring his relations with Brodsky, Etkind was attempting to impress writers and young intellectuals as a person of 'independent' views.

Etkind spoke in defence of Brodsky at his trial, defending, as he put it, 'the right of talented people to choose their own way of life'.

In March 1964, at a meeting of the Secretariat of the Leningrad section of the Writers' Union, the behaviour of E. and others, expressing itself in 'the thoughtless defence of the parasite Brodsky', was unanimously condemned. E., however, did not admit that his speech at the trial was harmful, and reacted negatively to the criticism of the Secretariat.

In this way Etkind, together with Heifets and Maramzin, took part in the preparation and diffusion of the ideologically pernicious verse of Brodsky.

E.'s hostile activity is also shown by the fact that he wrote and had distributed a letter entitled: 'Open Letter to Young Jews wishing to emigrate.' This letter gives a distorted image of the nationalities policy of the CPSU and contains appeals to Jews to struggle for change in the existing order not from abroad, but from within the USSR. In particular the letter says:

'The fact that you are enjoying foreign democratic freedoms will not introduce a multi-party system in your own country, nor will it bring back Pavel Litvinov[1] from exile.

'Foreign freedoms are not needed for the work you have to do. They will not help either you or your society.

'Struggle, but here, not there. One independent word spoken at home is worth more than big demonstrations outside the Soviet Embassy in Washington.'

[1] Physicist and well-known champion of human rights in the Soviet Union; he was sentenced to five years' exile in Siberia for taking part in a demonstration in Red Square on 25 Aug. 1968.

Further it has been established that Etkind uses his social position as a writer and scholar and teacher in an establishment of higher education in order to drag into his literary works views which contradict the principles of Marxism-Leninism.

In 1968 the Bureau of the Provincial Committee discussed the question of 'the gross political error committed by the editorial board of the "Poet's Library" in publishing the 2-volume *Masters of Russian Verse Translation* with an introduction by Etkind'.

The resolution of the Bureau notes that 'in 1968 the editorial board of the "Poet's Library" published a 2-volume *Masters of Russian Verse Translation*, the introduction to which, written by the Leningrad scholar and Doctor of Philology Etkind, contains not only tendentious judgements on particular poet-translators, but the politically pernicious allegation that social conditions in our country, particularly in the years between the 19th and 20th Congresses, did not allow Russian poets to express themselves to the full in original writing. Such statements by the author of the introduction are nothing but falsifications of the literary history of our country, and show a desire to put forward a false idea concerning the absence of freedom for artistic creation in the USSR, and to distort the objective picture of the development of socialist culture and blacken Soviet reality.'

In the resolution of the Bureau the administration of the Herzen Pedagogical Institute was asked to discuss this gross political error of Etkind's at a meeting of the Academic Council.

However, as is shown by the analysis of a number of Etkind's literary works, he has kept to his old positions, in spite of the criticism of his politically pernicious ideas and judgements. It is easy to find ideological and methodological errors in such works of his as *Talking about Verse*, *Four Masters*, and *Russian Poet-Translators from Trediakovsky to Pushkin*.

In 1972 in his book *Bertolt Brecht*, Etkind put forward a tendentious account of Brecht's work, distorting the true evolution of his world view. Thus he asserted that Brecht only came to the scientific understanding of the 'class structure of capitalist society' at the beginning of the 1930s and that 'in the earlier years Brecht's protest was purely speculative'. This tendentiousness in his account of Brecht's work caused Etkind to be criticized in *Literary Russia* (21.12.72, article by Dymshits).

Preventive and warning measures were repeatedly taken towards Etkind: in 1949 as a result of the methodological errors contained in his dissertation Etkind was relieved of his literary lectures and obliged to move to the Tula Pedagogical Institute; in 1964 he was subjected to criticism for his incorrect speech in favour of Brodsky; in 1968 he was rebuked at the Academic Council of the Herzen Institute for his tendentious accounts of individual poet-translators in his introduction to

Master of Russian Verse Translation; in 1973-4 various measures were taken in connection with Solzhenitsyn and his circle.

Etkind should have understood all this as a warning against inadmissible hostile activities. However, he drew no personal conclusions from it.

Thus, over a long period of time, Etkind has deliberately engaged in ideologically pernicious and hostile activities, causing considerable damage to the interests of our country. Being as he is a Soviet writer, a scholar, and a teacher in higher education, Etkind is acting as a political double-dealer and compromising these honourable titles.

In this connection it seems appropriate to consider the question of the impossibility of his working as a professor in the Herzen Institute and the inappropriateness of his continuing as a member of the Writers' Union of the USSR.

So much for the Report. Kholopov continues to speak on his own account, waxing indignant and quoting from Case No. 24, which has been shown him at the Big House:

'Look at the conspiratorial life led by Etkind. Here is another statement by Voronyanskaya (extract from Case No. 24): "After destroying my copy I met Etkind in his apartment and told him about Solzhenitsyn's instructions concerning his copies of *The Gulag Archipelago*. He informed me that he was aware of them and would shortly destroy his copies. Some time later . . . when I called on Etkind, I asked if he had destroyed the copy of *The Gulag Archipelago*. Etkind declared that all the copies had been destroyed and not a single page was left. I believed him and informed Solzhenitsyn of this." Here is another quotation, from the statement of L. A. Samutin to the KGB on 2.4.74: "The day after Voronyanskaya's funeral, knowing about her death, I telephoned Etkind. On the following day, August 30th, I met Etkind at the morgue and went with him in his car to the cemetery and there, when I was alone with him for a few moments, I told him about the confiscation of Voronyanskaya's papers. To his question about the fate of her private archive I answered: 'They've got it.' " '

Having read out these extracts from the secret files of the Big House, Kholopov continues:

'And now a few last words about the other document, entitled "Open Letter to Young Jews wishing to emigrate". The story of this letter is a curious one. It was sent to the Visa and Registration Department by a man who wrote that a letter to those wanting to emigrate to Israel was being passed around town. According to him the author was the writer Efim Etkind.

'In a conversation with Boborykin, Etkind admitted to being the author of this letter. The letter takes the form of a dialogue with erring souls. Etkind plays the part of the spiritual father or the shepherd putting his flock on the right path.

'What is it that he calls for, this man who owes everything to Soviet power and above all the honourable titles of scholar, professor and writer? He calls for a struggle against this power. "Struggle, but here, not there." And he gives this advice: "Emigration is only permissible in cases of extreme necessity, under the threat of physical destruction." '

(G. K. Kholopov finishes with a quotation from Brezhnev's speech at the congress of the Communist Youth League—the one about garbage.)

Having finished, he calls on each of the Secretaries to speak; they all have their say one after another, each in his turn.

Vasily Nikolaevich Kukushkin:
'It is saddening to have to deal with affairs like this. Etkind occupied a position of great trust, he was treated with respect in all our organizations. I am shocked by the incident involving the preface to the "Poet's Library", as a result of which many people were punished. What is the origin of all this? By his own actions and behaviour Etkind has placed himself outside our Writers' Union.

'All the letters which were written against Soviet power and the Party, were written from within the union group. Think of the affairs of Brodsky, Betaka, Ben, Maramzin, and Heifets. It is a very serious matter; things are not right in our union group. For instance Burov, Boitsov, Frantishev, all of them war veterans and experienced journalists, have been refused admission. I consider that Etkind has by his own actions placed himself outside the writers' organization.'

Mikhail Aleksandrovich Dudin:
'If one thinks of Etkind's introduction to the "Poet's Library" volumes and this letter to young Jews, it is clear that we have here a repulsive case of nationalism, from which it is a short step to fascism. This Zionism is visible in every line. It has nothing in common with the programme of the Writers' Union. Etkind by his own actions places himself outside our organization.'

Vladimir Vasilyevich Toropygin:
'Recently I returned from a visit to Canada and the USA. Journalists asked me a large number of different questions, including some about Solzhenitsyn. I replied that his activities were damaging to the policies of our state. Etkind's activities are like the dealings of Solzhenitsyn; this man should not be in the ranks of our Union of Writers.'

Vasily Grigorievich Bazanov:
'The main thing in my opinion is not the fact that Etkind used to meet Solzhenitsyn. Solzhenitsyn was a member of the Writers' Union and was published in *Novy Mir*.[1] When Solzhenitsyn became an internal émigré who sent his anti-Soviet productions abroad, that was when it became a serious matter. What shocked me was the letter to young Jews and the review of Heifets' preface. It is not our habit to be very strict with people if they go astray. But Etkind understood nothing. He was not stripped of his doctorate for errors in the preface to the "Poet's Library" collection, we tried to make him understand that he was wrong, and we printed his books—*From Trediakovsky to Pushkin*—his articles, etc. He remained a professor and a Doctor of Philology. These documents have made a powerful and very painful impression on me. I agree with the previous speakers that Etkind's actions and behaviour contradict the statutes of the Writers' Union and are incompatible with further membership of the Union.'

I. I. Vinogradov:
'I consider that this is a deliberate collective activity. Etkind shared the views of Heifets and even strengthened his anti-Soviet tendencies.

'The editing of the 5-volume Brodsky is a considerable blow in the ideological struggle. The letter to the young Jews is an astounding document. It seems that life is impossible for Jews here! It's a clear call to struggle here, not there.

'Etkind cannot remain a member of the Writers' Union.'

Gleb Aleksandrovich Goryshin:
'I share the views already expressed. The most unpleasant thing of all is the review of the preface to Brodsky's poems. Brodsky's poems are not worth the halo that is given them. We see here the insatiable ambition of Brodsky and Heifets, in which Etkind too had a part.

'We must not confuse Etkind's case with Solzhenitsyn's. Solzhenitsyn is rapidly being forgotten, he no longer really exists. It is a pity that Etkind is not here. Can we not meet him and tell him all this to his face? There is no doubt that he has placed himself outside the Writers' Union.'

I. I. Vinogradov:
'Shouldn't the union group be disbanded? It's like a union within the Union.'

Vladimir Nikolaevich Orlov:
'The thing that most depresses me in this affair is the moral aspect. A

[1] An important monthly literary review. The title means 'New World'. [Tr.]

great deal was done to help Etkind to understand. Take this "Poet's Library" incident—he ruined an important cultural undertaking. He was given the opportunity—a generous opportunity, more generous than he deserved—to reflect about our ideology. It is curious that Etkind thinks one thing but writes another; he writes one thing, and publishes another. By his own actions he has placed himself outside the Writers' Union; our only course is to expel him from the Writers' Union, since he is not a Soviet writer.'

Anatoly Nikolaevich Chepurov:
'The documents show Etkind in a very poor light. The letter and the article and the notes [?] all show that Etkind is our ideological adversary. Think how many people had to shoulder the blame for the errors in the "Poet's Library", while Etkind came out of it unscathed. He did not recognize his errors, but repeated them at greater length in his "Letter to Young Jews". This is deliberate activity, the work of a group.

'Etkind's continued membership of the Writers' Union is unacceptable.'

Semyon Vladimirovich Botvinnik:
'Not long ago we had a talk in the Secretariat with some young people who wanted to be published, but we explained to them that there was no point in publishing them. In general our work with young people has grown slack. Etkind is a teacher and he knows the measure of responsibility that a teacher bears towards the young. This is a direct infringement of the statutes of the Writers' Union. Even so it would have been better if Etkind had been present, and the rest of our respected Secretaries also.'

Boris Nikolsky:
'I was at the meeting of the Academic Council of the Herzen Institute, where Etkind's activities were vigorously and unanimously condemned. It was decided to relieve Etkind of his job and his professorial title. I was amazed at Etkind's letter to the Academic Council, where he speaks of "isolated slips and inaccurate expressions" in particular letters.

'Heifets, Brodsky, Ben, and Maramzin make up the union group—without them he would have had no one to talk to, they are his natural environment. Apart from our decision about Etkind, we need a recommendation on the union group. It should be disbanded.

'What most shocks me in Etkind's activities is that a certain fraction of our intelligentsia puts forward *its own* opinion as the opinion of a whole generation, a whole people. This is a deliberately chosen road of ideological struggle. I consider that Etkind should be expelled from the Writers' Union.'

The decision is unanimous.

Everything is clearer here than at the Institute; it had obviously been decided that the writers needed fuller information, whereas the professors would swallow anything that was put in front of them and the mere teachers in the Faculty would be satisfied with a brief résumé, with no quotations from 'Case No. 24' and no police reports. And they were quite right: the teachers swallowed the résumé, the professors the shortened version, and the writers licked their lips over the detailed report with its criminal details. (It's interesting to wonder what would have happened if it had been the other way round? Would they still have swallowed it? I think the result would have been exactly the same.)

Well then, the manly Dudin did not revolt after all, the educated Orlov did not quote Blok or Pushkin, the timid Botvinnik did not keep quiet, and Goryshin the lover of truth did not refuse to take part in the execution. It all went like a concert. Boris Andreev had no need to worry. Indeed, it's possible he didn't worry at all. It is only I, telling the story to the uninitiated, who have suggested this as the most likely hypothesis. But perhaps the KGB and Andreev are cleverer than I supposed in their stage management? They know the irresistibility of fear and the invincible magnetic power of words such as 'aiding him in his hostile activities', 'in the course of the verification of these facts', 'interrogated at the State Security Headquarters', 'a former Vlasovite, previously tried for treasonable activities', 'their collaboration in hostile activities', 'slander against the Soviet state and social system', 'carried out searches', 'the confiscation of many of the above-mentioned documents', 'the author slanders the internal and external policies of the CPSU', 'under questioning', 'to the detriment of the interests of the Soviet Union', 'falsification', 'a political double dealer'. . . . Indeed,

> Words such as these
> make coffins want
> To stride about
> On four oak legs.[1]

One must assume that the Secretaries, having taken Dutch courage, only heard 'words, words, words' and did not delve into their meaning. And what good could the meaning do them? The bold Dudin was obliged to gabble something, once the chairman had called on him and the people from the City Committee and the

---

[1] A quotation from the poet Vladimir Mayakovsky. [Tr.]

KGB were staring expectantly at him. What did he say then, the brave Dudin?

'If one thinks of Etkind's introduction to the "Poet's Library" volumes and this letter to young Jews, it is clear that we have here a repulsive case of nationalism, from which it is a short step to fascism. This Zionism is visible in every line. . . .'

It is visible in every line of this text that Dudin has not read anything, or even heard anything, and that he has clearly overdone the Dutch courage. He accuses me of nationalism and then, more precisely, of Zionism. On what grounds? On the basis of two documents mentioned in his speech (if that is the word for it). In the 'introduction' (i.e. the article 'Verse Translation in the History of Russian Literature') there could not be any trace of Zionist ideas, even if the author had been a fanatical Zionist; the Provincial Committee had accused the author of libelling Soviet poets by declaring that being in a certain period 'deprived of the possibility of expressing themselves in original work' they had chosen to translate the foreign classics. Where's the 'short step to fascism' and the Zionism here? The second document is the 'Letter to Young Jews' —I shall have more to say about this later. For the moment let me just say that even in the KGB 'Report' it is stated that the author dissuades Jews from emigrating to Israel. Are Zionists really opposed to the emigration of Jews? No, call it what you like, but not Zionism. Perhaps even anti-Zionism. At first I imagined that Dudin was deliberately talking nonsense so as to be more easily refuted and generally so as to make the whole meeting look like a parody. Perhaps he had discovered a new form of resistance, resistance by nonsense? Alas, no! Dudin has simply heard the word 'Jews' and probably 'appeal' as well, and the rest was the work of his half-drunk imagination.

In his verse Dudin paints a picture of himself as the fearless soldier, faithful friend, lover of truth, and devotee of virtue, justice, and honour:

> I want the thoughts and life-blood of my friends
> To flow through my uncompromising lines,
> That what I write should not insult with lies
> The consecrated silence of the grave,
> But like an equal join the honest ranks
> Of my good friends.

He constantly aspires—

> Like sinking stone
> Or soaring bird
> The battle done, to fight again,
> And to remain in the best sense
> True to myself,
> True to myself.

And so we see Mikhail Dudin being 'true to himself'.

Now he is a winner of state prizes, a deputy to the Supreme Soviet, a favourite subject of press panegyrics, a boon companion, and a Secretary of the Writers' Union—but has he remained a poet? Has he kept to the 'uncompromising lines' that so appealed to him in others when he aspired to join their 'honest ranks'?

It is hard not to recall another epigram, which, like all such popular sayings, goes straight to the heart of the matter:

> Union Secretary Dudin,
> Wrong is right and right is wrong;
> Son of Judas, Michael Dudin,
> Sell your brother for a song.

Professor Bazanov is cunning and chooses the noble part. Please to take note that he is not too concerned by the fact that Etkind used to meet Solzhenitsyn, who was a member of the Writers' Union and was published in *Novy Mir*. What made 'a powerful and very painful impression' on him were two documents—the 'Letter to Young Jews' and the review of Heifets' preface. He never set eyes on either of these. If he had seen them he would have known that they are not documents at all, but private letters. The first is a letter addressed to my son-in-law, who was intending to emigrate. The second is a hand-written letter to Heifets and it concerns not a 'preface', but a rough draft, yes a *draft* of Heifets' article about Brodsky's poetry (poetry, incidentally, which is completely devoid of any political content). Can a person be penalized for a letter, no matter what ideas it may contain? This would amount to penalizing thought. (Naturally this is a purely rhetorical question. We were not only expelled for letters, but put away and for long periods. The arrest of Solzhenitsyn and his correspondent Vitkevich in 1945, followed by spells in prison and labour camp, all this was the result of private letters. You may say the war and the Stalinist terror were to blame—neither of these exists today.)

Yes, in this letter it was asserted that Brodsky's generation was shaken by the 1956 events in Hungary, rather than by the 1968 occupation of Czechoslovakia. What is there that is criminal in this assertion? Agreed, I did not approve of the entry of Warsaw Pact troops into socialist Czechoslovakia. But, in the first place, no one approved of this occupation except the demagogues, who told lies at meetings knowing full well what they were doing, and the inveterate Stalinists (such as the dogmatist Cunhal and the literary pirate Sholokhov); we all remember the positions taken up by the Western communists, the Swedes, the French, the Italians, the British, the Spanish. . . . While not approving of this immoral deed, I remained silent. I remained silent because I had no desire to leave my native country. I expressed my opinion not in any wide-reaching propaganda, but in one private letter, in a single copy. What then made this deep and painful impression on Professor Bazanov? That people write letters to one another? That they permit themselves in these letters to say what he himself may think but dare not say aloud? I could understand Bazanov if his 'painful impression' were caused by the actions of the police, who in peace-time seize private letters, or by the actions of his colleagues who do everything the police tell them and pillory a writer for thoughts expressed in confidence to a third party. Does Professor Bazanov know that the French writer Louis Aragon expressed in public his indignant condemnation of the invasion of Czechoslovakia —in his article 'J'appelle un chat un chat'? And that this same writer Louis Aragon received from the Soviet government the Order of the October Revolution—several years after the article was published? Aragon is not a Soviet citizen, it is true. So this is the logic of it: if Aragon had been a Soviet subject he would have been expelled from the Writers' Union. But since he is a French subject he is rewarded with a decoration. And which decoration? The October Revolution. Bazanov knows all this very well, but he trots out the ritual speeches, playing the part assigned to him in the show and not worrying about the meaning of the words.

About the 'Letter to Young Jews' which also 'shocked' Bazanov, it has to be even more categorically stated that it provides no legal grounds for prosecution. In the first place it, too, is private. In the second place that one sentence which the KGB considered criminal has been given an arbitrary interpretation. I did indeed write: 'Struggle here, not there.' But what was I advising the young Jews to struggle for? For justice. Is the call to struggle for justice a criminal matter? Bazanov can say of course: 'Don't try and wriggle out of it, I know full well that there is no justice in our country and consequently you are calling on them to struggle against Soviet power.' Perhaps, but these would be Bazanov's words, not mine.

Perhaps this polemic comes a bit late in the day. I am writing from a safe refuge in France, looking out of the window at the magnificent and infinitely peaceful Savoy Alps. Isn't it a bit late to be arguing with Bazanov? What's more, my readers could say to me: 'You're in safety now. What's the point of talking in this roundabout way and presenting yourself almost as a supporter and defender of just Soviet power? You knew well enough that it is incapable of justice. In saying: "Struggle here, not there" for justice, you naturally meant "Struggle against Soviet power". In this case they were quite right to crush you. They were defending themselves and acting quite openly. Whereas you were being devious.'

This is a very important question. But it is not hard to answer.

Was I calling on the 'young Jews' to struggle for the overthrow of Soviet power? No. Was I a conspirator? No. My work was in literature, not politics. Is it my fault if every honest declaration in the Soviet Union takes on—against our will—an anti-Soviet meaning?

It is important to get one thing straight: I had not been acting illegally. To prove that I had would have called for solid legal evidence. Had I kept a copy of *The Gulag Archipelago*? Had I 'aided and abetted' the author? Perhaps. But the prosecution is obliged to provide evidence. There was no search; this copy was neither found nor seen by anyone. The testimony of the deceased Voronyanskaya is not proof; a confrontation between us was impossible. What if she was forced to give false statements? Even supposing that the KGB has tape-recordings of my conversations, the police do not have the right to use unlawful material of this sort. In any case, no tapes were ever produced. Even if I myself had confessed to being a conspirator, this would not have been enough for a condemnation, because, in modern times, even in the USSR, the personal confession of the accused is not accepted as proof. The only positive evidence is provided by my private letters. But all they tell us about is my opinions, not my actions. Indeed the police did not deal with me themselves, they preferred to act through the professors and writers. Neither the professors nor the writers, however, either demanded or obtained any proof—they simply took the word of the police investigators. The whole procedure is illegal. And it is this illegal, non-juridical punishment that concerns me. What was done to me yesterday by means of 'public opinion' can be done to anyone tomorrow. Behind me stood the shadow of Solzhenitsyn, behind this 'anyone' will stand another shadow—Nekrasov, Korshavin, Galich, now Etkind. Acquaintance, connections, aiding and abetting, reading works, passing them on to others. . . . No, I am not such an idealist as to appeal to the charter signed by the Soviet Union in Helsinki on 2 August 1975; in all probability this charter will remain a scrap of paper just like another charter previously signed by our delegates—the Declaration of Human Rights. Please God I turn out to be a bad prophet! At this point in my story I am not appealing for freedom of thought, but for something much less grand: a minimal respect for the proper legal procedure.

I am appealing, too, for one further thing: for my erstwhile compatriots to behave in a dignified way and in accordance with the demands of conscience. Let them at last realize that they are being shamelessly manipulated and that they have not only the right but the duty not to vote for something that they know nothing about, not to condemn what they have not read, not to pronounce sentence without calling for evidence. A multitude of professors, teachers, prose-writers, poets, and critics has filed past us. All of them without exception have let themselves be dragged into a criminally illegal trial grounded on the whims and dictates of the police. And yet each of them was a kind of juror at this trial. In countries such as France the public prosecutor has a hard time with juries: he has to convince them not so much by a display of rhetoric, let alone threats, as by systematic proof; he has to provide a convincing refutation of the defence, putting his more weighty evidence against theirs; he has to show them that the proposed punishment is appropriate and not excessively severe. The jury, after weighing up the pros and cons, gives its verdict. Such is the practice in democratic courtrooms.

The 'juries' we have seen are no more than a decoration. The verdict is given without consulting them—they are simply informed of the outcome; there is no proof, no defence, no accused even. Each of the 'jurors' has to pronounce judgement in public;

there is a sort of reciprocal guarantee, a blood-brotherhood between criminals. In such circumstances it does not matter what any one of the 'jurors' says; if he has not spoken 'against' this means he is 'for', and he too is bound by the blood-brotherhood. Vasily Kukushkin, Gleb Goryshin, and Semyon Botvinnik did not understand this devil's logic (perhaps they preferred not to understand it) when they agreed to speak, very decently too, more decently than the rest, but it was still speaking, they had fallen into the trap. No one wanted more from them than their recognition and participation. It is Pyotr Verkhovensky's old motto: 'bind the group with blood'.[1]

The 25th of April was nearing an end. From time to time came a short ring on the doorbell from one of my friends. Late that evening I left the house with a briefcase containing a toothbrush and a razor—it was unwise to stay the night at home and I decided to pretend to be leaving for Moscow, to turn up with a briefcase at the station, and then, by a side exit and side roads that I knew well, to make my way to the hospitable house where I had been offered a refuge. We all came out together, family and guests, and we were stunned by what we saw, even after our years of experience. The courtyard, with a little garden in the middle, was swarming with spies. One of them walked slowly towards me; he was an old friend of mine who was constantly hanging about under our windows or in the entrance hall, an elderly man with a stoop, a large flabby nose, and bags under his eyes—terribly easy to spot, you wonder why they take them on. I used to greet 'my' spy most days and sometimes on cold days I would invite him in for a cup of tea, but he, unabashed, would grunt something about his friend who would be out in a minute. 'Still waiting? Friend let you down again?' I would ask as I strode past, but he would just shiver and turn up his collar. This time he appeared out of the darkness, but I had no time to say anything to him because one of my companions laughed and pointed to another one scuttling off over the roof of the nearby garage; a third, a fourth, and a fifth were standing or walking to and fro at the entrance, round the corner and in the street. My daughter went off and got a taxi, one of them rushed after her, but we climbed in quickly and drove off, shaking off our pursuers. A few minutes later we were already at the inter-city telephone office telling our friends about the day's events. I had disappeared from home and was not to return there for some time—meanwhile the

In Dostoevsky's *The Devils*. [Tr.]

spies kept tags on my wife. For a few days I lived with friends, then I left for Moscow.

Such is the history of one day. There is a lot in it that the reader may not understand, so I shall recount a few episodes that preceded 25 April 1974. Then I shall return to what happened after this crucial day. If we regard this day as a given point on the axis of time, we shall first be moving left from it, into the past, and then right, into the future.

3

Justice (1963–4)

But I roam once again, sunk deep in thought,
down hallways, from the last interrogation
to the next one—toward that distant land
where there is neither March nor February.

BRODSKY, 'Sonnet', 1962, tr. G. L. Kline

Even before 1963 I had heard of the young poet Iosif Brodsky; the most inveterate sceptics were invariably enthusiastic about his poems. I had not yet seen anything he had written. In those days there was virtually no Samizdat. There were poems passed around by word of mouth (and thus inevitably sometimes in manuscript), but they were always political. Perhaps the best-known at this time were the strong and deliberately clumsy lines of Boris Slutsky, who in the name of a whole generation gave a poetic summing-up of the recent night of Stalinism:

> All were sleeping. Only sweepers
> Frenziedly worked,
> Tearing at the roots, scraping
> Deep down in the earth,
> As if to grub out
> From the calloused soil
> Of peremptory shouts
> And scribbled decrees
> The new traces of death
> And the older traces
> Of his thirty years' glory,
> Thirty years of disaster.

Brodsky was not a political poet; his poems were not copied out and passed from hand to hand. Once, however, I was given a few pages of his, and what I read made an immediate impression on me; for many days I could not get these bleakly monotonous, oppressive yet incantatory lines out of my mind:

> *The night-black sky shone brighter than his legs;*
> *He could not drift into dissolving dark.*
>
> That evening, sprawling by an open fire,
> We caught our first sight of the raven steed . . .
>
> So black was he that shadows made no stain;
> they could not dye him darker than he stood.
> He was as black as any midnight dark
> or any needle's fierce unfathomed heart—
> as black as the dense trees that loom ahead,
> as the tense void between the nested ribs,
> the pit beneath the earth where a seed lies.
> I know that here within us all is black—
>
> and yet he gleamed still blacker to our gaze!
> It was no more than midnight by my watch.
> He came no closer by the slightest step.
> Unplumbed obscurity lurked at his loins.
> His back had wholly vanished from our sight;
> no single spot of light now lingered there.
> The whites of his two eyes struck like twin blows.
> Their pupils were more terrifying still,
>
> with the strange leer of eyes in negatives![1]

Is it not astonishing that these terrifying lines about death are the work of a youth of twenty? That his imagination gave birth to such striking and paradoxical comparisons and metaphors? 'as black as . . . any needle's fierce unfathomed heart'. . . . A true poet! And what is more, he differed from every other poet I know in the modernity of his art; his writing followed on from that of Tsvetaeva, of Mayakovsky, of Khlebnikov, and above all of Mandelstam. He was solving new problems set by himself and the time he lived in. Soon I got to know other poems of his which were every bit as black as the raven steed:

[1] For this poem, as for the epigraph to this chapter, I am indebted to the translations of George L. Kline (Joseph Brodsky, *Selected Poems*, Penguin Books, 1973).

Death is both garden and gaol,
and all machines.
Death is all men on earth
with their hanging ties.

Death is the sum of our strength,
our labour and sweat.
Death is the blood in our veins,
our soul and flesh.

We'll not climb the hill again.
In our houses are lights.
We are not those who see them—
nor do they see us.

It cannot be said of such lines, as of the verse of many young poets, that they are riddled with literature, or at the other extreme that they stand outside all tradition. In them we see a mature combination of lived personal experience and thought with a subtle and concentrated literariness, an organic use of previous poetic forms. The poem dedicated to Anna Akhmatova demonstrated in a particularly powerful way this coupling of the momentary and the eternal, the classical and the deliberately contemporary, the musical and the conversational:

I have not seen, nor shall I see your tears,
I shall not hear the murmur of the wheels
bearing you off to trees and bay and through
a land that bears no monument to you.

In a warm room, without a single book,
no suitors there, for this is not their place,
resting your head upon your hand you'll write
in crooked lines about our troubled lives.

And you will utter these sad words: 'Dear God!
This curdled air is but the flesh of thoughts
that have abandoned their true destiny,
not a creation of Thy majesty.'[1]

---

[1] The translations (my own in the case of the last two poems) inevitably fail to match the quality of the originals. The English reader might get some idea of these by thinking of Yeats's late verse. [Tr.]

When the old Victor Hugo heard Baudelaire's poems, he exclaimed: 'Here is a new thrill!' In the rhythms, metaphors, and
sonorities of Brodsky there was this new thrill, the unfailing mark
of the true poet—there is no better word for it. Anna Akhmatova
heard it too; she chose the line 'in crooked lines about our troubled
lives' as the epigraph to her poem 'The last rose' (1962). This was
an honour accorded to few people; in the lyric poetry of her last
years her epigraphs came only from Horace, Pushkin, Annensky,
Blok, Tsvetaeva, and Baudelaire. What is more, her poem itself has
a deep meaning connected with the epigraph:

> Dear God! You can see I am weary
> Of reliving and dying and living.
> Take it all, but let me once more
> Breathe the freshness of this red rose.

A quatrain written in the same year is devoted to this same theme
suggested by Brodsky's line, the theme of the fate of the young
poets of the early 1960s:

> No more I'll grieve at my own fate,
> But God forbid I should see now
> The golden brand of failure set
> Upon a still unwrinkled brow.

Alas, this hope was not to be fulfilled: the unwrinkled brow was
soon to be clouded with bitterness, suffering, and despair. It was
stamped with the 'golden brand of failure', of reprobation.

It was in this way, in Akhmatova's epigraph, that the name Iosif
Brodsky first appeared in print, in the January number of *Novy
Mir*, 1963, apparently placed by Akhmatova on a level with the
names of her favourite poets. A few months later, however, it
appeared again, this time in the evening paper *Vecherny Leningrad*
for 29 November 1963. This was in an article entitled 'A Drone of
Literature', which began in this way: 'A few years ago a young man
appeared in Leningrad literary circles who called himself a poet.
He wore velvet trousers, and always carried the same briefcase
stuffed with papers. In winter he went around without a hat and
his red hair was sprinkled with snow. His friends called him simply
"Osya". But in other circles he assumed his full name—"Iosif
Brodsky".'

The article, signed by Lerner, Ionov, and Medvedev, depicts Brodsky as an ignoramus, a layabout and a parasite, who does his best to avoid socially useful activity, and spends the evenings in restaurants in the company of long-haired and dissolute young men and women, composing pessimistic little pieces about death or pornographic songs. He hobnobs with foreigners and riff-raff, he once attempted to steal an aeroplane and fly West, and he lives by sponging on his ancient parents. 'The likes of Brodsky', concluded the indignant authors, 'have no place in Leningrad.'

It was an ominous sign. Written in a not particularly well-educated or well-informed manner—for instance, the authors quote poems which are not Brodsky's work at all—the article was obviously inspired by circles close to the Big House, and contained charges concerning not only what one might call life-style, but also politics: the red-headed Osya should properly have been immediately arrested if he had really attempted to steal a plane and escape from the Soviet Union.

By this time I had already got to know him. Brodsky astonished me by his unceasing flow of short and long poems which he recited as if in a trance, his eyes half shut, and in such a deafening guttural chant that the windows shook. His delivery was as unusual as his poetry; it showed a frantic energy, the monotony was only rarely broken by a raising or lowering of the voice, but the gaps between stanzas were marked by an increased urgency. There was something symbolic in this: at the end of a stanza, where everyone else would have paused, Brodsky speeded up and achieved an effect of intermittency by the exact opposite of the usual procedure. It was the same not only in the reciting of poetry, but in everything else.

Iosif Brodsky appeared at one of the regular poetry readings entitled 'For the First Time in Russian' which I had been organizing for some years in the Mayakovsky Writers' House. Each of these evenings was attended by hundreds of people, with a predominance of young writers in the audience, and to this audience translators of every generation, from the heavyweights to the complete beginners, presented their latest unpublished work. It was a talented audience, eager for poetic discoveries. Brodsky's performance in front of this packed hall was unlike any other; his verbal and musical intensity had a magnetic effect. He was reciting his translations of poems by the Pole Konstanty Ildefons Gałczyński:

Bewitched droshky,
Bewitched driver,
Bewitched horse . . .

and the audience, too, was bewitched, although at first the inarticulate mass of guttural r's in Brodsky's recitation might even have seemed funny.

I already knew that Brodsky was not simply an exceptionally gifted poet, but also an unusually hard-working person: in order to translate Galczyński he had studied Polish, and in order to read in the original and translate John Donne and his other beloved metaphysical poets he had learnt English. His Russian John Donne is fantastic. And now this fanatic of the word, this poetic pioneer, was being called a parasite and a layabout! Such charges could be very dangerous; not long before, on 4 May 1961, the Supreme Soviet of the USSR had issued a decree concerning the struggle with parasites and their expulsion from large cities ('Concerning the intensification of the struggle against individuals who evade socially useful work and lead an anti-social and parasitic life'), and this decree had been confirmed and extended by the plenum of the Supreme Court on 10 March 1963. In itself the law was very necessary: the number of idlers living by thieving and various sorts of speculation had become frightening. The decree spoke of the large number of people living in large cities and taking on jobs for appearance' sake, to divert attention from their real and unsavoury activities. 'The parasitic way of life of these individuals is generally accompanied by drunkenness, dissolute morality, and disregard for the rules of socialist community life, all of which has a negative influence on the other members of society.' All this was much needed and entirely correct. But—the law against parasites had an ulterior motive. It made it possible to take away the job of anyone with unorthodox opinions, and subsequently on the pretext that he was not working, send him off to the tundra—as a parasite. So Brodsky was threatened with expulsion; he did not write political verse, but everything that he did, thought, or wrote was unorthodox. This was unforgivable.

I rushed to Brodsky's defence. In the Writers' Union the work of the 'young people' was the concern of a special committee headed by Daniil Granin. I was a member of this committee and as such I took the matter up with the chairman. 'It is not for us to intervene', he replied curtly. Not for us? But wasn't it our obvious duty? Before our very eyes they were hounding a young writer; who was to defend him if not us? Granin gave no reasons; he simply rejected the possibility and therefore the necessity of helping. A few days later Lerner, the author of the article in *Vecherny Leningrad*, spoke at the Secretariat of the Leningrad Writers' Union. Why was this allowed? I later found out that he had shown the poet Aleksandr Prokofiev, who was at that time in charge of the Leningrad section, some kind of document from 'Them' which sent him into a panic. Having seen this document with the stamp of the Big House, Prokofiev took up an 'At your service' attitude and gave in without the slightest resistance. So on 13 December Lerner arrived at the Union and treated the frightened Secretariat to a sabre-rattling speech. He gave them to understand that this boy Brodsky was a pernicious element, surrounded by the drug-addicts, alcoholics, hooligans, hippies, and currency speculators of the town, hob-nobbing with American tourists and doubtless peddling foreign currency and drugs, that he was the holder of anti-Soviet views, which had often been expressed in conversations (bugged) and letters (intercepted), an active Zionist, etc., etc. . . . All this was the product of Lerner's malicious imagination and a settling of some kind of personal score with Brodsky. I might say in parenthesis that Lerner is in his way a typical figure: until 1954 he was a captain in the MVD, then he became a member of the volunteer people's militia and patrolled the area round the European Hotel with an armband saying 'Member of the People's Militia'. A swindler and an adventurer, extracting large sums of money from currency speculators by blackmail, he was undoubtedly connected with the Big House even after his official retirement, but not openly: the document he waved around was most likely a fake. The KGB do not place too high a value on riff-raff of this sort; they use their services and even allow them to show some initiative, but then they throw them out by the scruff of the neck. This was the case with Lerner. The State Security Organization used his hands and tongue to organize the 'public indignation' around the parasite Brodsky, his trial, the press coverage, and all the necessary intrigues, and then washed its hands of him. Ten years later, in May 1973, Lerner was arrested and tried as a large-scale swindler (it should have been as a slanderer too) and was sentenced to six years in the camps. But this was much later. In December 1963 Lerner was the victor; the Secretariat of the Writers' Union decided with total unanimity to hand over Brodsky for trial as a parasite. The Secretariat consisted not of uneducated civil servants or irresponsible senile pensioners, but of writers: the poets Aleksandr Prokofiev and Nikolai Braun, the prose-writers Pyotr Kapitsa and Daniil Granin, critics, dramatists and others. And these writers took a shameful and unprecedented decision; at the demand of some crook behind whose back loomed the shadow of 'Them', they handed over a young poet to the courts. For me this action of the writers, the Secretariat of the Union, was not only ominous, but far more alarming than the arbitrary behaviour of the KGB, the whims of the volunteer militia, and the criminal stupidity of the Provincial Committee.

Brodsky was arrested. 'It was a very cold night. . . . I was walking along a street and three of them surrounded me. They asked for my name, and like an idiot I replied that I was "their man". They suggested that I should go somewhere with them, as they needed to talk to me. I refused—I was going to see a friend. There was a scuffle. . . . They brought up a car and twisted my arms behind my back. . . .'

We learnt that Brodsky was in the 'Kresty' prison and tried to muster public opinion in his defence and to see important officials in the Writers' Union, the Public Prosecutor's office, and the ministries. But it was too late: Brodsky was behind bars—or perhaps it was too early: what if he should be acquitted? Is it possible that a Soviet people's court should bring in a verdict of guilty without weighty evidence? Once you have been arrested, that means 'there's no smoke without fire'. And this 'no smoke without fire' has been the habitual pretext which over the past few decades has allowed many people to keep the illusion of a clear conscience while doing absolutely nothing.

Various supporters, however—and above all the poet Natalia Grudinina, with her fierce social conscience and high sense of responsibility—were casting about for a way of saving Brodsky and were trying to mobilize various writers, lawyers, and journalists. On one such day, when the position seemed quite hopeless, I wrote to our old friend Frida Abramovna Vigdorova in Moscow, giving her full details of the witch-hunt and asking for her support. Not that there was any doubt about her giving it—she threw herself headlong into any cases where justice had been interfered with and there seemed some hope of restoring it. She had powerful allies and numerous connections: for many years she had worked for the *Literary Gazette, Komsomol Pravda,* and *Pravda,* writing articles on questions of moral education. Her help was invaluable, and she did not need to be asked twice. From the day when she heard the details of Brodsky's case, it became her life's work, or to be more precise the work of her last year and a half.

I have kept one of Frida Vigdorova's letters from the beginning of her campaign on behalf of Brodsky; it is dated 17 December, four days after the decision of the Leningrad Secretariat to hand over Brodsky to the courts, and it mentions the following people: V. S. Tolstikov, the First Secretary of the Leningrad Provincial Committee of the Party and therefore at that time the effective boss of Leningrad (at present ambassador to China); Viktor Efimovich Ardov, the satirical writer and close friend of Anna Akhmatova, who had asked him to help; Aleksei Aleksandrovich Surkov, the poet and at that time Secretary of the Writers' Union of the USSR; David Yakovlevich Dar, the Leningrad prose-writer, an active participant in our campaign who had written to Frida Vigdorova about the Brodsky affair at the same time as me. Here is the letter:

. . . Just now Ardov and I were talking with Shostakovich. He is a Leningrad deputy to the Supreme Soviet, so it was natural to appeal to him. We had a very good conversation. He said that he would find Vasily Sergeevich Tolstikov at the meeting and have a word with him. Vasily Sergeevich is already in the picture—Ardov spoke to him yesterday.

On the 21st Shost[akovich] will be in Leningrad. If nothing has changed by then, make a point of going to see him and telling him that things are as bad as before. But I very much hope that a turning point has been reached in this hateful affair.

In addition, we yesterday sent all the material to Surkov and today he telephoned Anna Andreevna [Akhmatova] and said that he would have a word with the people in charge of your Union. That shouldn't do any harm, should it?

I am not writing to Dar, but my letter to you can serve as a reply to him. If it is not too inconvenient, could you pass on to David Yakovlevich all I have told you. . . .

December 17th, 1963.   Moscow.

This was only the beginning: Frida Vigdorova was indefatigable.

Her efforts brought three Lenin Prize-winners into the fight, Dmitry Shostakovich, Samuil Marshak, and Kornei Chukovsky, and with them poets, musicians, and academics. This was all a novelty at the time; there was no Samizdat then and no experience of collective campaigning. All this came later, as a result of the Brodsky affair.

But Iosif Brodsky was in prison. Shostakovich talked to Tolstikov and Surkov to Prokofiev, while in the offices of the Provincial Committee, the KGB, and the People's Court, telegrams piled up from Marshak, Chukovsky, Akhmatova, Vigdorova, and many more. Even Daniil Granin now realized his original mistake and sent a telegram to the Public Prosecutor of the USSR in which he expressed his indignation at the illegal actions of the Leningrad authorities.

But Brodsky sat in the 'Kresty' prison and things took their course, just as the scoundrel Lerner had wanted.

Not long before the trial Frida Vigdorova came to Leningrad. A group of writers met at the apartment of the well-known novelist Yury Pavlovich German to discuss possible (and impossible?) lines of action. Yury German himself, a moderate law-abiding man and a lover of peaceful solutions, was in a rage; this 'case' seemed to him unprecedented, absurd, grotesque, fantastic. He telephoned to the Militia Headquarters where he had long-standing connections, wrote letters in all directions, tried to woo the bureaucrats, and being naturally optimistic believed in the triumph of good over evil.

But Brodsky sat in the 'Kresty' and waited. The parallel lines did not meet.

A few days before the trial I went to see the President of the Leningrad City Court. He received me, one of the leading members of the translators' section of the Writers' Union and a member of the committee for work with young writers, with official and indifferent politeness. I tried to explain to him that someone who writes and translates poetry cannot be considered a parasite simply because he is not a member of the Writers' Union. The President listened carefully, nodded his head in silence, and then gave me to understand that parasitism was really only the formal charge and that there was other evidence against Brodsky. What sort of evidence? He had never been interested in politics. He was a metaphysical poet, concerned with questions of being, life and death, eternity and infinity. What sort of evidence could there be against someone like that?

He glanced through his files, took out a paper and handed it me. It was a rather improper and extremely malicious epigram on Aleksandr Prokofiev.

'Have you a lot of evidence as good as this?' I asked. The judge was annoyed: 'I don't see the need for irony.'

'It's an old epigram. Someone else wrote it and it has no connection with Brodsky.' (In fact, Dudin was the author.)

'We have other material', said the judge sternly, and showed no desire to continue the conversation.

The hearing was fixed for 18 February 1964. As we approached the District Court on Vosstanie Street we could see a crowd waiting at the entrance for the arrival of the accused. We went upstairs into a dark and dirty corridor; just then the emaciated Brodsky was led past us, he looked over in our direction and gave a barely perceptible smile. A few minutes later we—Frida Vigdorova, the writer I. Metter, the relations of the criminal and myself—were let into the court-room. A crowd of young people continued to wait noisily outside—the militia-men had not let them in on the pretext that there was too little room inside. The hearing was accompanied by a din of voices, it was hard to hear, every so often there was a fruitless attempt to quieten down the crowd. Frida Vigdorova sat with her notebook in front of her and as soon as she began to take notes she attracted the wrath of Judge Savelieva, a morose woman of about forty who was less like a judge than a concierge disgruntled at the noise made late at night by a gang of drunks. On either side of her sat the bored assessors, who had no very clear idea what was going on; they kept glancing in perplexity at the door behind which the young people were making such a din.

Here now is the first session of the court[1] in the transcript of Frida Vigdorova:

Judge: What is your profession?
Brodsky: Writing poetry. Translation. I think . . .
Judge: We don't want your thoughts. Stand up properly! Don't lean

---

[1] This was not a criminal, but an administrative court, since parasitism was not a criminal offence; such a court could apply 'administrative sanctions' such as resettlement and compulsory labour. The court is made up of a professional judge and two lay assessors who have no formal legal training. [Tr.]

against the walls! Look at the court! Answer the court properly! (To me.) Stop taking notes this minute or I'll have you removed from the court-room. (To Brodsky.) Do you have any regular work?

Brodsky: I thought that was regular work.

Judge: Answer nore precisely!

Brodsky: I wrote poems. I thought they would be published. I thought . . .

Judge: We are not interested in your thoughts. Answer me, why didn't you work?

Brodsky: I did work. I wrote poetry.

Judge: That doesn't interest us. We are interested in knowing what institution you were connected with.

Brodsky: I had contracts with publishers.

Judge: Did you have enough contracts to live on? What were they, when are they dated, how much are they for?

Brodsky: I can't remember exactly. All the contracts are with my lawyer.

Judge: It's you I am asking.

Brodsky: Two books were published in Moscow with my translations . . . (Names them.)

Judge: How long have you worked?

Brodsky: Roughly . . .

Judge: We are not interested in your 'roughly'.

Brodsky: Five years.

Judge: Where did you work?

Brodsky: In a factory. And on geological field-work . . .

Judge: How long did you work in a factory?

Brodsky: One year.

Judge: As what?

Brodsky: A milling-machine operator.

Judge: But what is your specialist qualification?

Brodsky: Poet. Poet-translator.

Judge: And who declared you to be a poet? Who put you on the list of poets?

Brodsky: No one. (Spontaneously.) Who put me on the list of human beings?

Judge: And did you study for this?

Brodsky: For what?

Judge: For being a poet. You didn't try to take a course in higher education where they train . . . teach . . .

Brodsky: I didn't think it came from education.

Judge: Where does it come from then?

Brodsky: I think it comes . . . (embarrassed) . . . from God . . .

Judge: Have you any request to the court?

Brodsky: I should like to know what I was arrested for.

Judge: That is a question, not a request.

Brodsky: In that case I have no requests.

Judge: Does the defence have any questions?

Counsel: Yes. Citizen Brodsky, do you hand over your earnings to your family?

Brodsky: Yes.

Counsel: Are your parents also earning?

Brodsky: They are on a pension.

Counsel: Do you all live together as a family?

Brodsky: Yes.

Counsel: Consequently your income went into the family budget?

Judge: You are not asking questions but drawing conclusions. You are helping him to answer. Do not ask leading questions.

Counsel: Are you an out-patient at a psychiatric unit?

Brodsky: Yes.

Counsel: Have you been an in-patient?

Brodsky: Yes, from the end of December 1963 to January 5th of this year in the Kashchenko Hospital in Moscow.

Counsel: Do you not think that your illness hindered you from working for a long time in one place?

Brodsky: Perhaps. Yes, certainly. I don't know though. No, I don't really know.

Counsel: Did you translate poetry for an anthology of Cuban poetry?

Brodsky: Yes.

Counsel: Did you translate Spanish *romanceros*?

Brodsky: Yes.

Counsel: You were connected with the translators' section of the Writers' Union?

Brodsky: Yes.

Counsel: I ask the court to take into consideration the testimonial from the translators' section, the list of published poems, copies of contracts, a telegram saying 'Please sign contract as soon as possible.' (Gives details.) And I request that citizen Brodsky be sent to medical experts for an assessment of his state of health and a judgement as to whether it was such as to hinder regular work. I further request that citizen Brodsky be immediately released from custody. I consider that he has not committed any crime and that it is against the law to hold him in custody. He has a permanent place of residence and can be called before the court at any time.

The court retires for deliberation. It returns and the judge reads out the decision:

To call for psychiatric evidence as to whether Brodsky is suffering from any mental illness and whether such illness constitutes an obstacle to his being sent to forced labour in remote parts. Considering that it appears from his medical history that Brodsky tried to avoid hospitalization, Section No. 18 of the Militia is charged with ensuring that he appears for psychiatric examination.

Judge: Have you any questions?

Brodsky: I have a request—I should like to have a pen and paper in my cell.

Judge: You must make this request to the Militia superintendent.

Brodsky: I did so and he refused. Please may I have a pen and paper?

Judge (softening): All right, I'll pass on your request.

Brodsky: Thank you.

When everyone came out of the court-room they saw a huge crowd, particularly young people, in the corridors and on the staircases.

Judge: What a lot of people! I didn't expect such a crowd!

A voice from the crowd: It's not every day they try a poet.

Judge: It doesn't matter to us whether he is a poet or not.

In the opinion of the defending counsel, Z. N. Toporovaya, Judge Savelieva should have released Brodsky from custody and ordered him to appear for examination on the following day at the psychiatric hospital, but she kept him under arrest and he was taken to the hospital under escort.

This then was the first hearing. The reader should not be surprised at the request of the defence lawyer; at that time we still knew nothing about the special psychiatric hospital-prisons in which dissidents are incarcerated. They only became known in March, when the eminent military theorist and serving general P. G. Grigorenko was declared insane. In February the defence counsel believed that by proving Brodsky's illness she was saving him from being sent to 'remote parts'. Brodsky was taken under escort to the psychiatric clinic. There he spent some three weeks during which he was subjected to a painful ordeal, but he remained mentally stable, thus proving his unusual firmness of mind. Lovers of poetry actually gained from this episode; we are indebted to it for the long poem 'Gorbunov and Gorchakov' which he wrote some time later. So in those distant and idyllic days, Brodsky was not sent to a mad-house by the psychiatric experts. (If he had been, he'd be there still.) Instead they concluded that he was fit for work and that administrative sanctions could be taken against him.

Less than a month after the first hearing the second one[1] took

[1] For a transcript of this hearing, see Appendix 1.

place in the large hall of the Builders' Club on the Fontanka next
door to the former domain of the chief of police, A. K. Benkendorf,
i.e. the 'Sixth Division of the Chancellery of His Imperial Majesty'
—the same building is currently occupied by the Leningrad City
Court (a curious coincidence, a poet being tried next door to the
building from which Pushkin, Lermontov, and Nekrasov were
persecuted). The second hearing was a long one—a full-length
feature so to speak. As I said earlier, there was an audience composed of seasonal workers specially brought in by the lorry-load;
they shouted and cheered for the prosecution and showered the
defence with taunts. There were a few writers there too—I will not
name them here. The same Judge Savelieva mockingly interrogated
the accused, trying to establish that he did not earn enough to live
on and was a parasite on society's back.

Judge: What have you done that is of value to the fatherland?
Brodsky: I have written poems. That is my work. I am convinced ... I
believe that what I have written will be of service to people not only now
but in generations to come.
A voice from the audience: Go on! You're kidding yourself.
Another voice: He's a poet. He's bound to think that way.
Judge: So you think your so-called poetry is of service to people?
Brodsky: Why do you say 'so-called poetry'.
Judge: We call your poetry 'so-called' because we have no other con-
ception of it.

This was honest at least; *they* had indeed no other conception of
poetry, in fact they had no conception of it at all. We were sitting in
this court-room surrounded by truculent seasonal workers and
shuddering at every remark that was shouted from the public gal-
lery. How easy it is to present a poet as a madman or simply a
parasite living on the people's labour! How easy to talk about 'so-
called poetry' and to persuade people who have to carry heavy
loads of bricks, mix concrete, and cover roofs with iron that a man
who sits all day at his writing table composing incomprehensible
rhyming lines and holding a mere pencil in his soft hand is a layabout and a good-for-nothing! In reality it is natural for a manual
labourer to respect every kind of work, including that of the writer.
But if the authorities set him on to the man with the pen, repeating:
'You work hard, but he has it easy. You earn your crust of bread by
the sweat of your brow, but he hangs about restaurants swigging

brandy. You get up at the crack of dawn and squeeze into an over-crowded bus, but he rots in bed all morning . . .'; if this sort of thing is repeated often enough, the labourer may in the end begin quite naturally to hate the privileged idler and in his anger be capable of joining in the pogrom. How is he to know which is the true writer who deserves his sympathy and which the scribbler who wants an easy life? Brodsky's trial was just such a deceitful setting of the workers against a poet, who was represented as an idler and a debauchee. The prosecution exposed Brodsky's 'use of other people's labour'—i.e. the use of plain prose versions for poems in languages he didn't know well. At this point the public roared with indignation: what, this layabout can't work himself and he exploits others into the bargain! The judge insisted that Brodsky was unwilling to do any work and simply amused himself by writing poetry. Brodsky repeated in a bewildered way that writing poetry was work too and not some sort of game or amusing pastime. His words were greeted by mocking laughter.

Judge: Brodsky, it would be better if you explained to the court why you did not work during the intervals between jobs.
Brodsky: I did work. I wrote poetry.
Judge: But that didn't have to stop you working.
Brodsky: But I did work. I wrote poetry.
Judge: But there are people who manage to work in a factory and still write poetry. Why didn't you do that?
Brodsky: But people aren't made the same way. Even the colour of their hair and their facial expressions are different.
Judge: We don't need you to tell us that. You'd do better to explain to us how we should assess your contribution to our great onward march to communism.
Brodsky: The building of communism is not just a question of working at a lathe or ploughing the fields. It involves intellectual work too, and . . .
Judge: Don't give us your high-flown phrases! We'd rather hear how you intend to organize your working life in future.
Brodsky: I wanted to write poetry and do translations. But if that is against some social norms, I'll take a regular job and continue writing poetry.
Assessor Tyagly: Everyone works in our society. How could you spend so long doing nothing?
Brodsky: You don't consider my work as work. I wrote poetry and I consider that to be work. . . .

What a fantastic dialogue! Re-read twelve years later, it seems a parody. But at the time, to those of us who were sitting in that huge hall, it was no joke. The Judge and Assessor Tyagly were not characters from a fairground farce, but representatives of state power, and the fate of a writer was in their hands. Brodsky is not Pushkin, but what if they had been trying Pushkin?

Witnesses spoke for the defence. The writer N. I. Grudinina stated that Brodsky was a talented poet and a hard-working translator, that 'the difference between a parasite and a young poet is that the parasite eats and does no work, whereas the young poet works, but does not always eat', that the use of a plain prose translation is not a form of exploitation but an accepted literary practice. Professor V. G. Admoni spoke of Brodsky's great culture and skill as a poet-translator: 'Miracles don't happen. Neither skill nor culture come of their own accord. They call for constant and unflagging work.' He described the charge of parasitism as an absurdity. I too spoke as a witness; I described Brodsky as 'a man of rare gifts, and, what is equally important, a conscientious and assiduous worker'; I spoke of his very wide knowledge of American, English, and Polish literature; I explained that the work of a translator of poetry 'calls for diligence, knowledge, talent . . . self-denying love of poetry and of work' and that Brodsky possessed all these qualities. I expressed my astonishment at the notice by the entrance gate: 'Trial of the parasite Brodsky'—was not this a violation of the presumption of innocence?

We were wasting our breath, however—the judges neither understood nor wished to understand us. One of the assessors, Tyagly, was a retired military man who sat there in a field shirt without epaulettes, making neither head nor tail of it all. I was talking about the strong impression made on me by 'the clarity of poetic expression, the musicality and passionate energy of the verse' in Brodsky's translations, and Professor Admoni was quoting Mayakovsky's 'For the sake of a single word you extract thousands of tons of verbal ore', when Assessor Tyagly suddenly asked: 'Where did Brodsky read his translations, and in what foreign languages did he read them?'

We were speaking different languages. 'The deaf summon the deaf before a deaf judge. . . .' Savelieva seemed to understand better than Tyagly what we were talking about. But her position was not particularly pleasant either: her orders were to condemn Brodsky to the most severe sanction allowed in an administrative court. No doubt she was rung up that very morning, whether by the Provincial Committee or the KGB I don't know. And as we all know, 'Justice is the consecration of existing injustices.'

Then came the witnesses for the prosecution. They had never seen Brodsky before or read a word he had written, but they were full of indignation. Here for instance is pipe-layer Denisov:

I do not know Brodsky personally. I only know him from what has been written in the press. [In what sense is the pipe-layer a witness? A witness of what?] I am speaking as a citizen and a representative of public opinion. After what the newspapers have written, I am indignant at Brodsky's work. I wanted to see what his books were like. I went to the library, and they didn't have his books. I asked my acquaintances if they'd heard of him. They hadn't. I am a worker. I've only changed jobs twice in my life. But what about Brodsky? . . . I want to express the view that as a worker I am not satisfied by Brodsky's activities.

(Always the same vicious circle: the newspaper, Denisov in the court-room, the newspaper again, public indignation, the court passes sentence.)

Writer Voevodin was no better than pipe-layer Denisov. He too did not know Brodsky and had not read his poetry, but quoted poems by other people, and presented the court with a report supposedly composed about Brodsky in the committee for work with young writers, but in fact written by Voevodin himself—the other members of the committee knew nothing about it.

Counsel: Does the report which you wrote on Brodsky represent the views of the whole committee?
Voevodin: We did not get the report approved by Etkind, who has a different opinion.
Counsel: But the other members of the committee are acquainted with the contents of your report?
Voevodin: No, not all of them.

Not all of them. Or to be more precise, no one besides Voevodin. To be even more precise, the official report transmitted to the court in the name of an official committee of the Writers' Union was a fake.

Then came the speech of the public prosecutor Sorokin, a speech full of pompous empty phrases and abuse. 'Brodsky is defended by swindlers and parasites, lice and cockroaches', he proclaimed (the defenders in question were merely Shostakovich, Akhmatova, Marshak, Chukovsky . . .), and added menacingly: 'we ought to scrutinize the moral character of his defenders . . .'.

During this speech there were two episodes, both involving my neighbours in the court-room. On my right was the well-known economist, historian, and diplomat Evgeny Aleksandrovich Gnedin. When Sorokin began insulting Brodsky's defenders, old Gnedin could not contain himself and shouted out: 'Who? Chukovsky and Marshak?' A couple of volunteer militia-men made their way over to him, lifted him out of his chair by force, twisted his arms behind his back and dragged him out of the hall. Later Gnedin told us how he had been bundled into a car, driven to the other end of town and left there. But he was used to this kind of thing—he has some twenty years in the labour camps to his credit.

On my left Frida Vigdorova was sitting taking notes. Suddenly, when the public prosecutor had nearly finished his speech, the judge shouted:

'Stop taking notes!'

Two volunteer militia-men made for Frida Vigdorova, obviously intending to take away her writing pad. I grabbed it, put it in my breast pocket and folded my arms across my chest. The militia-men saw such angry determination in my face that, not having permission to start a fight in the court-room, they went away again.

The defence lawyer, Zoya Nikolaevna Toporovaya, needed considerable courage to speak as she then did. She demonstrated the utterly unfounded nature of the charges, the unreliability of Voevodin's report, the incompetence of all the prosecution witnesses without exception (making statements as they did on the basis of some sort of unchecked documents obtained in a mysterious manner, or simply expressing their opinions in speeches of denunciation), and equally the incompetence of the judges themselves (since they were not specialists in 'questions of literary work'). She proved quite convincingly that

(*a*) the evidence for the prosecution was insubstantial or falsified,
(*b*) the accused was not a parasite.

Her speech persuaded everyone, even apparently the more unprejudiced and rational of the seasonal workers. The court withdrew. A verdict of guilty seemed impossible to us—it would be too flagrant a piece of injustice.

While the judges conferred, the public jostled in the corridors. Frida Vigdorova took notes of what she heard:

Conversations in the court-room

—Writers! They ought all to be kicked out!

—Intellectuals! They're on our backs!

—What's wrong with the intelligentsia? They work the same as everyone else.

—Go on! You've seen how they work. They exploit other people.

—I'll get hold of a plain prose translation too and start translating poetry!

—Do you know what a plain prose translation is? Do you know how a poet works with one?

—Oh, big deal!

—I know Brodsky. He's a good bloke and a good poet.

—He's an anti-Soviet. Did you hear what the prosecutor said?

—And did you hear what the defence said?

—The defence was talking for money and the prosecutor for nothing. So he must be right.

—That's right, all the defence wants is to earn as much as possible. They don't mind what they say, so long as they get the cash.

—Rubbish!

—Don't you talk like that to me or I'll call a militia-man. Did you hear the bits they quoted?

—He wrote them ages ago.

—So what, if he wrote them ages ago?

—I am a teacher. What sort of a teacher would I be if I didn't believe people could be educated?

—We can do without teachers like you!

—We send you our children, and what sort of stuff do you teach them?

—But Brodsky wasn't even allowed to defend himself.

—Shut up, we've had enough of your Brodsky!

—And you there, taking notes! What were you taking notes for?

—I'm a journalist. I write about education, and I want to write about this case.

—What is there to write? It's all as clear as day. You're all in league. Your notes ought to be taken away from you.

—You just try.

—What if I do?

—Just try. You'll see.

—You're threatening me, are you! Hey, militia-man, they're threatening me.

—He's a militia-man, not a policeman, he's not going to worry about every word that's spoken.

—Hey, militia-man, they're calling you policemen. You ought to be expelled from Leningrad, the lot of you, that would teach you, you parasites!

—Comrades, what are you saying! He'll be acquitted. You heard the defence, didn't you?

But he wasn't acquitted. The sentence was ready in advance—I don't know what the judges were doing all that time in their conference chamber. They repeated all the disproved arguments of the prosecution and gave their verdict: in accordance with the decree of 4 May 1961 Brodsky was to be sent to a remote part of the country for five years' compulsory labour.

Digression concerning Unbridled Form

But the oddest and most incomprehensible thing is that authors can choose such subjects. I confess it's quite beyond me, it's really . . . no, no, I really don't understand. In the first place it's absolutely no use to the nation, and in the second place . . . in the second place it's no use either. I just don't know why. . . .

N. V. GOGOL, *The Nose*

As we separated we felt crushed by the whim of brute force, by our feeling of powerlessness, and by the cynicism of this judicial show. It was like taking part in some fantastic scene where only the form counts. The court session had indeed taken place according to the rules; on a dais, on high-backed chairs carved with the emblem of the Soviet Union, sat the People's Judge, duly elected by secret ballot, and two People's Assessors, duly appointed by the appropriate social bodies. Everything was done in the proper manner: the interrogation of the accused, the statements of the defence witnesses and the prosecution witnesses, the speech of the public prosecutor and the speech of the defending counsel, the judges' conference in a special conference chamber, the solemn proclamation of the sentence—'In the name of the Russian Soviet Federative Socialist Republic . . .', even the public applause after the sentence and the exit of the accused under escort.

'All according to plan, but a bit hit and miss . . .'[1]

[1] From a song by Aleksandr Galich. [Tr.]

There was no real content, or if there was, it had no importance. The judge did not understand the basic issues. The assessors, whose role was to clarify details concerning the literary profession, had not the first idea what it was all about. The prosecution witnesses had witnessed nothing, since they knew neither the accused nor his writings. The public prosecutor based his speech on a fake report, someone else's poems, and some private letters and diaries of mysterious origin. The judges conferred, it is true, but this was pure form in as much as the sentence was dictated in advance and only had to be made public here in the court-room. The official form of proceeding can be filled out with absolutely any old content—no one will take any notice. The habit of being ruled by official form is so great that the form itself can become the content.

Mikhail Koltsov once wrote a piece about some provincial Party leader who all one day shouted the same revolutionary slogan to the demonstrators marching past the rostrum:

'Death to the enemies of capital! Hurrah!'

And all the thousands who marched past repeated enthusiastically: 'Hoo-rah!' No one noticed the content of the slogan, 'Death to the enemies of capital'. The hypnosis of the form was irresistible, the rostrum, the shared 'Hurrah!', the familiar words 'death', 'enemies', 'capital'.

And isn't the same *law of hollow form* the basis for many novels, poems, plays, and films? Everything is there, a beginning and an end, positive and negative characters, metre, rhyme, everything except a meaning.

> My dear, do you know that every day at evening,
> Before the dew has fallen on the leaves,
> The setting sun rests on my shoulder, calling
> To take the road that runs beyond the seas.
> I know that far beyond those bright blue waters
> And far beyond the distant forest rides
> Are women's eyes that shine with other heavens,
> But life for me is easy by your side.
> What if the cities far beyond the ocean
> Are miracles in groves of paradise?
> Though they are full of light and foreign radiance,
> I never felt the urge to make them mine.

My soul is in the white soul of the birches,
No foreign sun can warm my heart so well,
And nothing can wipe out the name of Russia
From memory, nor free me from her spell. . . .

There does not seem to be much connection between this poem
of Vladimir Firsov, written in 1965, and the trial I have just
described. But there is a link, if only indirect. The poem, too, is
an imitation, an example of empty form. It is a plaster cast, with
no content. There are all the external attributes of 'poetry': the
dew, the sun, the distant forest, the women's eyes shining with
other heavens, the groves of paradise, the white birches, the
soul, the heart, Russia. There are rhymes. There is five-foot
iambic metre. There are metaphors, echoes of folklore, allusions to Gumilyov and Blok. . . . Everything is there and the
result is a tailor's dummy. What's it all about? 'I don't want to
go abroad, I am happy in Russia.' That's all it is. Empty form.

How many books I have seen consisting of a binding, a
gleaming dust-jacket, and pages covered with typographical
signs! How many monuments representing some magnificent
figure of a democrat with a great-coat down to his ankles! How
many newspapers which were no more than large sheets of
paper with striking headlines and ersatz news! And how many
speeches I have heard that consisted of an elevated platform,
microphones, a monotonous voice and endless set phrases made
unintelligible by constant repetition. . . .

It's all a mirage.

And we continued to exist in this phantasmagorical world of
tailor's dummies. The court had pronounced sentences not only on
Brodsky but on us, the witnesses for the defence; a 'special report'
had been made on each of us and sent both to the Writers' Union
and to our place of work. 'X. has shown political short-sightedness,
lack of vigilance, and ideological illiteracy.' Soon afterwards we
were summoned to a meeting of the Secretariat. The pig-like
Aleksandr Prokofiev, his face red with anger, shouted at us lengthily
and incoherently. It would be impossible to reproduce these shouts
here. His voice was breathless and hoarse with rage; the other
Secretaries listened in silence with different emotions on their faces,
from sycophancy to barely concealed ironic contempt. The essence
of Prokofiev's grunting was that we, as members of the Writers'

Union, had taken the liberty of attending the court without asking the authorities' permission, that our speeches contradicted the decisions of the Secretariat, that we were politically immature and short-sighted, that the Provincial Committee of the Party was extremely dissatisfied with our behaviour.

We tried to answer him. Professor Admoni spoke of Brodsky's talent and the need to treasure gifted people and approach them with tact and understanding. N. I. Grudinina recounted once again how Brodsky had worked in her seminar for young poets and what hopes she had placed in him; in addition to this, with her characteristic impetuosity, she exposed the fraud committed by Voevodin in presenting the court with a report on Brodsky containing moral and political criticisms and supposedly emanating from the committee for work with young writers when in fact it was unknown to all the members of the committee except its author, Voevodin—the sentence had been based precisely on this fake document, which for the court had represented the opinion of the Writers' Union about Brodsky.

In my speech to the Secretariat, I stuck to juridical arguments: 'Yes, we took part in a court session without the Secretariat's permission. But we had been summoned as witnesses by the court. You could criticize us or even bring us to justice if we had committed perjury, but no one accuses us of that. We told the court what we had in fact witnessed. We did not lie. The liar was Voevodin, but no one thinks to blame him for it. Since when have witnesses had to ask the consent of the authorities before making statements? A witness testifies under oath—as we all know, he swears to tell the truth, the whole truth, and nothing but the truth. We did not break our oath. Perhaps our truth was inconvenient to some people. But it is the truth and you can't alter that.'

Then the Secretaries spoke. I remember the speech of Pyotr Kapitsa, a servile prose-writer, who was obviously trotting out the cynical arguments he had heard in the Provincial Committee:

'There you were, naïvely refuting the charge of parasitism against Brodsky, but do you really think that's what it was all about? He is an anti-Soviet, he slanders Marx and Lenin in his letters and diaries, and the business of hi-jacking a plane in Samarkand was not just a funny story. You are sympathetically disposed towards Brodsky. But would it really have been better for him to have been tried not for parasitism but for anti-Soviet activities and statements?

What if his trial had been openly political? According to the existing law he would not be a free man in some northern village, but a prisoner in a strict regime camp, and he wouldn't thank you for that! He was lucky, they were kind to him—the KGB agreed to be indulgent—and let him be tried by an administrative court, so that only an administrative sanction was applied to him. Administrative, not criminal. Surely you see the difference. And yet there you are, the three of you, turning up at the court and upsetting everything. You start trying to prove that Brodsky can't be tried for parasitism. That means that you want him to be tried for anti-Sovietism and sent to a camp. It's lucky for you that Voevodin came to the rescue.'

This caused an uproar. We kept repeating that a people's court was not the place for these sorts of machinations; that if it was known that someone had committed a murder one could not be indulgent and try him for pickpocketing; that the argument about indulgence was false since 'They' were not given to this sort of humane approach and if they did not try Brodsky for anti-Soviet activities, this meant they had nothing against him; that the prosecution had only one piece of evidence, and this was a series of unverified phrases taken from a very old diary and from some letters which the investigators had come by in some mysterious way; that private letters were not grounds for a criminal prosecution; that we had spoken at a real trial which had really taken place, and not at an imaginary one existing only in the minds of some mysterious impresarios.

Then Granin give a short speech. He condemned Voevodin's deceit, which had been most offensive of all to him, Granin, the chairman of the committee in whose name the report was written. He gave his support to us, the defence witnesses, and agreed with our arguments.

But Prokofiev was the boss. On the basis of the private report of the court, all three of us were given a reprimand 'for political short-sightedness, lack of vigilance, etc. . . .', but in reality for having made statements in court which corresponded to the truth and not to the desires of the Provincial Committee and thus of Prokofiev.

A couple of days later the committee for work with young writers met. There was a speech from Voevodin, the secretary, and one from me with an account of the trial and the fake report;

Granin as president closed the discussion by demanding the immediate removal of Voevodin from the committee on the grounds
that he had betrayed the trust of society, misused his position, and
deceived the court. Voevodin was unanimously expelled from the
committee. The same day the Leningrad Writers' Union split into
two factions; one of them, the reactionary one, was led by Aleksandr Prokofiev, the other by Daniil Granin.

Prokofiev was far from isolated. The Moscow leadership were
dissatisfied with the ugly and stupid 'Brodsky affair', but considered
it their duty to support their blundering subordinates and put a
good face on things. In December 1964 A. B. Chakovsky, the
editor of the *Literary Gazette* and Secretary of the Writers' Union
of the USSR, was asked the following question by journalists in
New York:

'Do you believe what happened to Brodsky is organically linked
to the Soviet system? Will it hurt the cause of freedom of expression in Russia?'

The crafty Chakovsky replied: 'Brodsky is what we call a *podonok*
("riff-raff", "scum")—a plain and simple *podonok*. He was tried
in open court under the established procedures of our law; he
defended himself; the judges heard all the relevant testimony from
literary experts and from Leningrad public opinion—and then
came to the conclusion that he should be banished from the city
and given some honest work. I think it is simply amusing that you
can work up so much self-righteous indignation about the so-called
"Brodsky case" when here bombs are thrown into churches, young
girls are killed and the killers allowed to go free.'

This historic interview with A. B. Chakovsky was published in
the *New York Times Magazine* on 20 December 1964. He didn't
say anything like this in Leningrad—he had to be more careful.
But in far-off New York the odd lie is nothing to be ashamed
of.

At the next election of officers the Leningrad writers kicked out
Prokofiev in a secret ballot, elected Granin in his place and made
all three of us—Grudinina, Admoni, and myself—members of the
executive. The first meeting of the new Secretariat reconsidered
our case in our presence; there was a unanimous decision to clear
us of the unjust reprimand and Daniil Granin, the new leader of
the Union, solemnly apologized to us on behalf of the Secretariat.

All this happened while Brodsky was still in his northern village where 'God does not live only in icon corners'.[1] Naturally this increased the value of our victory. We had not expected such a complete and unconditional triumph. The enemy suddenly vanished; even Pyotr Kapitsa, it seemed, had always known that we were in the right; even Nikolai Braun, who in the previous Secretariat had supported Prokofiev in his stern and ostentatiously honest way, was now in no doubt about our rightness and appeared to have forgotten that he had previously voted for a public reprimand.

A few months went by, Iosif Brodsky was brought back to Leningrad and rehabilitated, and the court sent an unprecedented paper to the Writers' Union in which it admitted that the private reports on us were erroneous.

This was in 1964. Just ten years later, in 1974, in the KGB report on me and my anti-Soviet activities, the Brodsky affair floated back to the surface in its original form, as if nothing had happened in between and as if the sentence, the private report, and the public reprimand were still valid and had never been rescinded. And the 1974 Secretariat remembered nothing, refuted nothing, asked nothing.

Such is justice.

---

[1] See Brodsky, *Selected Poems*, tr. G. L. Kline, Penguin Books, 1973, p. 81.

4

The Sentence Affair (1968–74)

A writer who is incapable of flexibility must go to work with a briefcase if he wants to earn a living. In our day and age Gogol would have spent his time in the theatrical section, Turgenev would undoubtedly have translated Balzac and Flaubert for 'World Literature', Herzen would have lectured to the Baltic Fleet, Chekhov would have served in the Ministry of Health.

E. ZAMYATIN, *I fear*, 1920

In 1968, in the 'Soviet Writer' publishing house, a two-volume anthology entitled *Masters of Russian Verse Translation* was about to appear in the famous 'Poet's Library' collection founded by Gorky. I had made the selection and written a sizeable introductory article, 'Verse Translation in the History of Russian Literature', together with a large body of notes. It had been a difficult job, calling for lengthy research in archives and libraries on my part and demanding great care from the publishers. The manuscript had been thoroughly read, and more than once, by Ksenia Bukhmeier, who had impressed me by her thoughtfulness and conscientiousness; she had collated the poems with their first published versions in journals and collections of the eighteenth and nineteenth centuries, had pointed out all the careless mistakes and contradictions in my introduction and notes, and had forced me to improve awkward turns of phrase and obscure expressions. The proof-readers had read through the galleys and the page proofs several times. The chief editor of the publishing house, Mikhail Smirnov, also a conscientious and educated person, had read the book from cover to cover, as his post obliged him to. The censor too (or, to give him his correct title, the representative of Glavlit, the central literary organization) had read it, and not having found anything forbidden in it (no 'state secrets') had placed his magical stamp on the title page. And finally the book had been 'approved for publication' by the president of the 'Poet's Library' editorial board, Vladimir Orlov, who had already signed over two hundred similar volumes. As is usual in Soviet publishing, all this had dragged on for many months. But now it was all done, and there on the table lay the final copy of the book which the author only reads so that he can if necessary make a list of errata. The printing was complete and 25,000 copies were waiting in the stores for authorization to be sent out for sale, when suddenly . . .

Calling in at the publishers' office, I found everyone in a state of commotion. The previous evening there had been a 'phone call from 'high up' in Moscow, ordering that all work on the book should stop immediately. No one knew what had made the Moscow people hold up a book that seemed so inoffensive, academic, and remote from political passions. They were expecting trouble from other books awaiting publication in the 'Poet's Library': the poems of Mandelstam, Vladimir Solovyov, or Vyacheslav Ivanov might well cause considerable problems. But surely not a collection of verse translation! And think how many pairs of eyes had read it, how carefully they had scanned it, how many readers' reports had been written about it! Nevertheless the storm warning was up; it looked like a real political row.

Before long the director of the Leningrad section of 'Soviet Writer', G. F. Kondrashov, returned from Moscow and called his subordinates to a meeting. Someone 'high up' (the Central Committee? the KGB? the Leningrad Provincial Committee?) had noticed one sentence at the very end of the introduction; discussing the unprecedented flourishing of verse translation in the Soviet period, the author had written: 'The social causes of this phenomenon are comprehensible. During a certain period, particularly between the 19th and the 20th Congresses, Russian poets were deprived of the possibility of expressing themselves to the full in original writing and spoke to the reader in the language of Goethe, Orbeliani, Shakespeare, and Hugo.' In this one sentence there was ideological sabotage.

The machine began to turn more and more quickly. The editorial staff were called in one by one to be questioned by the director: how could they have let through such an obviously slanderous, politically harmful and anti-Soviet statement? N. B. Lesyuchevsky, the general director of the whole of 'Soviet Writer', came from Moscow (Leningrad was only a branch) and stormed about, threatening expulsions and demanding to see the author.

My meeting with the Moscow director took place in the office of the Leningrad director, Kondrashov, on the third floor of 'Book House', the former headquarters of Singer sewing machines, which was hymned in the twenties by Zabolotsky (he must be mentioned now, for reasons which will become clear before long):

> There in the night the Nevsky Prospect,
> Brilliant and gloomy, its pigments changed,
> A hairsbreadth from a fairy story,
> Unfearing, blowing in the wind.
> And, as by some wild fury seized,
> Through petrol, gloom and foggy sky,
> Over the tower a winged globe reared
> And raised the name of Singer high.

Apart from Lesyuchevsky and Kondrashov, there was only Orlov in the office. The reader is already acquainted with him, but I must introduce the two directors.

Nikolai Vasilievich Lesyuchevsky is a typical man of his time. For many years he has been in charge of the most important Soviet publishing house and the one that publishes the greatest number of contemporary authors. His services to Russian literature are considerable: he is the author of denunciations on the strength of which many writers were arrested and liquidated between 1937 and 1953. There is documentary proof of his part in the arrests of Boris Kornilov, who was shot in 1938, and of Nikolai Zabolotsky, who died a natural death after being rehabilitated, but spent eight years in the camps. An eminent historian of Russian literature, the Pushkin scholar Yulian Oksman, once refused to shake hands with Lesyuchevsky at a ceremonial gathering in memory of Pushkin on the stage of the Bolshoi Theatre. There were representatives there of various bodies, such as the Writers' Union and the Literary Museum, and when he saw Lesyuchevsky, Oksman asked in a loud voice: 'Who are you representing here? The poets' murderers?' When what was hidden came to light after 1956 and denunciations were made public, several writers demanded that Lesyuchevsky be brought to justice. He sent a written statement to the Party Committee of the Writers' Union (I have seen this fantastic document), in which he explained how he had always been a devoted son of the Party, religiously believing in its infallibility and the correctness of its general line, and how, when in obedience to the Party he had

written his denunciatory commentary on Kornilov's poems, he
had been convinced that in writing of wild beasts the poet had had
the criminal intention of secretly depicting Soviet society under a
zoological disguise. In 1937 and 1938 he, Lesyuchevsky, had been
an ardent, uncompromising Young Communist, and his only
crime had been to be too unswerving in his devotion to the high
ideals of communism. Apparently he did not defend his denunciation of Zabolotsky, but after all it was only too easy to charge the
author of *Scrolls* and *Ladeinikov* with counter-revolution. It was
enough to quote the lines:

> Ladeinikov listened carefully; the garden
> Crept with the murmur of a thousand deaths,
> And Nature, now appearing an inferno,
> Performed her business calmly, without fuss.
> Bugs ate the grass, then by the birds were eaten,
> And the birds' brains were sucked out by the stoat.
> And with uncannily distorted features
> Nocturnal creatures from the grass looked out.
> The never-ending grinding wheels of Nature
> In one club brought together death and being,
> Only the mind of man had not the power
> To reconcile these two great mysteries . . .

and having quoted them to say that 'Nature' should be understood
as 'Soviet society'. Soviet society was the 'inferno' and the 'never-
ending grinding wheels'. By chance Zabolotsky escaped execution
—the trumped-up charge against him was too ridiculous (that he
had buried a tank in a Leningrad courtyard). His terrorist organization was supposedly headed by two writers from the 'Serapion
Brothers', Tikhonov and Fedin; when he was in the prison latrines
Zabolotsky came across a scrap of newspaper with the name of
Fedin, who was by that time an important figure in Soviet society
(whereas until then Zabolotsky had thought that both Fedin and
Tikhonov had been executed). He was saved by this piece of newspaper, which allowed him to protest at his continuing imprison-
ment, but Lesyuchevsky did all he could to ruin him. And now
there he sat in front of me—'representing the poets' murderers'.
There he sat in the office of his Leningrad henchman Kondrashov.

Georgy Filimonovich Kondrashov, unlike Lesyuchevsky, had no
literary pretensions. (He might have done well as a writer of
denunciations, however.) He had come into the publishing house

by way of the City Committee of the Party, where he had occupied the very serious post of secretary. He had made some blunder and had been kicked out, but not trampled underfoot—he wasn't a nobody, after all! So the disgraced Kondrashov was sent to run the publishing house, on the understanding that the more he had offended the authorities, the more gratitude he would show for his new job, even if it was not the most brilliant, and the more he would be vigilant, obedient, and unforgiving. As for his achievements in the field of denunciations, I have only one document to refer to, but it is a good one: Kondrashov's letter to the Provincial Committee denouncing his own subordinates. Sensing that my 'sentence' threatened danger to him and that he ran the risk of being kicked out again (and he wasn't far off retirement!), he composed the following missive:

To the Chairman of the Cultural Department of the Leningrad Provincial Committee of the CPSU, Comrade G. P. Aleksandrov

The libellous assertion of E. Etkind concerning the development of our literature during the Soviet period in his introductory article to the book *Masters of Russian Verse Translation* cannot but cause me profound indignation.

I can find no justification for the action of Comrade Smirnov, chief editor of this section of the publishing house, in approving Etkind's manuscript for printing in December 1967 without reading it thoroughly.

Although since January 1968 the 'Poet's Library' collection has not been my concern as far as the scrutiny and editing of manuscripts is concerned, as a Communist and as director of this section of the publishing house I have no right to defend my non-intervention on legalistic grounds. There is a political and moral duty on every member of the Party to struggle by all possible means for the purity of our ideology.

Naturally strict administrative measures will be taken by the directors of the publishing house against those who were directly responsible for letting through Etkind's anti-Soviet attack, but the chief conclusion to be drawn, the most important point, is that educational work in the publishing house must be raised to a level corresponding to the decisions of the April Plenum of the Central Committee of the CPSU, and the slightest possibility of views foreign to the socialist ideology of our society finding their way into published works must be eliminated.

G. F. Kondrashov, Director of the Leningrad Section of the publishing house 'Soviet Writer'. 11.10.68

Even the most gifted writer could not have composed a text so characteristic of the Soviet civil servant, toady and demagogue. Nothing is missing: there is the swipe at the author ('libellous assertion'), the careful omission of the nature of his libel (what if Kondrashov should later be accused of repeating it? This is why he writes vaguely: 'concerning the development of our literature during the Soviet period'), the betrayal of his own colleague and chief editor ('I can find no justification for the action . . .'), the suggestion that he himself is 'legalistically' not concerned ('the "Poet's Library" collection has not been my concern . . .'), the noble self-criticism ('as a Communist . . . I have no right to defend . . .'), the sacred oath ('to struggle by all possible means for the purity of our ideology'), and finally the promise of punitive action against his subordinates ('strict administrative measures . . . against those who were directly responsible for letting through Etkind's anti-Soviet attack'). The most interesting word here is 'directly'. These are the people to be punished, those directly responsible—not me. This is all very remote from me, I am not to blame, 'the "Poet's Library" is not my concern . . .', but I am a communist, and I myself, freely and of my own accord, want to admit my responsibility. . . .

All the European languages have taken over from present-day Russian not only the word 'Sputnik', but also 'apparatchik'. The word is often used in the West without being fully understood. Well, here he is, the apparatchik, he is called Kondrashov. A comic figure, but frightening too. He kept his promise and sacked those 'directly responsible', four of his most valuable staff, the editor Ksenia Bukhmeier, the editorial director of the 'Poet's Library' Irina Isakovich, the chief editor Mikhail Smirnov, and a little later Vladimir Orlov, chairman of the editorial board of the 'Poet's Library'. On what grounds? As Kondrashov himself put it in the document I have quoted, they were all 'directly responsible for letting through Etkind's anti-Soviet attack'.

Such were the people I had to talk to. Behind his large desk, thin as a post, with a long neck and a long, gloomy, respectably greying head, sat Kondrashov. Lesyuchevsky stalked about the room, his great fat neck and bald head flushed with emotion, his dark hair sticking out in all directions and growing out of his nose and ears, his voice choking: 'You are slandering the Soviet system . . . driving a wedge between the Party and the writers. . . . When were poets not allowed to talk freely? When were they forced into translation? Your sentence is an ignorant lie . . . a lying piece of slander. . . .'

I said nothing. In my head, and just asking to be spoken aloud, were the lines of a very young poet:

> From Goethe as from a ghetto speak
> The burning lips of Pasternak.

I had been permanently struck by these lines, and even today they seem to me the work of a genius. They contain in a compressed form all that I could say in long pages of prose, and all that I had timidly whispered in my feeble 'sentence'. But I remained silent, and then asked quietly: 'Surely you don't deny that there was a personality cult?' What a stream of indignation, what a burst of fury that caused! I could no longer make out what Lesyuchevsky screamed as he rushed over to the window on his short legs. Only one thing I remember: 'You are speculating on the tragedy of the people', he shouted. I stared at him in astonishment—he seemed to be having a fit. Orlov uttered some meaningless words of reconciliation, Kondrashov from time to time put in something about the purity of our ideology. After waiting a few moments, I poured oil on the flames, and such oil that it seemed Lesyuchevsky would have a stroke. I mentioned Zabolotsky.

'You keep on denying it,' I said, 'but look at the facts: between 1948 and 1956, over a whole decade, a poet of the stature of Zabolotsky only published a bare five or six poems. But those were the very years when he wrote his best poems, "Gurzuf", "The Last Leaves are Falling", "Parting with Friends", "A Dream", "The Poet", "The Failure", "On the Beauty of Human Faces".... In those years he published not only his innumerable translations from the Georgian—Vazha Pshavela and Orbeliani—but also from the German, the Hungarian, the Tadzhik, the Uzbek. He translated everybody. Zabolotsky returned from the camps in 1946, but he didn't begin to be published as an original poet until 1956. Surely this means something? And what about Pasternak? Or Akhmatova?'

Lesyuchevsky didn't answer, he didn't even seem to be listening. Orlov tried to raise objections ('Zabolotsky and Pasternak did translations because they recognized that they were participating in a multi-national Soviet culture'), but Lesyuchevsky continued his furious monologue. The name of Zabolotsky had been a red rag to a bull. In the end he calmed down and gave me to understand that too much money had been spent on the edition, so that unfortunately it would have to be published, but that the editorial committee had been told to get rid of all the Gumilyovs and Khodaseviches and that I was to rewrite the introduction 'in the light of the Party's indications'.

'Baron' Lesyuchevsky never forgave me for that conversation. The insurmountable obstacles put in the way of my books in the 'Soviet Writer' publishing house were consequences of my audacity. I had dared to remind the all-powerful director of his victims.

A Bitter Digression

> And he cast down the pieces of silver in the temple, and departed, and went and hanged himself.
>
> Matthew 27:5

You, my colleagues in the West, have so many sources of information that you could know and understand everything. But these sources are too many in number; you haven't the energy to keep up with them all, and in the end you lose interest in them. And in any case you might well not be surprised that Nikolai Lesyuchevsky has retained an elevated place in the State hierarchy in spite of the repellent role he has played for so many years. He is not the only one. Even yesterday you could meet in the Gorky Institute of World Literature one Yakov Efimovich Elsberg (previously published under the name of Sheperstein-Lerts), a solid academic, and the author of many works on the theory of satire and the history of Russian literature—on Herzen for instance. This impressive professor was a pathological scoundrel; I do not know the total number of his victims, but there were a lot of them. Here is an episode from his life. In 1949 they arrested the historian, Indian specialist, and historical novelist Evgeny Lvovich Steinberg; during his wife's first prison visit he shouted to her through double bars: 'Yakov'. In the evening Elsberg used to come and play cards, and being a bachelor he spent many hours in his neighbour's pleasant home. Of course he didn't know that his victim's wife knew about his denunciation; after Steinberg's arrest he kept on calling in and asking worried questions about his friend. . . . In the end Tatyana Akimovna Steinberg lost patience and showed him the door.

The respectable Herzen scholar had many such victims. In his time, like Lesyuchevsky, he had been threatened with expulsion at least from the Writers' Union, and like Lesyuchevsky he had written a long letter denying nothing, but insisting that he had followed the Party in the mistakes he had made. He was forgiven and allowed to remain not only a member of the Writers' Union but also the chairman of the theoretical section in the Institute of World Literature. He had had a complicated life story: in his time he had been Lev Kamenev's private secretary, and had survived. Naturally he didn't just survive like that, by chance, he obviously had to pay a high price for his life—and this price included the life of his closest friend Evgeny Steinberg.

But still visitors came from all over the world to the Gorky Institute of World Literature, and Elsberg greeted them hospitably, shook them by the hand and they too shook this bloody denunciation-writing hand. We usually avoid murderers. But in Soviet conditions denunciation meant murder; on the strength of denunciations people were shot or at best put behind bars for long periods.

Germany has been ridding herself of vermin for many years now. The USA has recently seen the need for self-purification. Alas, the people of the Soviet Union know all this, but they can only mutter:

'There are murderers in our midst.'

The day after this meeting in Kondrashov's office, the wife of my friend N. rang up in a disguised voice to tell me that in an hour's time he would be waiting for me on the little bridge in front of the Petropavlovsk Fortress. When we met, N. led me out to the very middle of the empty square and, having checked that there were no witnesses, said that in two days' time there would be a meeting of the Bureau of the Provincial Committee to discuss my subversive action. Tolstikov (the secretary of the Committee) was furious and would demand that I be stripped of my doctorate; I must therefore take steps to prevent this. And indeed the next day I was summoned to the Provincial Committee. Two important officials— Aleksandrov (to whom Kondrashov had sent his letter) and his assistant Vvedensky—explained to me for a full two hours in a reasonably polite manner that I was mistaken in my views and must perform the necessary self-criticism; this, they claimed, was my only chance of saving the large number of people who were threatened with severe reprisals. Naturally 'the sentence' was brought up against me, but also a number of other crimes; why for instance had I praised Pasternak so extravagantly in my introduction? Everyone knew that Pasternak was an anti-Revolutionary poet and had died unrepentent of his act of treachery in having *Doctor Zhivago* published in the bourgeois West, and that he was a bad translator who imposed his own obscure style on all his foreign authors. . . . Nor was there any reason for speaking so highly of Marshak; he was a good children's poet, but not everyone was so keen on his translations. Both of them repeated several times the assertion that I extolled one group of translators at the expense of another and quite unjustifiably neglected the merits of such poets as Lugovsky, Surkov, and Prokofiev. I tried to object, saying that Pasternak had translated all the main tragedies of Shakespeare, Goethe's *Faust* and Verlaine's lyric poetry, that Marshak's translations of Shakespeare's sonnets and Burns's songs had become a fact of Russian literature, that Pasternak and Marshak had nothing in common except that their names ended in -ak, and in no way formed a 'group'. I genuinely did not understand what they were talking about until, turning to the second volume of the anthology, they were equally violent about Osip Mandelstam, Ilya Ehrenburg, and David Brodsky. Only then did I realize that there was another charge in addition to anti-Soviet subversion: Jewish nationalism. All the poets they mentioned were Jews. 'One group' meant a Jewish group; I had extolled 'my' Jews at the expense of the Russian poets. But all this remained unspoken, so it was hard to combat, as it always is when the enemy puts up a smokescreen. All I could do was to suggest in a roundabout way that I had written about various groups, or rather tendencies; one of them was represented by Valery Bryusov and Mikhail Lozinsky (Russians) and also included to a certain extent Georgy Shengeli (a Jew); Aleksandr Blok (a Russian) belonged to another tendency, and Boris Pasternak (a Jew) was connected with this one. . . . Of course these notes in brackets were not spoken out loud, and even now as I reproduce my own train of thought, I am ashamed of myself. Why did I allow myself, without even saying so aloud, to agree that Mandelstam, Pasternak, Marshak, and Ehrenburg are nothing but Jews? They are also Russian writers and creators of Russian culture just as I am, who supposedly lumped them all together in a special 'group' of Jewish translators. We are all Jews by blood and Jews for the racialists, the anti-Semites, the savages.

In his autobiography Ilya Ehrenburg declared: 'I cannot speak Hebrew, but I have often been reminded of my Jewishness by people who obviously believed in special racial characteristics. I am not a racialist, but as long as there are still racialists about the place I shall answer the question about my nationality with the word "Jew".' This was written in 1959, ten years after the anti-Semitic campaign against cosmopolitans, six years after the quashing of the case against the Jewish doctors ('murderers in white coats'), three years after the Twentieth Congress. Ehrenburg knew that there were 'still racialists about the place', and not just about the place but in his own native land—it wasn't long after the appearance of his autobiography that Evtushenko's poem 'Babii Yar' was published and then answered by another poem by Aleksei Markov, who accused Evtushenko of forgetting his own people and behaving like a rootless cosmopolitan. Evtushenko had had the effrontery to recall the tragedy of the Jews who were shot at Babii Yar in Kiev, and had identified himself with the victims of mass murder. ('I am every old man who was shot here. I am every child who was shot here.') Markov couldn't forgive him that:

> How can you call yourself a Russian
> When you forget our people's tears?
> Your soul is narrow as your trousers,
> And empty as a flight of stairs!

So begins his poem 'About "Babii Yar"', and it ends:

> As long as cosmopolitans
> Can tread our graves under their feet,
> I say: 'I am a Russian man!'
> And in my heart the ashes beat.

In his 'Reply to Markov' (unpublished in the Soviet Union), Evtushenko rightly brands his opponent:

> Yes, Evtushenko aimed at anti-Semites,
> But shot a member of the WU.[1]

When these responsible members of the Leningrad Provincial Committee of the Party suggested to me that there was a special

[1] The Writers' Union.

'Jewish' group of poet-translators, who were alien to Russia and the Russian language, they were speaking entirely in accordance with the spirit of the times, and Aleksei Markov had given forceful expression to their ideas in his racialist doggerel. It is no accident that his poem was published, whereas all the many replies to it were confined to Samizdat, later finding their way West. In 1968, when my 'sentence affair' blew up, the Jewish question had arisen in a peculiarly acute form; the official Soviet press was writing quite openly that the propagators of the 'Prague heresy' were Zionists—Goldstücker, Kriegel, etc. . . . It is now known that during the meeting at Čierna nad Tisou P. Shelest, a member of the Politbureau, shouted at the old communist Dr. Kriegel: 'Galician yid!' and that the other Soviet participants in the 'talks' supported him.

I am ashamed that I said nothing to these people, even though I understood what they meant by this 'one group' which I was supposedly extolling 'at the expense of another'; I said nothing and thus made a sort of compromise with them.

Yes, I am ashamed to remember even these inner concessions, let alone the outer ones, for at the end of this talk which I am describing I agreed to write a 'self-critical' statement addressed to the Bureau of the Provincial Committee. It went like this:

Dear Comrades,

Knowing that on October 23rd the Bureau of the Provincial Committee will be discussing a question connected with the book *Masters of Russian Verse Translation* edited by me in the 'Poet's Library' collection, I consider it my duty to make the following statement.

In the introduction to this book, in the last paragraph, I have given an incorrect account of the development of Soviet poetry. I now realize that the sentence about poets who could not 'express themselves to the full in original writing' and so became professional translators, reads objectively as politically erroneous. It is expressed so imprecisely and in such a general way, that it might have created a false picture of the development of Soviet literature and misled the reader—if the book had gone out in its present form.

I had no intention of suggesting such far-reaching political conclusions. However, I admit that, whatever my original intentions, I have committed a serious error, for which I must bear responsibility.

October 19th 1968

If here in this book I have decided to print this shameful piece of compromise, I have done so for two reasons: firstly, so as to be honest and not give an idealized picture of myself; secondly, so as to show my reader to what depths of degradation and servile dependence people are brought in Russia. And particularly literary people.

It is time I asked myself the inevitable question which is on the reader's lips: why in fact did you write that ill-omened sentence; was it out of naïvety or short-sightedness, or just by chance? Or was it written with a deliberate political intention, in the knowledge that it was opposed to the official ideology and could explode and cause a lot of damage?

My answer is that I simply wrote the obvious truth. Of course I realized its political explosiveness—if my reasoning was taken to its logical conclusion. But I used a tactic which is normal in Soviet conditions, that of innocent understatement—you never know, it may slip by unnoticed. If it does slip by, it will give the careful reader something to think about. And if it doesn't, well, it'll just be struck out without more ado. And after all I wasn't so far out in my calculations: 'the sentence' had got past all the obstacles, everyone had let it through, even the censor. And why? Why had it been spared by the censor's red pencil? Because until very recently it would have been not only permissible, but quite inoffensive—just think what got printed during Khrushchev's thaw! I had been counting on the inertia of liberalism, which had still not been officially rejected. And it turned out that they had pounced on my book as a pretext for getting rid of the last pitiful remnants of this liberalism. The violent measures which began in 1968—during and after the 'Prague spring'—were greeted by many of the victims above all with a feeling of surprise: what have I done wrong? Only a few months ago more outspoken and radical things were being said, and not in dark corners but on the platforms of Party Congresses. . . . And they weren't being said by just anybody, but by the very people who govern us today. What has happened? . . . What had happened was something that is incomprehensible not only to foreigners, but also to Soviet people themselves if they are looking for logic and consistency. What had happened was that the very same leaders from the very same platforms and in the very same newspapers were using the very same words, but with exactly the opposite meaning. So you didn't notice when this strange about-turn happened, when the same words in the same mouths and the same newspapers took on the opposite meaning? Then watch out! Most Soviet people only read the papers in order not to miss this change and become the victims of their own slowness. But if you fall into the trap, there's only one thing for it: confession of sins.

There is, however, one further consideration which few Westerners understand, but which everyone understands in the Soviet Union, and which gives some justification for letters of this kind. Let me refer—with due acknowledgement of the differences between the writers in question—to Boris Pasternak's tragic statements refusing the Nobel Prize and refusing to go and live abroad, and to various letters written by Bulat Okudzhava, Varlam Shalamov, the Strugatskys, Aleksandr Tvardovsky. . . . They were usually occasioned by the need to preserve the right to an active life within one's own country. It is humiliating to have to spit in your own face, but each of the people I have named accepted this humiliation in the hope that they could continue writing and publishing in their own society, with their own readers, their own language, and their own culture. Such letters are less and less common, but they will undoubtedly continue to appear in the newspapers, not to mention all those which are not published and remain in the safes of the Writers' Union, the Academy of Science, and the universities. The life of the honest Soviet man of letters consists not only in the writing of books, but in the daily struggle to get them published. The authorities have a number of ways of severing the links between an author and his readers: he can be politically discredited, so that his name cannot be printed; each individual manuscript can be rejected under a variety of pretexts, sometimes serious, but more often ridiculous; books can be published for appearance' sake in a tiny printing and then not distributed, or even destroyed; the author can be ground down by poverty so that he has no time or energy left for writing; or finally one can get rid of him, either by declaring him insane or by sending him off to the ends of the earth where no one will be able to hear him. The confessional statements I am talking about are the writers' feeble attempts to protect themselves from the all-powerful monopolizing state and to use the unreliable and unrespected rules of the game in order to defend their own interests and those of their readers.

Luckily my statement to the Bureau of the Leningrad Provincial Committee remained unpublished, but it did me no good either.

On 22 October the meeting took place under the chairmanship of Tolstikov himself, who, according to witnesses, was in a ferocious mood. An account of the anthology and the introduction was given by Pyotr Vykhodtsev, professor at the University of Leningrad, who was liberal with his political criticisms and insults. The members of the Committee unanimously condemned the offending author and the editorial staff of the 'Poet's Library', widening their charges to cover other books, including the volumes devoted to Andrei Bely,Vladimir Lugovsky, and Ilya Selvinsky (this last one as yet unpublished). Tolstikov called for energetic administrative sanctions against the editorial staff, and when he named the author of 'the sentence' literally stamped his feet with rage and declared that he must be stripped of his academic degrees.

The resolution of the Bureau of the Provincial Committee was unusually brutal:

. . . in the introductory article by the Leningrad literary scholar and Doctor of Philology Etkind, together with tendentious evaluations of the work of particular poet-translators, there is the politically pernicious allegation that social conditions in our country, particularly in the years between the 19th and 20th Congresses, did not allow Russian poets to express themselves fully in their original work. Such allegations are nothing other than a falsification of the literary life of our country, and show the desire to spread an erroneous opinion concerning the absence of freedom for artistic creation in the USSR, to distort the objective picture of the development of socialist culture, and to show Soviet reality in an unfavourable light.

Clearly my unfortunate sentence must have gone in deep if it could provoke such a storm, and if a few quite ordinary words could give rise to so many charges: 'falsification of the literary life', 'erroneous opinion concerning the absence of freedom', 'desire . . . to distort . . . the development of socialist culture', 'unfavourable light'. For crimes like these an author deserved to be burnt at the stake! And he hadn't even—so far—been expelled from the Writers' Union. The temperature remained a degree lower in the Union than in the Party organization; in Moscow they were obviously surprised by this storm in a teacup.

Some time later the question of the 'Poet's Library' (as a whole, for appearance' sake) was discussed at a meeting of the Secretariat of the Writers' Union of the USSR; Orlov only just escaped with his job—and that only for a short time. Even in the stiff official lines of the resolution you can sense that the meeting was a turbulent one:

. . . In recent years the editorial board and the editorial staff have grown lax towards the ideological and political approach and the aesthetic value of publications. As a result several introductory articles have shown a marked tendency towards a biased and superficial interpretation of phenomena, glossing over ideological and aesthetic contradictions, and the analysis of literary works has at times not been related to the social position of the poet (articles of T. Khmelnitskaya, L. Anninsky, V. Ognev).

The diminished sense of responsibility and the failure to work collectively led to serious errors in the preparation of the collection *Masters of Russian Verse Translation*. Insufficient thought was given to the choice of material. The introductory article by the literary scholar Etkind contained a series of false, subjectivist and unscientific judgements, and in one of its theses there was a gross political mistake.

As was shown by the examination of the case by the directorate of the 'Soviet Writer' publishing house, and confirmed by the discussion of this question at the Leningrad Provincial Committee of the CPSU, the collection *Masters of Russian Verse Translation* was not read through by a single member of the editorial board. The chief editor V. Orlov, who approved the collection for publication, bears personal responsibility, together with a number of editorial workers, for the errors contained in it.

. . . The Secretariat has ordered the chief editor V.Orlov to increase his vigilance and pay particular care to the choice of authors.

> (Information Bulletin of the Secretariat of the Writers'
> Union of the USSR, 1969, No. 3–4, p. 4)

The last sentence means that for all his 'personal responsibility' Orlov was not being kicked out for the time being. This was to happen shortly afterwards, when the collection *Lenin in the Poetry of the Peoples of the USSR* came out. You would have thought this volume had everything: Lenin, the peoples, and even, as an exceptional feature, a showy dust-cover to show the special importance of this book and the respect due to it. But all this did not help Orlov. In the introduction to this volume was found a sentence (once again a sentence!) to the effect that the sources of Russian writing about Lenin were to be found in Mayakovsky, Tikhonov, and Pasternak. How can one speak in the same breath of Mayakovsky, the author of 'Vladimir Ilich Lenin', and Pasternak, the

author of the obscure and suspect poem 'Lofty Malady'? No one
mentioned the prophetic lines in 'Lofty Malady', but they were
undoubtedly in people's minds:

> From many generations' ranks
> Someone steps forward, all alone.
> Genius announces privilege
> And going, leaves oppression's yoke.

Not that the poetry mattered. Orlov had to go, and his dismissal
had already been decided on 22 October 1968 at the meeting of the
Bureau. They didn't want it to be connected with my sentence, so
they found another one. They weren't frightened of looking stupid
—and this time the stupidity was even more obvious. Just imagine:
a chief editor, who has published hundreds of volumes, is given the
sack for a sentence, not even written by him, in which Mayakovsky
and Pasternak, contemporaries, friends, and allies, are named side
by side. It is particularly absurd when you think that it was Mayakovsky who published Pasternak's 'Lofty Malady' in his journal
LEF in 1924. And Mayakovsky presented his poem 'Good!' to
Pasternak with the inscription: 'Volodya to Boris with friendship,
affection, love, respect, comradeship, habit, sympathy, admiration,
etc., etc., etc.', not dreaming that forty years later Orlov would be
removed from the editorship of the 'Poet's Library' for daring to
print side by side the names of these two people who loved and
respected one another.

It was explained to Tolstikov that neither the Provincial Committee nor even its Bureau had the right to strip anyone of academic
degrees. Incidentally, in 1968 there had still been no government
decision to strip people of academic degrees and titles for 'anti-
social activities'; it was made later, as a result of the misdemeanours
of Academician Sakharov. (In fact they didn't actually take away
his title of academician—after a powerful artillery barrage they
didn't have the courage and retreated.) In any case, the Rector was
insisting that the Institute should be allowed to decide for itself,
in its own Academic Council, how to deal with its professor. Having
received permission for this (the fury was abating), he began to
prepare the Council meeting. I have already described how this is
done. This time, however, those in charge of the Institute wanted
to go no further than a show; they obviously thought that Professor
Etkind could still be of some service. Although he had 'driven a

wedge' between the Party and literature, he was still giving lectures, running seminars, supervising graduate work, examining theses, and he had been doing all this without a hitch for nearly twenty years; students didn't cut his lectures, his graduate students produced their theses successfully, and he published articles and books —this too was useful for the Institute's reputation. All in all it was better to keep him than kick him out. I imagine the Rector had all this in mind as he got to work on the speakers for the Council meeting. He also spoke severely to me, threatening me with an uncompromising discussion of my ideological mistakes, but exhorting me not to be too obstinate: if I behaved myself modestly and tactfully things might turn out all right. I was attached to the Herzen Institute, I had grown accustomed to it over many years, I thought highly of my students and colleagues alike, and I had therefore no intention of asking for trouble. After all, I knew quite well that the ritual of the *prorabotka* called for certain responses—I had seen enough of them in my time.

Linguistic Digression: 'Prorabotka'

> Look, with unaffected greatness
> Bending over piles of files,
> Clearly it's some private matter
> They're discussing—see their smiles.

ALEKSANDR TVARDOVSKY, *Terkin in the other world*

> Not to the crown of thorns
> By execution,
> But like a blow on the face
> By resolutions.

ALEKSANDR GALICH, '*To the Memory of Boris Pasternak*'

Prorabotka is a Soviet word and does not exist in a single non-Soviet language. At the end of the thirties it was still a neologism, as was indicated in the *Dictionary of the Russian Language* by B. Volin and D. Ushakov, who define the related verb *prorabotat*: 'to subject to severe or hostile criticism', adding the note: 'iron., joc., neol.' (vol. 3, 1939, col. 987). More than two decades passed and the *Dictionary of the Contemporary Russian Literary Language* produced by the Academy of Science showed a change of usage; the word was defined as 'to subject to severe criticism' (vol. 11, col. 1302–3), 'hostile' had disappeared, and the previous note was replaced by 'familiar'—in 1961 the word was no longer perceived as an 'ironical, jocular neologism'. There was nothing to joke about now. Between 1939 and 1961 even the lexicographers had realized that this was a serious matter and that there was nothing ironical left in the word *prorabotat*. The 1961 dictionary gives two examples of the word:

1. 'He has made a nuisance of himself and doesn't repent. We must give him a going over (*prorabotat*) at the shop and factory Party meetings, and it wouldn't be a bad thing to stick a little satire in the paper.'   (Popov, *Molten Steel*)

2. 'Public criticism was powerless; after the *prorabotka* the lathe operator did not change his attitude to people or to work.'
(Uksusov, *After the War*)

What a terrible literature that can provide such sentences, but what a terrible word! How can I explain it to people in the West? It is based on the verb *rabotat* (to work), which can change its meaning with the addition of various prefixes. The prefix *pro-* gives the verb a feeling of completion or perfection, and this is present in the case of *prorabotat*. But there is another shade of meaning which is present for instance in the verb *propustit* (lit. 'to let through', 'put through') as used in the Russian expression for 'to put through the mincer'. A *prorabotka* is the 'correction' of an individual personality by the group. It means a meeting set up in advance at which an individual is exposed and criticized by a series of speakers. The aim of such criticism is to bring out into the open the failings of such and such a theory, a scientific school, or an artistic or moral principle, and to oblige its victim to comply with the demands of the meeting, in other words to 'correct himself'. The aim is in no sense to elucidate the truth—it is not a discussion. It is distinguished from a discussion by the inequality of the participants; the subject is wrong from the outset; he may resist, but no one is likely to support him and 'place themselves outside the group'. The *prorabotka* is intended as an *exposure* of the individual by the group, involving the re-education or the expulsion of the individual; at certain periods in our history, before the war, for instance, re-education was more common, at others expulsion.

I well remember how my university teachers were put through this process. Both variants were applied to them. In 1936–7 in the Faculty of Philology of Leningrad University there was the *prorabotka* of the formalists, closely followed by that of the 'vulgar sociologists'; then in 1946–7 came the decadents and modernists, and from 1948 on the cosmopolitans, worshippers of the West, comparativists and anti-patriots. They all followed the same stereotype, the established ritual: first there was a speech from the secretary of the Party organization or the special representative of the Party Bureau, then came a few speeches from apparent volunteers who had in fact been recruited in advance and who divided up the subject between them, trying not to repeat one another. What was prized above all was the surprise attack which stunned or paralysed the victim; this might be some devastating quotation from a private letter once written by the victim and now placed before him and the whole meeting, or perhaps there would be an unexpected witness who would report the defeatist statements of the victim during the German advance, or again some close friend or disciple—or best of all his former wife—would suddenly appear on the platform and the victim would go pale, crushed and speechless. All these ornaments gave class to a *prorabotka*, making it irresistible and out of the ordinary. If it was just a routine going-over, it was reckoned a failure. The spectators were supposed to be thrilled by the humiliation of the victim and particularly by the theatrical effects which produced this humiliation. Therefore one other important condition was desirable at the *prorabotka* of an academic or a writer: as far as possible, the victim should be popular or, better still, famous. The crushing of a notable victim is a particularly voluptuous experience. There were all sorts of professors in the university during the thirties, but the *prorabotka* was the prerogative of those who were particularly popular with students: the historian Evgeny Tarle, the literary scholars Viktor Zhirmunsky, Grigory Gukovsky, Boris Eikhenbaum, Vladimir Propp. It wasn't an easy business; they were all brilliant debaters capable of dealing crushing blows to their attackers, and what's more you needed to be very knowledgeable to criticize them. For instance, Zhirmunsky was a specialist in a number of different areas: German, English, and Russian literature; German dialectology and grammar; the theory of verse; the history and theory of epic. His *prorabotka* called for a dozen speakers who had at least some idea of what they were talking about. At first they went for him as a formalist, then as a sociologist, and later —after the war—as a cosmopolitan and a disciple and partisan of Aleksandr Veselovsky. Gukovsky suffered the same fate; he was not such a polymath, but he could be beaten with the same three sticks as Zhirmunsky. At the time we, the students, did not fully understand that these shows could have a bloody dénouement; we found them interesting, followed the tournaments with excitement—in the thirties every beating looked like a battle—and did not yet see any direct connection between these shows and the arrests of 1937 and 1938—perhaps indeed there was no connection. Later, incidentally, I understood that there was something in common between the castigation of popular professors and the Moscow show trials; the aim was to discredit those who were strongest and most eminent—only to discredit them for the time being; it was later that they began to be liquidated.

The history of the *prorabotka* ought to be written; someone must have kept records of these meetings, the precursors of similar events in the Chinese Cultural Revolution.

I myself was more than once a victim of this ritual procedure. Not at all because I was popular, let alone famous; at the end of the forties I had not had time to set the authorities against me with any such crimes. I had taken my first degree at the very beginning of the war, in June 1941, had taught in the remote provincial towns of Kirov (Vyatka) and Yaransk, and had then fought in the war from April 1942 to the final victory; I had remained an officer until 1948 and had been vivaed for my candidate's degree (on 'Zola's novels in the 1870s and problems of realism') in battle-dress. Thus I had not yet any academic achievements or publications to my credit; I was giving lectures, it is true, but they were rather descriptive and not particularly original (this is always obvious to students) and in general my ideas about literature, style, and methodology were still relatively unformed. I was far below the level of our teachers, and if I was picked out for public castigation this was not for anything

I had done, but precisely because of my teachers. 'You're always showing off about having had Zhirmunsky and Gukovsky as teachers', said the secretary of the Party Bureau at one of these shows; 'you should have had Lenin and Stalin.' This was in 1949, when I was being accused of cosmopolitanism and anti-patriotism in the Leningrad Institute of Foreign Languages. One of my loyal colleagues had denounced me because in a lecture on *The Story of a Real Man* by Boris Polevoi (the story of a war-time pilot who returns to his unit in spite of having lost both legs) I had referred to Jack London's story *Love of Life* as a model for Polevoi. The zealous speakers assured a shocked and silent audience of teachers and students that Etkind disparaged and slandered Soviet literature, seeing in Soviet writers pitiful imitators of Western bourgeois authors, that he prostrated himself to the West, licked its boots, etc. I in my innocence insisted that Jack London was not at all a bourgeois writer, but rather an anti-bourgeois one, and that I had not presented Polevoi as an imitator but merely drawn a legitimate thematic parallel. I did not yet understand that no arguments could save me, since my fate had been decided in advance and my crime, like that of the other cosmopolitans, lay not in anything I had said but in the fact that I was a Jew. Not long after this *prorabotka* the Rector, A. M. Komarov, summoned me to his office and told me that I was dismissed—for cosmopolitan and anti-patriotic mistakes, for erroneous lectures, for propagating decadence and modernism, and for something else that I have forgotten. The students were sorry for me, but were not inclined to rebel; no doubt they thought that if our government was fighting against cosmopolitanism, even to the extent of renaming French buns as city buns, the 'Nord' café as the 'Sever'[1] and Limburg cheese as Kostromsk, then Soviet power was indeed threatened by the anti-patriots who crawled to the West, and that perhaps their teacher was in fact guilty of this, since he lectured with excessive enthusiasm about Rousseau and André Chénier, Stendhal and Anatole France; I had no right even to breathe the names of Baudelaire, Rimbaud, or Valéry, and the fact that I had nevertheless talked about these 'decadents and modernists' was an additional proof of my anti-realist sympathies and propaganda for the decadent

---

[1] *Sever* is the Russian word for North. [Tr.]

literature of the degenerate West. In those days there was also a straw man that the demagogues made great use of—the 'theory of the single stream'; teachers guilty of this crime failed to distinguish between the progressive realists and the reactionary anti-realists. Gukovsky, for instance, was castigated for idealizing the poetry of Zhukovsky, who was a courtier, the enemy of the Decembrists, the poet of decadent, twilight, Christian, anti-revolutionary moods and in a word a reactionary, in spite of which Gukovsky had placed him in the vicinity of the progressive Pushkin.

Even before being thrown out of the Institute of Foreign Languages I had had a *prorabotka* in Leningrad University, where, even if I didn't lecture, I had presented my thesis in 1947. At an open meeting of the department—i.e. with invited guests—I had been given a going-over for my faulty methodology and pernicious ideas. This was in the Department of Western European Literatures (already renamed 'foreign', so as to avoid the taboo word 'West'), a department run for nearly thirty years by my supervisor Viktor Zhirmunsky, who had made of it the best department in the Soviet Union. Zhirmunsky had already been drummed out of the University and his chair was occupied by his young and as yet academically undistinguished pupil T. Vanovskaya, who kept her pleading dark eyes fixed on me, her former class-mate ('don't blame me, it's all their doing'), while the pale Aleksei Lvovich Grigoriev, a historian of recent French literature, spoke about my thesis (which had recently been accepted by the same university). He too found the whole business not merely disagreeable but repulsive, but not being the bravest of men he was obediently carrying out the instructions of the Party organization. In my work on Zola he had noted some significant shortcomings which revealed ideological weaknesses: formalistic lay-out, including even formulae and diagrams (the word 'structuralism' did not yet exist, so they made do with accusations of formalism); revisionist approach to Marxism, expressed in criticism of an article by Marx's son-in-law Paul Lafargue about Zola's *L'Argent*; cosmopolitan anti-patriotism, as for instance when, speaking of the depiction of the working masses in recent literature, I had presented Zola as a precursor of Gorky. This was really *lèse-majesté*: fancy suggesting that our proletarian classic Gorky could have learnt anything from their naturalist Zola! Fancy forgetting that naturalism is a reactionary substitution of heredity for social laws and of Social Darwinism for Marxism, and betraying the Russian Gorky in order to exalt some semi-decadent Westerner! The members of the department, having been trained by Zhirmunsky, tried to mutter something sensible, but it was an open meeting and the guests did what was expected of them. I recall the vigorous speech of A. V. Zapadov (once one of Gukovsky's favourite pupils, but the first to betray him); in a shower of flowers of rhetoric he went into details about the anti-patriotic distortions in my thesis, and spoke of the mistake committed by the Academic Council in awarding its author the degree of candidate (meanwhile many members of this Council—Academician Alekseev, Professors Derzhavin and Smirnov—were sitting there terrorized and speechless) and of the need to rectify this mistake. However, they didn't take away my degree then and I kept it until April 1974.

So that is what a *prorabotka* means in university life. But it is a big subject and, as I have said, it deserves special treatment. Here I must be content with this short but necessary digression.

So now I was facing another *prorabotka*, this time apparently for my own good: the ritual might appease the bloodthirsty Tolstikov, and the more savage the speeches were, the better it would be. The victim himself understood that the harder he was beaten, the greater his chances of survival.

On 28 November 1968 a lot of people turned up at the meeting, which was to be an imposing one; sparing neither time nor energy, two Academic Councils were to discuss my 'sentence' at the same time. I sat with my back to the hall and made notes; a line from a parody song very popular at that time in intellectual circles kept running through my mind. Since childhood we had sung at demonstrations, without thinking over-much about the meaning: 'We're born to make fables come true, To conquer distance, vanquish space . . .'. The parody ran: 'We're born to make Kafka come true . . .'. This then is what I was thinking about as I waited for the meeting to start. Franz Kafka was a man of unparalleled imagination—in *The Trial* a fearful law case arises out of nothing. But he didn't imagine anything like my 'sentence'. After all, 'nothing' is less of an absurdity than 'the sentence'; 'nothing' can be given all sorts of meanings and colorations, it can be blown up to gigantic proportions and it will offer no resistance. K.'s case took on a nightmarish appearance and could assume any size or shape because it was built on emptiness, on 'nothing'.

My case was not the product of fantasy, it was founded on material reality, on this one 'sentence'. Any normal person who is not blinded by fear, ambition, or fanaticism will look at 'the sentence' and shrug his shoulders. So what? Russian poets did translations, they couldn't write their own stuff, so they translated. That's a fact isn't it? And now they've started writing their own stuff – that's a fact too. And they do less translating. And a good thing too.

Far from it. For several months on end the Writers' Union in Leningrad and Moscow, the 'Soviet Writer' publishing house in the same two cities, and the Herzen Pedagogical Institute had all been in turmoil; dozens of people had lost their jobs and were thus on the brink of despair; dozens more people in editorial offices and printing shops had watched the fruits of their labour being destroyed and had gloomily started all over again . . . and all this because of 'the sentence', because of just one sentence which someone (I still don't know who) had misread into the bargain.

I did a little sum: the discussion and condemnation of 'the sentence', together with the repairing of the damage it had caused, had occupied no less than 400 (*four hundred*) people, each for 2½ hours on average (some for no more than an hour but others, such as the editorial staff or the members of the Councils, for 5 or 6 hours); thus 'the sentence' had cost the state approximately 1,000 (*one thousand*) man-hours involving highly paid writers, professors, and publishers. And think how much money had gone on the printing of the first version, its destruction and the printing of the second version (two volumes, printings of 25 thousand, 50 thousand volumes in all)! Verily, verily: 'We're born to make Kafka come true . . .'.

The meeting begins. The Rector speaks first. On this occasion he is severe to the point of rudeness. On the desk in front of him is the ill-fated blue book, which by some miracle is still in existence; he leafs through the introductory article and on every page finds cause for mockery and insult. I listen in amazement; he really is overdoing it! Later they will be able to say that his criticism and the whole *prorabotka* were mere parodies, so they will be able to reopen the case and that will be my ruin. He quotes some words of mine to the effect that the *dolnik*[1] in Russian verse first appeared in translations from Heine, and that this subsequently had a certain influence on Mayakovsky and his verse reforms. 'It's a lie!' exclaims the indignant orator. 'It's a lie! Mayakovsky's poetry was born of the Revolution, not of translations from Heine!' In another passage the author says that poetry in translation should be looked at in the same light as original poetry; this assertion infuriates the Rector, who chooses a particularly offensive word for it—it is 'intellectual prostitution' he shouts. Why does Etkind claim that the history of verse translation is particularly important for Russian poetry? Does he want to demonstrate our feebleness? He lists all the verse forms which came into Russian poetry from the West— the alexandrine, the iambic pentameter, the free verse of the fable —does he want to imply that we had nothing of our own and borrowed everything from the West?

This was the Rector's first line of attack. The second was the criminal overestimation of Pasternak. 'If we are to believe Etkind, Pasternak translated Shakespeare using modern images and language. There's nothing good about that. Pasternak's version of Shakespeare is squalid and badly written. Take the 73rd sonnet— Pasternak gives us a lot of gibberish about "bare ruined choirs" and so forth. It might just as well be by Captain Lebyadkin!'[2]

The Rector had got all worked up; he was in an area he knew nothing about and he hurried to finish, prophesying that Pasternak's sordid and unfaithful translations would occupy the same sort of place in Russian literature as the idiosyncratic translations of Balmont (someone else must have written all these denunciations for him, he wouldn't have thought of Balmont for himself, let alone Captain Lebyadkin!). And here finally was 'the sentence': politically pernicious conception . . . falsification of the whole process . . . of the whole development of Soviet literature. . . . To say this is to deform . . . to distort . . . to smear . . . We, workers on the ideological front in a pedagogical institute, must bear full responsibility. . . .

The Rector sat down and called on Antonia Nikolaevna Shishkina, head of the Department of Soviet Literature. Shishkina, an honest

---

[1] The *dolnik* is a form of verse combining feet of two syllables and feet of three syllables.

[2] Captain Lebyadkin in Dostoevsky's *The Devils* is the author of some trivial and vulgar poetry.

and decent woman, was obliged by her position to speak first, but when it came to a *prorabotka* she was neither skilled nor enthusiastic. In this excellent introductory article—she said—there is a contradiction between the basic conception of the author and one of the conclusions contained in the last page. The allusion to a 'contradiction' allowed Shishkina to give a circumstantial and eulogistic account of the article as a whole, speaking of its wide view of literature in translation as a part of the spiritual life of the nation. The author took a variety of phenomena into account—she continued—but devoted adequate space to the great masters of translation and their contribution to Russian culture, and revealed the relation between their original writings and their activity as translators. At the centre of the author's conception lay an interest in Russian poetry and in translation, and a long unbroken tradition which laid the foundation for the flourishing of this art in the Soviet period. The Soviet translators had taken over and developed this tradition. . . . This was the basic line of Etkind's article. . . .

As A. N. Shishkina developed her thesis, I glanced from time to time at the Rector—he was frowning: why did we get all these people together if we were only going to hymn the praises of an article condemned by the Provincial Committee? Obviously Shishkina is going to tear it apart, but isn't she praising it too highly first? But before long his face brightened up—a different note could be heard in the speaker's voice. This was the transition from thesis to antithesis. Shishkina continues in a different tone—

'. . . and suddenly, against the background of this fertile and correct conception, on the last page there is a blunder. It does not spring from the material in question, nor is it connected with the method of investigation, and of course, it is at variance with reality. In its categorical dogmatism, Etkind's peremptory conclusion contradicts the principles of scientific research. It is also mistaken from a political point of view. Soviet literary scholarship does not shy away from complex problems, but these must be solved by means of deep and comprehensive analysis, and not on the apolitical ground of pure science.

I feel like some abstract scholar, who out of absent-mindedness forgets about the earth and politics. . . . This is unpleasant, but it's safer to be an academic wool-gatherer than a political saboteur.

'The demands on a Soviet scholar are first of all responsibility for every thesis proposed by him, and complete clarity of conception. Etkind, however, constructs his concluding generalization on random data which are outside the scope of his work and on material with which he is not sufficiently familiar. This conclusion of the author deserves severe condemnation. He needs to give more thought to the damage caused by such half-baked conclusions.'

Yes, A. N. Shishkina is a decent honest person. Does she realize that she is not telling the truth? She does. But during a prorabotka *the point is to compose your speech in such a way as to show unflinching Party severity towards the author of the article, but without hurting him. In order to satisfy the Provincial Committee he must be held up to shame, but at the same time he must be protected from the Committee. This can best be achieved by showing that 'the sentence' is an accident that contradicts the whole drift of the article, that it is a consequence of the author's apolitical attitude, his excessive scholarliness, or even stupidity. Such is our life; what concerns us is not truth but tactics.*

The second speaker was Professor Boris Fyodorovich Egorov, the head of the Department of Russian Literature; his position was complicated by the fact that he was a member of the editorial board of the 'Poet's Library' and at the same time was obliged by his post at the Institute to take an active part in the *prorabotka*. He too was neither skilled nor enthusiastic. He hastily agreed with all that had been said, described 'the sentence' as 'politically irresponsible and thoughtless', said that it had arisen out of the author's desire to explain the upsurge of the translator's art in the Soviet period (that is, out of the best patriotic motives!), but that this phenomenon could be explained in another way—by reference to the rich tradition in Russia; not only could the author have dispensed with this fallacious conclusion, but his article would have been all the better for it. And he finished by making the point that this sad story contained a lesson for us all, and particularly for the members of the editorial board. Mistakes must be spotted in time and articles containing them must be stopped . . . the 'Poet's Library' was founded by Gorky . . . Collective leadership . . . joint responsibility . . .

Egorov's speech petered out in these vague and generally friendly remarks, and he was followed on the platform by Elena Nikolaevna Knyazkova, the head of the Department of French Language—she was my immediate superior. Stylish and in her advancing years still a very handsome woman, Knyazkova did not understand the first thing about politics—nor indeed did she find science particularly appealing. Since 1952 she has been working side by side with Professor Etkind, and has a lot to say in his favour—knowledgeable, an excellent lecturer—but now it turns out that he is a political illiterate. How can this be? 'What is the explanation for such a strange contradiction? No doubt it is because in recent years Professor Etkind has cut himself off from the social activity of the faculty and stopped attending meetings of the Party education network. Worse still, he has left the Union and gone over to the Writers' Union, completely neglecting the raising of his ideological and theoretical level. [At the 'education network' I should naturally have had explained to me that the Russian poets were free to express themselves to the full!] Professor Etkind attends neither Union meetings, nor open Party meetings, and concentrates all his social activity in the Writers' Union, so we have no chance of educating him. It must also be said that he has become excessively arrogant and self-sufficient, avoiding formal gatherings and only rarely appearing at our comradely receptions on the occasion of Soviet holidays or thesis examinations. . . .'

Here Knyazkova was really laying it on a bit too thick. Her image of the arrogant anti-social professor is artistically convincing, but goes against the well-known facts: the professor never steered clear of friendly banquets.

'All this,' concludes E. N. Knyazkova, sighing sadly, 'all this must have led Professor Etkind to political illiteracy.'

Madame Knyazkova belongs to another world, she is not used to Soviet phraseology; it is only with difficulty and even with obvious repugnance that she can bring herself to use these lumpish expressions: 'cut himself off from the social activity of the faculty', 'neglecting the raising of his ideological and theoretical level', 'open Party meetings'. . . . On her ladylike lips all these linguistic monstrosities sound like blatant pastiche. Otherwise her speech is blessedly empty. The words sound hostile, but what do they really contain? That Etkind does not take part in theoretical activities, does not 'raise his level'? That he is not a member of the Institute Union? Well, that's all right, he can go to the meetings and join the Union, that's easily put right. The prora-botka *is slipping away into nothing and losing its teeth, that's why the next speaker is—*

Professor Sofronov, head of the Department of Party History. Now things are getting serious—the pastiche is over. On the plat-form stands a little hunchback with a rapacious face and a rasping voice. I know the type, an uncommon one, the fanatic who is pre-pared to go through fire and water for his Provincial Committee. Not that we should forget that this fanaticism is handsomely paid. Is it worth giving his speech in detail? You can find plenty of similar vulgar banalities in any copy of the *Literary Gazette* be-tween 1946 and 1955. However, this was all happening in 1968 and that changes everything; what's more, Sofronov's speech repre-sents the crowning glory of the 'theatre of the absurd' that the reader is witnessing in these pages.

'I am not a specialist,' grates Sofronov, 'but the author has stung to the quick every Soviet man or woman, and I consider it my civic duty to say what I think about a series of issues of general scientific principle which are raised by this article. No,' he suddenly ex-claims, turning to Knyazkova, 'no, it's not just a question of not attending the seminars of the Party education network. [A threaten-ing metallic ring enters his voice.] It is more serious than that. Why does Etkind not have a unified methodological approach to the study of translation? Why, in considering the past, does he dispense with Marxist analysis and the relationship between the writer's work and social processes? But then, as soon as he reaches the con-temporary period, why the sudden appearance of references to the personality cult? Why does the author fail to see the upsurge of the whole of Soviet literature caused by the Great October Revolution? There is more in this than meets the eye. Doesn't the Leninist principle of Party spirit in literature apply equally to translation? Don't the Russian translations of Marx's *Capital* bear witness. . . .

I have several times had occasion to work as a simultaneous inter-preter; I would sit in a box in front of a microphone and listen to the speeches of Soviet delegates over the headphones. Those members of the audience who knew both languages were often perplexed: how can he

*translate in advance, not waiting for the speaker to finish one sentence
or begin the next? And how does he manage to avoid mistakes when he
works by anticipation? It was really the simplest thing in the world:
speeches of that kind run easily along a track of familiar old clichés.
You know in advance the train of thought, the vocabulary, and the
succession of commonplaces.*

'. . . Literary translation is a crucial sector of the ideological front.
One can never detach the authors of original works and the authors
of translations from the social reality determining their world view.
The author gives a confused and methodologically unsound account
of Pasternak's work. He quotes Gumilyov's *Translator's Precepts* of
1919. But isn't it obvious that after the Great Socialist October
Revolution it is not the counter-revolutionary Gumilyov's precepts
that matter, but those of the great Lenin to the effect that by no
means everything can or should be translated. In the present international situation one should not quote Gumilyov's *Precepts* but
insist on Lenin's far-sightedness when he taught us that to play at
democracy is to clear the way for counter-revolution.

Here we can see the typical escalation of the prorabotka; *you start
with the alexandrine and the iambic pentameter, but before long you
reach the heights of playing at democracy and counter-revolution!*

'Yes, for counter-revolution. What does it mean to say: "Russian
poets could not appear in the original"? [Another typical gambit:
Sofronov has invented his own sentence and now he is going to
launch an offensive against it.] Which poets? Which writers? If
we're talking about Pasternak, then his *Doctor Zhivago* could not be
translated here . . .' [Shouts from the hall: 'Published, you mean.']
'Don't interrupt, I know what I'm talking about: translated. [From
what to what? But I say nothing and write it all down—the stupider
the better.] In fact it is only because of him, Pasternak, that this
sentence is there at all. In the article this Pasternak is served up to
us as a star of the first magnitude, his name is put side by side with
that of Marx. The article needs to be looked at more closely; it also
contains another idea, rapidly expressed it is true: "In the Soviet
Union the level of translation rose even higher than in Germany,
the land of translation." Could Etkind be talking about the Germany of the thirties? The Germany where progressive poets were
consigned to the flames? The Germany of Hitlerite fascism? . . .'

Further escalation: by now the author is being accused of preaching Hitlerism. Breaking off on this menacing note, Sofronov gathers up his papers and, looking triumphantly round the hushed room, leaves the platform. But it would be against the rules to finish the prorabotka *on this note, or indeed with a Sofronov; there is still the 'eminent scholar' number to come. So on comes our old friend—*

Professor Aleksei Lvovich Grigoriev, head of the Department of Foreign Literature, the same Grigoriev who twenty years earlier had given the University an account of my candidate's thesis. But times have changed and Grigoriev too; then he felt ashamed, but now. . . . Now he has mastered the tactics of the *prorabotka*. Yes, he agrees that there are contradictions in the article, but so there are too in the whole personality of Professor Etkind. After all, Etkind takes a direct part in our literary life, he translated the realistic and satirical plays of Brecht, how then could he of all people write an article with such a deeply mistaken political conclusion? He will doubtless give an explanation and a correct assessment of his erroneous judgement. His notion that Soviet poets took refuge in translation 'not having the possibility . . .' is simply wrong. Our time is one of an unprecedented flowering of the translator's art. Can one speak of 'taking refuge in translation'? This is where the author's mistake lies. Where did the authors take refuge? After all, they didn't translate some mere Ezra Pound, but Dante, Shakespeare, and Goethe, the highest values of European culture. And it is Etkind who is saying this, Etkind, who has himself made such a contribution to literary translation. . . . Or take Marshak—can one say that Marshak took refuge in translation . . .

Here the Rector cannot contain himself—they won't be pleased in the Provincial Committee!—and interrupts Grigoriev: 'It's not a question of an unfortunate turn of phrase, but of Etkind's whole conception. Don't you understand?' This throws Grigoriev—the Rector is displeased and the Provincial Committee will be angry, but to return to 1948. . . . No, he can't stoop as low as that.

Grigoriev hurries to a muttered conclusion: 'Etkind's mistake is all the more surprising in that in his books and articles he wages systematic war against formalism and anti-historicism. And yet here he can commit such a grave under-estimation of Soviet literary translation! He needs to study in depth the problems of Marxist–Leninist aesthetics.'

With this A. L. Grigoriev descends from the platform. He is old, weak, and ill; why submit him to this ordeal? He has survived it honourably, if you take account of the terrorist atmosphere. But if our Western colleagues want to know why Soviet academics die so frequently of heart attacks, let them put themselves in the place of Professor Grigoriev, a peaceful researcher who is continually called on to undergo this moral torture.

The last speaker is Professor Boris Ivanovich Bursov.

Bursov's name is known in the West; he is the author of numerous books about Tolstoi, Dostoevsky, Belinsky, Chernyshevsky, and Gorky. He is a long-standing member of the 'Poet's Library' editorial board, chairman of the critics' and literary scholars' section of the Leningrad Writers' Union, and an old communist. How could he refuse to speak? He is one of the strongest cards in the hands of the organizers.

B. I. Bursov: 'The "Poet's Library" does an important cultural job, it has published more than two hundred books which constitute a serious contribution to our culture, but it has also suffered more than most. . . . Previously the members of the editorial board read all the manuscripts before publication; this time, however, they remained on the sidelines, neither reading nor discussing Etkind's work. If everyone had done his duty conscientiously, this unfortunate event might never have happened. What is the cause of Etkind's political mistake? Various explanations have been offered, for instance that Etkind deserted the Institute Union for the Writers' Union. . . . But the Writers' Union is not some kind of almshouse [loud laughter in the hall]. The Writers' Union never let such things through unnoticed. Etkind will get a telling-off there too. But once again, how could this have happened? Etkind knows a lot of things, but he is not a specialist in Soviet literature, it is a field he is not really familiar with and he has been misled by the statements of a certain number of poets. As Mayakovsky said, "literature is not for those with weak nerves". The most disagreeable thing in such affairs is superficiality. Take me for instance; not long ago I published a book called *The National Individuality of*

Russian Literature in which I say something about Voltaire and Balzac. I am not a linguist, and have not studied French literature, so the result is superficial. Similarly Etkind does not have a thorough knowledge of Soviet literature and he is superficial when he tries to discuss it. We all have the same problem. It is extremely distressing for me to have to condemn my old comrade. But in pronouncing the severest judgement I am convinced that there were no evil intentions on his side, and that his error was not so much political as professional.'

B. I. Bursov's speech needs no comment; even if not entirely sincere, it is humane and the main thing is that Bursov has tried to set against the ferocious unforgiving tone of Sofronov a tone of calm discussion and thus remove the absurd and dangerous accusations which could only lead the victim straight to the stake.

Then the victim himself was allowed to speak. I expressed my profound regret that my 'sentence' had caused so much harm to my friends and colleagues who had worked unselfishly on the very complicated *Masters of Russian Verse Translation*, that this 'sentence' had brought such disaster on the 'Poet's Library', which I had always considered one of the most important facts of our cultural life and for which I felt deeply honoured to have worked, and finally that my negligence had led to such a waste of time and energy by so many people.

I then attempted to give the Academic Council a relatively convincing interpretation of 'the sentence', showing that the counter-revolutionary meaning had been put into it not by the author but by the unknown but influential reader who had started all this row. These were my words:

'I wanted to explain the high level of verse translation in our time by the fact that a number of eminent poets became professional translators, something that had not happened previously. How was this to be explained? We know that during a certain period of our development lyric poetry was not particularly in favour—let me remind you for instance of Mayakovsky's line: "Lyric poetry we've attacked more than once with bayonets fixed", and his words, "I mastered myself and trod on the throat of my own song". Mayakovsky was able to create a new poetry, fusing civic passion with the lyrical impulse. The lines I have quoted are

Mayakovsky's meditation on his own poetic past; he overcame the rift between the social and the personal in poetry without any outside help. His words "I shall stride over slim volumes of lyrics" do not at all mean that he had abandoned lyric poetry, but that he had rejected "pure" lyricism which was devoid of social passion and washed clean of politics.

'Mayakovsky was able to fuse civic and lyric poetry: "We opened each new book of Marx, as we fling open shutters in our house." Not everyone was so lucky. At a certain stage in their poetic careers Pasternak, Akhmatova, Zabolotsky, and even Marshak were unable to do this. Let me remind you that Marshak, a wonderful children's poet and a political satirist, was only able to publish his *Selected Lyric Verse* in 1962. This collection does not contain a single politically suspect poem, but the fact remains that until this time Marshak only very occasionally managed to publish his poems about poetry, nature, or love in journals, and that in his *Selected Writing* of 1947 there are only 20 such poems. In *Selected Lyric Verse* (which won a Lenin Prize in 1963) there are 92 of them.

'From 1942 to 1960 Marshak published 35 books. Out of this number only four small volumes contain short cycles of lyric poems. Probably Marshak himself did not consider these poems his most important work in the conditions prevailing at that time; on the other hand his lyrical gift found expression in his translations of Shakespeare, Blake, Burns, and Heine. Something comparable could be said of Pasternak, Zabolotsky, and Akhmatova. We know for instance that between 1947 and 1952 Zabolotsky composed many of his best lyrico-philosophical poems, but he published only eight of them, four in 1947, three in 1948, one in 1949, and none at all from 1950 to 1952. In the same period he put out a huge quantity of translations, mainly of classical Georgian poetry, epic and above all lyric. Zabolotsky's philosophical lyrics were published for the first time in 1957 (64 poems, including 17 written in 1948!) and the first more or less complete edition appeared in 1960—including for instance the cycle "Last Love", written in 1956 and 1957. Arseny Tarkovsky wrote:

> Why, O why have my best years
> Been given to other people's words?
> My head aches from translating you,
> Poems and songs of Eastern bards!

Let me remark in passing that my list of foreign poets through whose lips the Russian lyric poets spoke is not some rhetorical metonymy but should be taken literally: Goethe is Pasternak, Orbeliani is Zabolotsky, Shakespeare is Marshak (the sonnets), and Hugo is Martynov and Akhmatova.

'I am explaining all this not so as to justify myself but so as to make clear what precisely I had in mind: not some general laws of the development of Soviet poetry, but concrete facts from the biography of particular poets. Furthermore, I was interested not in the political but in the aesthetic problems of a given period in the history of Soviet literary translation.

'Who could have got the odd idea that I meant to say that Russian poets, not having the opportunity of expressing anti-Soviet views directly, used translation from the foreign classics to this end? It is enough to consider the absurdity of the question when it is put in this way, in order to lift the political charges against my article. I am naturally to blame for any negligence of expression which gave rise to this sort of misunderstanding, and negligence can acquire a political dimension if it leads to misinterpretation.'

The Rector closed the *prorabotka* with a ready-made conclusion. Once again he laid into the victim, who had presented his 'sentence' as a piece of negligence—that is an accident—whereas in reality, he thundered, it was a 'deliberate and premeditated mistake, as the collective should have been told'. What's more, Professor Etkind should be clear about his own position: 'Whose side are you on? What is your class position? This is a more serious matter than slovenly editorial work. The basic conception is at fault!' (That ought to satisfy the Provincial Committee.) But even so, let us show our confidence in Etkind one more time. Let him remain here, but remember that your common task must be to educate him in a communist spirit.

How long did this meeting last? I cannot remember, but it was so long that the smokers were pining for cigarettes and the old men stifling for lack of air. Though it seemed unending, it did come to an end at last, but the 'sentence affair' dragged on. It took on various shapes, but it still had a long way to go. Indeed it went on so long that it gradually acquired all the marks of truth. Everyone forgot that the 'sentence affair' was ridiculously trivial, they even forgot what it was all about, and just remembered that there was some ominous crime committed for some reason by somebody. One Leningrad writer whom I bumped into in the street one day said: 'Listen, you can set off bombs in private, but not in a museum; why sabotage the "Poet's Library"? It's not right, you know.'—'But do you know what it was all about?'—'Not really', answered the writer; 'there are all sorts of rumours. . . .'—'And do you remember the affair of the eighty thousand bales of hay?' I asked.—'No, I don't. But you acted badly. The "Poet's Library" does an important cultural job and you got it into trouble.' I listened to him sadly, and kept thinking of the affair of the bales of hay.

Seventy years ago Anatole France wrote a fantasy, *Penguin Island*, in which he tells how the Jew Pyrot, an officer in the Penguin army, is accused of the theft of eighty thousand bales of hay. There was in fact no hay and nothing to steal, but nevertheless the accusation against Pyrot had a great success with the government officials. 'No one had any doubts,' writes Anatole France, 'because people's total ignorance of the case left no room for doubt, which needs reasons; just as one cannot believe without reason, so one cannot doubt without reason. No one had any doubts because it was repeated on all sides, and for the public, repetition is proof enough. No one had any doubts because people wanted Pyrot to be guilty and people believe what they want to believe, and finally because the ability to doubt is rare. Only very few minds contain the seeds of it, and these only develop if they are cultivated. It is a strange gift, exquisite, philosophical, immoral, transcendental, monstrous, malignant, harmful to persons and property alike, contrary to the good order of states and the prosperity of empires, fatal to humanity, destructive of the gods, and abhorred by Heaven and earth. The Penguin multitudes were unacquainted with doubt. . . .'

Then Anatole France tells how Pyrot (whose prototype was Dreyfus) was 'tried in secret and found guilty. General Panther went immediately to inform the Minister of War of the outcome of the trial.

' "Fortunately," he said, "the judges were in no doubt, for there was no evidence." '

What a brilliant legal discovery! The best case of all is the one for which there is no evidence. Later, under the influence of the demands of the Penguin masses, General Panther begins to accumulate enormous piles of documents to prove the guilt of Pyrot, and then the War Minister Greatauk makes the following memorable speech. It is so similar in essence to the 'sentence affair' that it seems necessary to quote a passage from it here:

'I fear that Pyrot's case will lose its beautiful simplicity. It used to be pellucid; as with rock crystal, its value lay in its limpidity. Even with a microscope you could not have detected the slightest defect in it, not a flaw, not a crack, not a spot. As it left my hands, it was as clear as daylight; it was itself a source of daylight. I give you a pearl, and you turn it into a mountain. Evidence! Of course it is good to have evidence, but it may be better not to have it. . . . As I created it, the Pyrot case was beyond criticism; it had no weak points. It defied attack; its invulnerability lay in its invisibility. But now it is wide open to debate. . . .'

Greatauk had a good many disciples—he was far from imagining what powerful people would one day adopt his methods.

Let us return, however, to the *prorabotka* and questions of self-defence.

Digression on How not to Live by Lies

. . . you wouldn't always have to conceal the truth from free people: with a tyrant you can only speak in parables, and even that roundabout route is dangerous.

VOLTAIRE

I have prisoner's habits, habits of the camps. They amount to this: if you sense danger, anticipate the blow; spare no one; be prepared to lie, wriggle your way out, put up a smokescreen.

SOLZHENITSYN, *The Calf and the Oak*

The years have passed, nearly seven years. Everything around me has changed; I am writing these lines far from the land of the *prorabotka*, the Party educational network and the open Party meeting. I should like now to give a moral evaluation of the 'sentence affair'.

First of all it is a typical example of ideological despotism, Soviet style. Someone, somewhere (and how revealing that we do not know who, or where) detected sedition in one sentence of a two-volume book . . . or to be more precise this someone dreamt up this sedition . . . or to be even more precise, someone thought that this ambiguous sentence would allow him to earn the applause and gratitude of the authorities, to rise one rung higher, to obtain another contract for a book; in a word, to make a career for himself. And thus the avalanche is set in motion and carries with it more and more layers of snow. Of course everyone knows quite well that it is no more than a new version of the 'bales of hay' affair. But everyone has to say something, so one person repents and confesses, another exposes and denounces, a third analyses, while a fourth calls to action. And they all start from the assumption that 'the sentence' is anti-Soviet, because this is the order they have received.

Yet it was possible to say, for instance: 'We are living in the year 1968. Only four years ago you, my respected colleagues, were yourselves denouncing the personality cult (if you were brave, you may even sometimes have mentioned Stalin). Is it not true that literature was stifled and left to rot in gaol? Isn't this what our Soviet newspapers and magazines were writing only a short time ago? Even *Izvestia*, even *Pravda*? "The sentence" doesn't even go so far, it merely says that poets resorted to translation. What else could they have done? Died of silence and hunger?'

But no one said even that. I did attempt something of the sort with Lesyuchevsky, but I didn't keep it up. I shall have more to say about the consequences of that attempt. Could and should I have carried on?

If only all four hundred unwilling participants in the 'sentence affair' had got together and decided 'not to live by lies'! If only the members of the Academic Council of the Writers' Union had agreed to act together! But this did not happen. And in 1968 it could not happen, as we can see quite clearly now. But even six years later in 1974 it still did not happen.

At that time, during the 'sentence affair', I too acted deviously. I denied the political meaning of a text which possessed such a meaning. I repented—as far as decency would permit. And why? So as to protect my right to communicate with an audience of students, listeners, and readers, my right to work within my culture, my language, and my country. Not merely to live there, but to work, to take part in the education of the people to whom I belong. It was after the 'sentence affair' that my book for young people, *Talking about Poetry*, was published in an edition of 100,000 copies. This is in no way a political book, but it gave its readers a large collection of poems by the best

Russian poets from Pushkin to Akhmatova, including some authors whose work was difficult or impossible to obtain: Mandelstam, Pasternak, Tsvetaeva, Andrei Bely, Mikhail Kuzmin, and many others. In addition to this I published after 1968 a book on Brecht, a book on Russian poet-translators, several anthologies, and a large number of articles. And indeed that very two-volume book which started all the uproar, *Masters of Russian Verse Translation*, was also published. They threw out Gumilyov, Khodasevich, and Zhabotinsky—alas! But a lot was left, not only Krylov and Pushkin, Kurochkin and Pyotr Veinberg, but also Mandelstam, Pasternak, Voloshin, Tsvetaeva, Akhmatova. Was this not worth fighting for—even at the cost of some concessions?

My Soviet colleagues are in a tragic position; they are constantly being called on to solve insoluble moral problems. Insoluble—and yet some solution is usually found—all too often, alas, by way of compromise. As for instance in 1968, in my 'sentence affair'. Or else it is not found, as in my other affair, in 1974, when the three syllables Kay-Gee-Bee petrified even the most courageous.

What is one to do? Accept a compromise, that is a deal with the authorities and in a sense with one's own conscience, or resist to the death? The moral imperative 'not to live by lies' has been put forward by a man of heroic character, who knows neither weakness nor compromise. He is certain that 'oppression can only exist on the basis of lies, and lies only exist thanks to oppression'. And so the simplest, easiest, and most obvious 'key' to liberation is *'individual refusal to participate in lies'*. 'Our road is this: *in no way give conscious support to falsehood.* Step back from this gangrenous frontier!' Do not teach or write or vote or speak or read newspapers or listen to speeches, in so far as each of these actions is bound up with deliberate lying. 'When there are thousands of us, there will be no stopping us; when there are tens of thousands of us, our country will be unrecognizable.'[1]

This is the teaching of Aleksandr Solzhenitsyn.

'A programme like that', his imaginary opponent will say, 'is all very fine, and at first sight may even seem feasible. But it

[1] The quotations here and in the following paragraph are all taken from Solzhenitsyn's tract 'Not to live by lies', published in February 1974. [Tr.]

was announced a long time ago now, in February 1974. More than two years have passed and only a handful of saints have taken this road, the sort of saints who were around even before the manifesto. Solzhenitsyn's appeal has remained a voice crying in the wilderness. This may be depressing, but it is a fact. In more than two years there has been no moral revolution, in spite of the exceptional spiritual authority of the writer and champion who proclaimed this programme as the only one possible. But why has nothing come of it? I will tell you. In his manifesto Solzhenitsyn declared that anyone who did not follow the path laid down by him could simply say to himself: "I am a doormat and a coward—anything to be warm and well-fed." And a little before this Solzhenitsyn says on behalf of all these nonentities: "Anything as long as we don't have to leave the herd and take a step on our own—we'd lose our white bread and our gas geysers and the right to live in Moscow." So Soviet citizens are only held back from this manly resistance by cowardice and selfishness. What feeble despicable self-seekers! Is that really how it is? Solzhenitsyn's mistake lies in the unswerving and unconditional nature of his judgement, and in the merciless severity of his condemnation. Of course there are cowards and self-seekers, plenty of them. But they are not the ones who count. In the last two years or so, out of 250 million people, there have not been tens of thousands, not even hundreds, who were willing to resist to the death. Why? Is it because "the lash, the yoke with bells are their inheritance, From generation unto generation"? Not at all.' And the opponent continues:

'Take the case of a man who teaches literature in a school. If he stays in his job, he will still have the chance to teach the children something worthwhile, but if he decides "not to live by lies" and gets himself thrown out, he will be replaced by some stupid careerist or corrupter of souls—what is he to do? What is the average man of letters to do, the critic, the literary historian, the translator? What about the journalist? They are all aware of their responsibility to Russian culture. Are they simply to turn away and become (as some have already done) nightwatchmen or market porters—anything so as "not to live by lies"? Or should they pay the price of acceptable compromise and continue to play their parts in the culture of the country,

refusing to hand over their pupils or their readers to the waiting
bandits? If we choose the first course we shall be humouring
our conscience, and keeping it clean, but the general cause of
our national culture will be the loser. If we choose the second,
our conscience will certainly nag us, but our pupils and our
readers, both present and future, will be the gainers. What are
we to do?

'Remember that behind the back of every decent, serious,
and well-educated teacher or lecturer or research worker there
lurks a bandit who is just waiting to step into his shoes. And once
he has done so, he will never make way for anyone, he will
retain his chair or his office for years on end and use it to soil the
minds of our young people. Can we let these bandits in? Can
we surrender without a struggle? Surrenders of this kind will
only make our enemy all the stronger. Would not such behaviour be like abandoning our lines without a fight?'

The 'Solzhenitsynite' will object: 'If we recognize compromise-
ise as a proper and moral form of behaviour, are we not opening
wide the door to endless deals with conscience? You claim they
are made in the name of culture, enlightenment, and the future,
but in reality they simply help you to retain your privileges, to
climb the social ladder, and to make sure of an easy life for
yourself. Isn't this encouraging the sort of demagogy we know
so well in Russia, the demagogy that hides self-seeking under a
cloak of fine phrases about the general good? Isn't it giving
approval to careerism? Surely it is better to oppose this immoral
flexibility, this spineless realism, with an absolute refusal to
compromise, an unconditional devotion to truth, and an open
defence of human rights and truth. Each new compromise is a
new lie, another step on the road to injustice. Any member of
the Academic Council or the Writers' Union Secretariat you
were talking about earlier can justify his action on the grounds
of the necessity or even the desirability of compromise. They
can say that there were bandits waiting behind their chairs
ready to take their places. Even someone like S. Mikhalkov can
claim that he took part in the Pasternak witch-hunt because if
he had refused to do what the authorities told him he would
have been thrown out and replaced by some hardened villain.
In this way he was protecting society from the real extremists,
the incorrigible witch-hunters. Every little tyrant justifies his

lawless behaviour by saying that he would only be succeeded by someone even more ferocious. Krylov has a fable, "The Frogs who wanted a King", in which Jupiter lectures the frogs who are dissatisfied with their ravenous monarch, the Stork:

> You didn't like the quiet king I gave you,
> And in your pool raised a furore.
> Your present monarch is a lively fellow—
> Put up with him for fear of worse in store.

For the Stork can only be succeeded by an even more insatiable king. This is the Stork's argument; "I am here to save you from worse." But you must not give in to him, you must display a total refusal to accept any of his dealings.'

It is hard to refute this moral extremism; the opponent's position is weaker, it lacks an attractively clear outline. All he can say is:

'I know our society from within; it is not yet ripe for change, it is not capable of unified collective action. It might have been prepared for this by a political party, but there is no such party. A purposeful general resistance could have been led by literature, but literature is half stifled and it is manipulated by the state. The political, artistic, and spiritual self-awareness of the people will one day be reborn, but this won't happen all at once, nor most probably in the immediate future. It must be preceded by a process of enlightenment; this may come from underground and by way of Samizdat and Tamizdat, but that will not be enough. After all, literature is only half stifled, it continues to exist and—within the limits of legality—to do its job. The journalists too, though they cannot tell the whole truth, manage to say something—they write about education, schools, art, law cases and even, indirectly, politics. And the teachers educate people—in spite of all the plans and instructions. And the poor persecuted universities are constantly being reborn and producing new people—a new generation better than the old, honester and freer. This must be our immediate task then: to teach, to educate, to enlighten. In order to take part in this essential activity—truly the only important activity today—it may be necessary to conceal one's thoughts, to make concessions, and at times to manœuvre—within the normal limits of social morality of course. In battle one has to manœuvre.

Naturally it is much more impressive to march straight ahead, standing one's full height, but is it always possible to advance bare-chested against machine-gun fire? Isn't it a sacrifice of the infantry to order them to do this? And we have no tanks, only infantry. Indeed Solzhenitsyn's book *The Calf and the Oak* teaches us how to manœuvre; did the author of this book always advance head high against the big guns? Now he can tell the whole truth without lowering his voice. But what about the time when he was teaching school-children? Or when he published his stories in *Novy Mir*? Or when he gave way to Tvardovsky, and others too? Or when he wrote his letter of 25 April 1968 against the Western publishers, a letter which the *Literary Gazette* was happy to publish? ("An innocent little letter and sent to a communist paper too", comments the author—just as he tells the customs officials: "It was against those bandits the Western publishers and it was addressed to an Italian communist paper. Why did you stop it? . . ." Isn't that a manœuvre?) The need to manœuvre is annoying, humiliating even—but what is the alternative? Did not Pushkin manœuvre when he appealed to the Tsar to intervene against the censors and when he appealed to the censors in order to bypass the Tsar? Was he not acting deviously when in his "Epistle to the Censor" of 1822 (addressed to A. S. Birukov) he with comic grandiloquence set against the stupid censor the supposedly enlightened monarch (who was in reality repugnant to Pushkin as the "enemy of labour"):

> Say, are you not ashamed that Holy Russia
> Thanks to your obstinacy still stands bookless?
> If once they start to talk about this business,
> The Tsar, who loves both Russia's fame and reason,
> In spite of you will set the press in motion.

No, of course Pushkin didn't believe that the "balding fop" really loved "Russia's fame and reason", but even in this poem, which remained in Samizdat, he was willing to make a tactical move, to manœuvre. He did this for the sake of the cause, for the enlightenment of Russia. Pushkin manœuvred with the cheerful impudence of his French masters, Voltaire and Beaumarchais. France in the eighteenth century and Russia at the beginning of the nineteenth century were no more agreeable than the Soviet Union today, but the authors of *Mahomet, The Marriage of Figaro*, and the *Gabrieliad* were able to make fools of their opponents with virtuoso wit and without going in for grim iconoclasm. All the educated people in France laughed at Voltaire's manœuvre when he managed to give his anti-Christian tragedy *Fanaticism, or Mahomet the Prophet* an anti-Muslim appearance and even dedicated it to the person against whom it was first and foremost directed, Pope Benedict XIV. "Perhaps your Holiness will deign", wrote Voltaire in his dedicatory epistle of 1745, "to forgive the audacity of one of the humblest but most devoted admirers of virtue in dedicating to the head of the true religion a composition directed against the founder of a false and barbarous sect. To whom could I more properly send a satire on the cruelty and delusions of a false prophet than to the representative and follower of the God of peace and truth? I trust your Holiness will deign to permit me to place at your feet both the book and its author. I make so bold as to implore your protection for the one and your blessing for the other. . . ." And lo and behold! Benedict XIV had to reply to Voltaire: "Some weeks ago we received your most excellent tragedy of Mahomet, which we read with the greatest pleasure. . . . It remains to us to send you our apostolic blessing." And Voltaire returned his thanks and in conclusion, with mock humility, kissed the holy feet of the father of the Church. Was this a crafty manœuvre? Naturally. But the tragedy, against which Voltaire's enemies had mustered all their forces ("Such a play could only be the work of a scoundrel who deserved burning", wrote the Public Prosecutor, Joly de Fleury, to the Lieutenant of Police on 13 August 1742), was now invulnerable, it could even be performed, and it played an immense role in the struggle of the *philosophes* against feudal tyranny and the Catholic Church. All of France repeated the last line of the tragedy, Mahomet's words:

> Mon empire est détruit, si l'homme est reconnu.
> (My empire is destroyed, if man is recognized.)

It is well known how much Voltaire contributed to the transformation of French society which took place during the revolutionary years after the fall of the Bastille. Would this have been remotely possible if he and a few dozen of his contemporaries had devoted themselves to self-perfection, pitting a passively Christian "rejection of lies" against the violence of the regime and the catholic tribunals? Voltaire and his allies realized that it was not simply a question of the self-perfection of the individual, but also of the creation of a rational society. This was understood equally by Rousseau, who produced the *Social Contract* as well as a doctrine of the individual personality.'

To all these arguments the other side will reply, quoting Solzhenitsyn: 'Society is not made up of "social strata", but of individual people. The key to social problems is the doctrine of the individual personality. The best individuals strive "to purify themselves in soul and to preserve a similar purified radiance around themselves". And again, "Such a corrupt and degraded society, which has participated in so many crimes over the last fifty years—by its lies, by its joyful or reluctant servility, by its eager collaboration or cowardly inactivity—such a society can never recover its health or purity unless it passes through a spiritual filter. And this filter is a fearful one with a mesh as fine as the eye of a needle and room for only one person at a time. The door to the spiritual future is open only to individuals, who must squeeze through it.

'"By deliberate, voluntary sacrifice."' ('The Half-Baked', in *From Under the Rubble*, ed. A. Solzhenitsyn.)

And then it is the opponent's turn again:

'This sort of idea—the reform of society by the spiritual self-perfection of each individual member—has been proposed in the past too, but so far it has never come to anything. Solzhenitsyn starts from the assumption that society is made up of separate individuals rather than classes. It may be so. With the passion of an Old Testament prophet he denounces the Marxist theory of society. He may be right. He resolutely rejects the view of history as the struggle of social classes. However, even if Marxist theory looks dated and obsolete, it is a recognized scientific theory (I am not talking about the vulgar simplifications but the real thing). I do not say that it is true, but that it is scientific, based on the study of economics and the laws governing the replacement of one socio-economic formation by another. Can a theory be refuted by intuitive conviction, science by faith, reason by feeling? The social theory of historical and dialectical materialism (if we can take these words seriously) may be wrong, but this has to be demonstrated. Marxism must be disproved not by the revulsion it inspires as the so-called ruling ideology of the Soviet Union, but by the arguments of contemporary science: sociology, history, philosophy, political economy. In this strictly scientific debate religion can have no part, any more than poetry or music, however deeply they may express the essence of the human spirit.

'This is the trouble: the programme of purely moral resistance to the communist regime by the best people is based on a conception of society as the arithmetical sum of individuals. Such a conception will not find much favour in the Soviet Union: we should not exaggerate the number of Orthodox believers or underestimate the number of materialists. The latter will have to be convinced, but this will never be done by even the most vigorous exclamations or the most passionate invectives.

'Solzhenitsyn's supporters will not agree that a scientific theory cannot be refuted by faith, because from their point of view it is utterly mistaken and pernicious to impose our primitive rationalist ideas on history—"a philosophical system which appears clear and elegant can be built on error and falsehood; it is not immediately obvious how much is concealed or distorted" (Nobel Prize speech, 1970). History does not follow the rules of elementary arithmetic, it is "unfathomable" and cannot be fitted to the Procrustean bed of simple logic. Perhaps, comes the answer, perhaps, but this position too needs to be demonstrated and not simply asserted. Solzhenitsyn's claim that Marxism no longer exists, is a self-deception. In his speech in Washington on 30 July 1975 he declared: "Marxism has fallen so low that it is a subject for jokes and general contempt. There is no one at all serious in Russia now, not even students and school-children, who can talk about Marxism seriously and without irony or mockery." This assertion is made all the more dangerous by its peremptory tone, just as any under-estimation of an opponent is dangerous. Solzhenitsyn only knows the people he knows; he has neither the necessary information nor the logical foundation for such generalizations. It looks as if here too intuition has taken the place of scientific knowledge.'

In spite of all this, there is one crucial argument on

Solzhenitsyn's side. Who knows, perhaps the total refusal to participate promises a general renewal and a national revival some time in the distant future? But does not participation, which is necessarily in some degree a compromise even if it is not a crime, both strengthen the regime and make permanent the present morally intolerable state of society? Can this last argument be refuted?

I was forced to rewrite the introductory article containing the ill-fated 'sentence'; the politically harmful passage had to be replaced by another one which was tacked on to my article, so that even the inexperienced eye can see how alien it is to the author and how dissimilar to all that comes before and after it:

Original	*Revised version*
In the Soviet period there is a surprising turn of events, when a series of major poets become professional translators. This is the case with B. Pasternak, S. Marshak, A. Akhmatova, N. Zabolotsky, L. Martynov, P. Antokolsky (to confine ourselves to the older generation). The social causes of this phenomenon are comprehensible. During a certain period, particularly between the 19th and the 20th Congresses, Russian poets were deprived of the possibility of expressing themselves to the full in original writing and spoke to the reader in the language of Goethe, Orbeliani, Shakespeare, and Hugo. Whatever the reason, the 30s, the 40s and the 50s were fabulously productive for the development of verse translation in the USSR. This art reached a level in Russia which is unequalled in any other country.	In recent times many major poets became professional translators, and professional translators . . . attained a very high level of poetic culture. Verse translation became an inseparable part of Russian poetry, which today cannot even be imagined without this —quantitatively very significant— branch. One of the most important stimuli for the development of the translator's art in the USSR was the multinational character of the Soviet state and Soviet literature. The mutual exchange of poetic treasures became a natural form of existence and a law of our literature. Only after October did the rich and ancient literatures of many peoples of the USSR become a possession of the Russian reader. As early as 1929 A. M. Gorky remarked in a letter to A. I. Yarlykin that 'literature is the best and easiest way of making one nation acquainted with another.

This is confirmed by the fact that
in no Western European country
are so many books translated from
foreign languages as in the USSR'
(*Collected Works*, vol. 30, p. 115).
In the Soviet period the art of
verse translation reached a level in
Russia which is unequalled in any
other country.

The text for the 'Original' column is copied from a book entitled
Masters of Russian Verse Translation, vol. 1—it is bound in the
same blue cloth and from the outside it is indistinguishable from
the new version.

Digression concerning Gulliver and the Lilliputians

We can never forgive our neighbours the wrong we have done
them.

LA ROCHEFOUCAULD

Three or four days after the Academic Council meeting I had
an unexpected visit from a young man, who introduced himself as a printing worker and handed me a small parcel with the
words: 'Take it, it's more use to you.' The parcel contained
both of my volumes in their original form—all the rest of the
25,000 had been destroyed and I would perhaps never have
seen a copy had it not been for this anonymous well-wisher.
Here are one or two passages for the reader to compare.

In the first place, Nikolai Gumilyov had completely disappeared—as if no Russian poet of this name had ever existed.
Vladislav Khodasevich and Vladimir Zhabotinsky had disappeared from the anthology and therefore from the introduction. The passages in the introduction assessing Pasternak's
work as a translator had been rewritten as follows (the words in
italics had been deleted):

'A lyric poet of great personal force and strong individuality,
he was at the same time a professional verse translator, *who
worked with unparalleled productiveness*. . . . Certain critics who
were close to the school of Bryusov and Lozinsky refused to
give the name of translation to Pasternak's translations, and
considered them a manifestation of his original poetry. *However, the shortcomings of Pasternak's work are accompanied by*

great achievements; many of his verse translations have all the qualities of living Russian poetry, and thus re-create in the eyes of the reader the prestige of foreign genius. . . .'

Original	Revised version
. . . this great lyric poet, who in becoming a professional translator lost none of his characteristic all-conquering and absolutely individual lyricism, created immensely valuable works in the field of verse translation.	. . . this important lyric poet, who in becoming a professional translator lost none of his characteristic lyricism, created genuinely valuable works in the field of verse translation.

You wouldn't have thought the authorities needed to concern themselves with the evaluation of Pasternak as a translator. If I had quoted the lines I mentioned earlier ('From Goethe as from a ghetto speak the burning lips of Pasternak') they might have had something to complain about. But as it was . . . No, what our masters could not forget was the idiotic persecution of our best lyric poet in 1958 ('We can never forgive our neighbours the wrong we have done them'), and then the lines with which he had branded them:

> We've killed the cult of personality,
> But in their fortieth year
> The cults of evil and monotony
> Are still alive and well.

> And every day brings its dull load—
> It's more than I can bear—
> Of endless photographic groups
> With the same swinish stare.

And so, not being able to forgive their own persecution or his poem, they had avenged themselves, as the Lilliputians once took vengeance on Gulliver; he was not 'great' but 'important', his lyricism was not 'all-conquering and absolutely individual' but just 'lyricism', and the works he created were not 'immensely' but 'genuinely' valuable. As for a quotation from an article by the poet Andrei Voznesensky about Pasternak as a translator, the Lilliputians simply cut it out. In it Voznesensky wrote:

'The scale of Pasternak's work as a translator is astonishing. Never has Russian or world poetry seen anything like it. There are volumes and volumes. It plays a great educational role. He left behind him the example of translation as a heroic exploit. His career demolishes the myth of the poet as idle shepherd-boy. As a poet he worked day and night, like a gardener, and on his broad back brought home the culture of humanity, just as he carried our culture to the rest of humanity. And all this was done in a notably lofty and self-sacrificing spirit.'

We ought to be proud of all he did for the glory of Russia, and proud of being his contemporaries. And all we think about is how to cut him down to size, reducing him from 'great' to 'important', and then to mediocre, and unimportant . . . and in the end to Captain Lebyadkin.

The poet Ilya Selvinsky, a perfectly decent fellow be it said, disgraced himself by his speech against Pasternak during the *prorabotka* at the Writers' Union. At one time he had greatly admired him and even called him one of his masters—alongside Pushkin. After that shameful speech of his an epigram appeared which I should like to use to conclude this digression about Gulliver and the vengeance of the Lilliputians:

On Ilya Selvinsky

> And all my masters
> From Pushkin to Pasternak.
>
> . . . I never yet drove in a single nail.

I. SELVINSKY

> It's all done now, the shame and glory,
> Mere spite and jealousy remain.
> Now they have crucified the Master
> *You* come and drive in your first nail.

I kept up the struggle for a long time. I defended Khodasevich's translations, insisting that the description of the work, which had been widely distributed in the free publisher's prospectus, contained the words: 'The verse translation of the beginning of this century will be represented by the work of Bunin, Balmont, Sologub, Bryusov, Annensky, Khodasevich, Blok and others. A

considerable amount of space will be devoted to the Soviet masters:
Pasternak, Zabolotsky, Tsvetaeva, Tynyanov, Lozinsky, Marshak,
Akhmatova and others.'

Having promised Khodasevich in the prospectus, how could we
not print him in the anthology? There would be letters from irate
readers who had ordered and bought the book on the strength of
this description.

'Don't worry', they answered. 'Much better get a few dozen
letters of complaint than publish the work of the émigré Khodasevich with his translations of Zionist Jewish poets. And anyhow
what were you thinking of, how did that description ever get published in the prospectus? What a list—the émigré Bunin, the decadent Annensky, the émigré Khodasevich . . .! Only Bryusov and
Blok are mentioned in our textbooks. And what about the second
list—"the Soviet masters"? It's even worse: the traitor Pasternak,
the prisoner Zabolotsky, the émigré Tsvetaeva, the aesthete Lozinsky, the instigator and classic of Russian formalism Tynyanov, the
internal émigré and author of *Requiem* Akhmatova, the Jew Marshak. . . . Why, this list of yours only shows how right they were to
put you through a *prorabotka*!'

This—more or less—was what I was told by the senior officials
of the publishing house, often with a cynical leer, as if they were
not speaking on their own behalf but quoting what someone else
might have said in a similar situation.

I continued to defend Gumilyov, thrusting down people's throats
a report which I had produced after a lot of research and which
seemed to me unanswerable. 'Look,' I kept telling those in charge,
'there's a long article about Gumilyov in the second volume of the
Shorter Literary Encyclopedia, and it even says that "several aspects
of Gumilyov's work—his vivid ornamental descriptiveness, poetic
clarity of language, romantically theatrical gestures and vigorous
intonation—exerted a definite influence on the work of Soviet
poets . . ."; it's not so long since this was written, only four years
ago, in 1964, what has changed since then? [I knew quite well what
had changed: for instance, this article had been written by Andrei
Sinyavsky, who was doing a term in the camps during this "sentence
affair", but I kept quiet about this]; there are translations by
Gumilyov in the anthology *Foreign Poetry in Russian Translation*
which has only just come out in Moscow this year [incidentally,
the editors of this volume made a blunder and printed someone

else's translation of a *ballade* of François Villon under Gumilyov's name]; in P. Gromov's book *Blok, his precursors and contemporaries*, published as recently as 1966 in this very same Leningrad section of "Soviet Writer", there is a detailed twelve-page analysis (pp. 538–50), of Gumilyov's poems, and his own poems what's more, not his translations; Gumilyov is in all the textbooks and anthologies; in the university manual *Twentieth Century Literature* he is given two pages, in *The Theory of Verse* (1968) he is quoted on pages, 62, 92, 93, 101, 225. . . . What have you got against him? He died in 1921; he hasn't been in a position to commit any new crimes. In this report I quote accounts of Gumilyov from the book I have just mentioned by Pavel Gromov:

' "In these same years Gumilyov increases enormously in poetic stature, he becomes a major literary figure . . ." [p. 539. What's more, he is discussing the collection *Pillar of Fire*, published in 1921!]. Or again: "the new artistic quality which gives Gumilyov a place among the leaders of Russian poetry, is linked to a feeling of tragic unrest . . ." Or: "such masterpieces of Gumilyov as 'Memory' and 'The Run-away Tram'. . . ."

'These are all quotations from a book published in 1966. Does that mean that this was allowed two years ago, but not today? Not long ago it was correct, but now it has become incorrect? What has happened?'

Incidentally, I was not the only one who suffered—Efim Dobin's book *The Work of Akhmatova*, which came out at the same time in the Leningrad section of 'Soviet Writer', was all messed up—it even seems they destroyed a printing of ten thousand copies and reprinted the book in order to keep Gumilyov's name from sullying the pages. Thus, for instance, there is the following passage in Dobin's book about the 'Guild of Poets' which was led by the 'syndics' Gorodetsky and Gumilyov: 'The "Guild" was led by three "syndics", including Sergei Gorodetsky. They ceremonially opened and closed meetings . . .' (p. 30). 'Three' is a mistake, there were only two of them, but you can't write: 'two "syndics", including Sergei Gorodetsky'. How shameful!

I had also had translations by Gumilyov cut out of the proofs of another book, a bilingual anthology entitled *French Poetry Translated by Russian Poets*; all my appeals to conscience and logic were of no avail. It was a pity, too. I wanted to publish for the first time —from a manuscript I had come across by chance—Gumilyov's translation of Rimbaud's sonnet about the colour of the vowels. A few weeks later Academician Viktor Zhirmunsky complained to me that he had been forbidden in advance to mention Gumilyov in the article he was planning for the large 'Poet's Library' edition of Anna Akhmatova. 'Who on earth can I say Akhmatova married?' lamented Viktor Maksimovich. 'Some nameless leader of the Acmeist movement?'

Moreover, I repeated to all and sundry, in my *Masters of Russian Verse Translation* Gumilyov appears in his most inoffensive role, as the translator of Théophile Gautier and French folk-songs; what ideological damage could be done by 'Malbrouk s'en va-t'en guerre'?

It was all in vain. No one took any notice of me or read my reports—'we can do without Gumilyov!' Even though his removal from Dobin's book cost the state many thousands of roubles!

Various rumours were going about. They were saying that the top authorities had heard about the poem written just before his death by Gumilyov, and currently circulating among intellectuals —it includes such lines as:

> I do not fear, without a tremor
> I, a soldier, poet, sailor,
> Brave the bloody butcher's lead.
> Let me be branded as a traitor,
> I know that for the sake of freedom
> The black clot of my blood I'll shed.

But why should this annoy the authorities? You can't expect radiant verse from someone who is about to be shot. And is it so wrong to call a butcher a butcher? This didn't seem a likely hypothesis to me; perhaps someone, reading these terrible lines, had remembered Gumilyov and outlawed him as the victim of a revolutionary tribunal which had had him shot without cause, but was it worth reviving the memory of those bloody days?

There was another possibility. Shortly before the 'sentence affair', in 1967, Irina Odoevtseva's book *On the Banks of the Neva* had appeared in the West. In this book the author remembers how one day she was sitting in the house of Gumilyov, her teacher and friend, and happened to open a drawer stuffed with English banknotes; also she claims he showed her a revolver destined to . . . This is what she writes:

'If I am asked whether Gumilyov was in a plot or whether he was the victim of a quite unmotivated accusation, I can answer with certainty: Gumilyov was undoubtedly involved in a plot.

'Yes, I knew that he was involved in a plot. But I did not know that it was the conspiracy of Professor Tagantsev . . . (p. 430).'

Then comes the episode with the desk drawer stuffed with bank-notes:

'. . . And he, after swearing me to silence, told me that he was in a plot. This was not his money, but money for the salvation of Russia. He was in charge of a cell and distributed money to his members (p. 431).'

And to cap it all comes a dialogue. Gumilyov speaks to his guest, the almost twenty-year-old Iraida Geinike (who will later become the writer Irina Odoevtseva), a girl with a big black ribbon, as follows:

'—Forget all I have told you. Do you understand?

'I nod.

'—Do you swear?

'—I swear.

'He gives a sigh of relief.

'—That's all right then. I have told you nothing. You know nothing. Remember—nothing at all. No-thing! Now calm down and wipe your eyes. . . .

'But from then on I knew that Gumilyov was really in some sort of plot and was not playing at conspiracy (p. 432).'

This semi-fantastic story (what if Gumilyov was boasting to the girl in the black ribbon? What if Irina Odoevtseva is not accurately repeating what Iraida Geinike heard?) was enough to deprive Russian literature not only of the poet but of the translator Gumilyov. Enough to have him punished for the second time. In short, Odoevtseva managed to do what no one else had been able to do for half a century; she gave positive, or at least eye-witness, evidence of the guilt of Gumilyov, showing him to have actually taken part in a counter-revolutionary conspiracy. Her book began a second investigation of the Gumilyov affair. One must be careful; even here, in the West, where there is no censorship, one must weigh the possible consequences of one's words. As we have seen, they are incalculable. And they are particularly unfortunate when there is no certainty about the facts. Not to speak of another side to this strange episode; even supposing that it is all true and Gumilyov was not putting on an act in front of the little girl, telling her that his money was 'for the salvation of Russia', he did after all swear her to silence. Who released her from her promise? The passage of time? As we have seen, Gumilyov was wrong to breathe 'a sigh of relief'. His pupil gave him away. She kept her peace for half a century, then gave him away.

Odoevtseva's possible guilt does not make the 'sentence' business any saner. It still looks like a scene from the Theatre of the Absurd; the intonations, gestures and positions of the characters are lifelike, but once you listen to the dialogue, you realize that it is quite meaningless. Remember:

—I can buy a penknife for my brother, but you cannot buy Ireland for your grandfather.

—We walk with our legs, but we warm ourselves with electricity or coal.

—You can sit on a chair, if there is no chair.

5

Talking About Poetry (1973-4)

He . . . must have sorrowed unspeakably over the ruin of the country and the people he loved. His last photographs show the features of a martyr; he became what he had wished not to be.

THOMAS MANN, *Genesis of a Novel*, tr. Richard and Clara Winston, London, 1961, Ch. 14, pp. 158–9

The 'sentence affair' was not to end there. When it blew up, I had already been working for more than a year on a book about Russian poetry, originally called *The Art of Poetry* and later *The Material of Verse*. This was an important event in my academic and literary life; the book contained many ideas that I had been wanting to communicate for a long time, and I knew too that there were new things in it, particularly in the field of poetic analysis and in the interpretation even of well-known works. It had also a polemical side to it, and this called for rapid publication, since arguments date quickly. In the periodicals, both Soviet and Western, there were debates about structuralism, and *The Material of Verse* was full of the fire of these debates; in two or three years it would all have cooled down and my polemical tone would look dated if not positively old-fashioned.

My original informal agreement with Mikhail Smirnov was rendered useless when he was dismissed as a result of the 'sentence affair'. Thus when the book was finished in 1969, I began a protracted chess-game which was to end in the board being overturned in April 1974. My main opponent was the director of 'Soviet Writer', N. Lesyuchevsky, who could not forgive me for what I had said to him during the 'sentence affair'. The moves went as follows:

(1) The Leningrad section of the Writers' Union discusses the

manuscript. All those present are strongly in favour of publication (June 1970).

(2) The stylistics section of the Institute of Russian Language in the Academy of Science discusses the manuscript. Their opinion is equally favourable (June 1970).

(3) I present the manuscript to the Leningrad office of 'Soviet Writer'—the chief editor now being A. Chepurov (July 1970).

(4) I receive a packet from 'Soviet Writer' containing a part of my manuscript, but no explanation (February 1971).

(5) I demand a reasoned decision (March 1971).

(6) The manuscript is sent to a reader, Yury Andreev (March 1971).

(7) I am shown the reader's report which is largely favourable to publication, but criticizes the book's 'tendentiousness' and lack of 'Party spirit' and calls for some revisions (May 1971).

(8) Still having received no decision, I write to Kondrashov stating that I regard Andreev's report as an expression of the opinion of the editorial board (July 1971).

(9) I receive an official decision not to publish the book; this is allegedly based on Andreev's report (July 1971).

(10) I appeal to the judicial committee of the Writers' Union (November 1971).

(11) The Secretariat of the Writers' Union asks for another report, this time from the distinguished scholar N. L. Stepanov (November 1971).

(12) Stepanov praises the book and recommends publication (December 1971).

(13) I receive a letter from V. M. Karpova, chief editor of the Moscow section of 'Soviet Writer' and subordinate of Lesyuchevsky, asking to see the manuscript. I am advised by the judicial committee of the Writers' Union to comply (March 1972).

(14) I receive an official letter from Karpova rejecting the manuscript. This is based on a hostile report, supposedly by Professor L. I. Timofeev, in fact by a young colleague of his, which criticizes me for anti-historicism, lack of system and subjectivism (December 1972).

(15) Having sent copies of my reply to this report to many critics and scholars in the Soviet Union, I appeal to the Secretariat of the Writers' Union, sending them the complete file (December 1972).

(16) The Secretariat asks for two more reports from specialists,

D. S. Likhachev and M. L. Gasparov. Both recommend immediate publication (March–April 1973).

Clearly by now the author was victorious. But this victory was known only to his supporters and *The Material of Verse* remained unknown to the public. The leaders of the Writers' Union had no time to look into the matter properly; they were too busy going to international congresses, holding plenums and conferences, giving their erring colleagues a *prorabotka*, pillorying Solzhenitsyn, expelling Lidia Korneevna Chukovskaya from the Union. Or, to be more precise, they had no desire to enter the lists against Lesyuchevsky.

I attempted one or two more moves. But then, a year later, came the thunderbolt of 25 April and everything I had done until then was obliterated at one stroke. I had fought four years for *The Material of Verse*. Now it is going to be published in the West.

Meanwhile, in 1970, my book *Talking about Poetry* had been published in 100,000 copies by the 'Children's Literature' publishing house. It sold out in a matter of days; a week later I was unable to buy a copy, even though I asked acquaintances in all parts of the country. The book's success in terms of its large printing and rapid sale was confirmed by reviews in the newspapers and periodicals, and above all by the number of letters I received. They came from all sorts of people, youngsters, aged specialists, and ordinary readers remote from the world of books. I have published a good many books, but have never had a response like this—this must mean that I had achieved my aim in some degree at least. The aim was to bring poetry closer to young readers by writing about it in accessible and not excessively academic language. Books about literature today are becoming increasingly complicated, with an ever more specialized terminology, but I have long been convinced that even difficult and subtle questions can be discussed simply and clearly.

In school literature is taught in a way calculated to put people off it for life; the children are bored and repelled. Poems are artificially chosen for them, as if with the deliberate intention of permanently impoverishing the young readers' artistic world (perhaps indeed it is done deliberately?). My idea was to widen their horizons and offer them not only comprehensible analyses of poems, but also a whole anthology of poems that were hard to find. This applied

above all to recent poetry, the work of Anna Akhmatova, Khlebnikov, Mandelstam, Pasternak, Tsvetaeva, and even Mayakovsky,
who is taught in a tendentious and politically biased way. But much
of classical Russian poetry is equally unfamiliar to young readers:
Baratynsky, Tyutchev, Aleksei Tolstoi, and Fet are only names to
them, if that! I saw my moral duty as being to educate my readers
by bringing art closer to them. An article appeared in the Institute
newspaper by a very young first-year student called Elena Baev-
skaya, who confessed simply and sincerely: 'When you have read a
book like this you want to read poems for yourself and to learn to
see in them what you never noticed before. I think this book will
bring a lot of people to a thoughtful and profound reading of
poetry and will set a few people on the road to a terribly interesting
science, the science of verse.' (*Soviet Teacher*, 1 June 1971.)

The publishers were happy; they kept receiving grateful letters
and requests for a new edition. A hundred thousand copies had not
been enough. So the editorial board asked the author to prepare a
second edition with such additional material as he thought fit.
Having written a few new chapters and revised the existing ones, I
handed over a volume which had nearly doubled in size. *The
Material of Verse* had had a rough ride, but everything had gone
smoothly for *Talking about Poetry*; during the three years in which
my 'main book' was being thrown from one reader to another and
entangled in a web of intrigue, *Talking about Poetry* had been published and acclaimed by readers and press alike, and was now all
ready to appear for a second time. There was not a cloud in the sky;
it seemed as if 'Children's Literature' was on another planet, or at
the very least in another country, from 'Soviet Writer'. The problems raised by the new edition of *Talking about Poetry* were the
placid ones that every author enjoys: What size of page? How big
should the margins be? What sort of lay-out? Where should the
page numbers go? There were arguments about the cover: should
we keep the old one, but change the colour, or have a completely
new one? We agreed on the latter and my brother, who is knowledgeable about book production and a talented designer, had already prepared two mock-ups. In short, everything was going
smoothly, so smoothly that I was beginning to be apprehensive;
could I forget that a few blocks away from 'Children's Literature'
was 'Soviet Writer' and that my children's publishers had their
offices on Dzerzhinsky Square just opposite the Lubyanka?

The cover was finally approved and the page size agreed on. The manuscript had been returned to the editorial offices after copy-editing. . . . And I was following the whole process, following it impatiently and thinking: 'Hurry! Hurry! If only something doesn't go wrong and we can get it out in time!'

In time? Was something due to happen? I don't know, but I never stopped thinking about getting it out in time. In time for what? Before my enemies got wind of the new edition of the book and took steps to block it? Before the blow fell, which I was bound to receive some time from somebody? I knew of nothing threatening me, but I had got used to living in a Kafka nightmare. Nevertheless, 'Children's Literature' was an island, a patch of dry land amidst the whirlpools; there they neither knew nor wished to know about 'the sentence', the Provincial Committee, and the *prorabotkas*, and my *Talking about Poetry* seemed to them no more dangerous than any other book (for the Soviet publisher every book may conceal a mortal danger, and he fears it as a soldier fears an unexploded bomb; a second edition of a book which has already won approval and not blown up in the face of its publishers is always safer than a new one, which may contain some unknown explosive).

This easy passage was deceptive; not for nothing had I felt these vague premonitions.

On my next visit to Moscow at the end of March I went to the 'Children's Literature' offices and immediately sensed the embarrassment of the woman who received me. She averted her eyes and then took a paper out of the desk drawer and handed it to me, saying: 'Here is the control report we have just received from the Committee for Publications. Read it.'

Digression concerning Dignity and Freedom of Choice

We have indeed set up a record of subservience. Rome of old explored the limits of freedom; we have plumbed the depths of slavery, robbed even of the interchange of ideas by the secret police. We should have lost our memories as well as our tongues had it been as easy to forget as to be silent.

TACITUS, *Agricola*, tr. H. Mattingly, 1948, p. 52

Wahl is Qual.[1]

German proverb

[1] Choice is torment.

The Committee for Publications is in fact the supreme authority in the world of books; it has the right to veto any publication. Of course there are many people who can ban a book or at least hinder its progress. From the bottom up we have:

The editor
The head of the editorial staff
The chief editor
The first reader
The second reader
The director
The censor (or 'employee of Glavlit')
The District or Regional Committee of the Party
The Committee for Publications of the RSFSR
The Committee for Publications of the USSR
The Propaganda Section or the Cultural Section of the Central Committee of the Party
The KGB

Twelve Scyllas and Charybdises lying in wait for a book! The most amazing thing is that any books manage to squeeze through. Soviet writers have grown used to their Charybdises; maybe we should even find it tedious if danger did not lurk at every step:

> All threats of danger and distress
> Contain for mortal hearts a taste
> Of pleasure inexplicable . . .

'Pleasure inexplicable' indeed! But there *is* excitement in constantly walking on the brink of the precipice. The game against a hidden opponent spurs you on. And on each card there is the highest stake possible: all you have. Yes, every time I risk all I have, no less.

Dear French colleague, not long ago you were telling me how X did not want to publish your book even though you had a preliminary agreement with them. Having quarrelled with X you went off to Y. That didn't work either, because your ideas and taste conflicted with those of the person who had read your manuscript; you tried Z, but were no more successful there. Not having found a home in France, your book is going to be published by a Swiss publisher (it might equally well have been a Belgian or a Canadian). Throughout all these negotiations you appeared light-hearted, carefree, and cheerful, and as always you never for a moment lost your characteristic gentlemanly dignity. Go crawling back to X! The thought never entered your head, you deal with publishers as equal to equal, you have your pride and above all you are a free man. You come and go as you please. They say that when Yury Tynyanov had published his first historical novel *Kyukhlya*, Mayakovsky greeted him with the words: 'Tynyanov, let us speak as one power to another.' In the same way you, dear colleague, are a 'power' and no one can encroach on your rights or your dignity. Whatever happens you possess one basic freedom, the freedom of choice. (Oh, I am quite well aware, my friend, that you are far from free—there is always your economic dependence. One of your compatriots had good reason to say to Soviet writers in 1974: 'Your bold spirits are gagged; ours are subjected to a commercial, financial, economic boycott. . . .' But we have that as well; that sort of boycott is not the end, there are ways round it. When in addition there is a non-economic police boycott, then there is no way out, and the writer is a slave.)

Do you understand, my friend, do you really understand how the Soviet man of letters differs from you? He goes to see his publisher, Lesyuchevsky in this instance, and as soon as he crosses the threshold of the director of 'Soviet Writer' his dignity is gone—he has no choice. Lesyuchevsky has just to toss back his manuscript, grunting 'Too pretty!' or 'Too pessimistic!' and he is lost, his manuscript is doomed. Of course he can always appeal to the Regional or Central Committee, to the Writers' Union or the Academy of Science, but they all value Lesyuchevsky more highly than some scribbler; why should they go offending a powerful director? Your Soviet colleague is condemned to humiliation from the outset. He is well paid, better than you are, but he is totally and irretrievably dependent on the whim of his publisher, who represents for him Soviet power. And then, even if the boss is willing to turn a blind eye, he is successively or simultaneously dependent on all the other individuals or bodies listed above. The opinion, or rather the caprice, of each of them can determine the fate of a book which may have cost him years of work. I recall with bitter sadness the faces of writers I have met in publishers' corridors; they bore the mark of secret toadying, of deliberately gruff dignity or of forced cheeriness. Of course there are those who are above such things; Mikhalkov does not depend on the publisher, the publisher depends on Mikhalkov.[1] The relationship is different in that the individuals have changed places. But what remains unchanged is the sycophantic expectancy on one side and the capricious impunity on the other. One face shows power, the other subordination.

Sometimes Western observers—including those who are sympathetic to our intelligentsia—think that the lack of freedom of the Soviet writer is to be blamed on censorship and that once that has been removed the age of freedom will dawn. Alas, it is more complicated than that. We have a multi-level censorship, carried out by all twelve bodies mentioned above and, most important of all, by the first censor, or if you prefer the thirteenth, the writer himself, who excludes from his manuscript everything he thinks is unprintable—this is the so-called 'self-censorship' under the slogan: 'It'll never get through anyhow.' So there's not much left for the censorship proper (Glavlit) to do. In the history of nineteenth-century Russian literature there were periods when it was precisely this 'domestic' censorship which did most damage to literature. S. N. Glinka, who was a censor in the days of Pushkin, did not bother to read manuscripts and proofs; he signed everything without looking. He liked to repeat: 'Give me a pile of blank paper, I will sign every sheet as censor and you can write what you please on it! I do not believe there is a man capable of abusing the trust placed in him by the censor, particularly when in any case he has to answer for what he writes.' And Glinka was right; for a certain time his authors did not let him down and the 'domestic' censorship worked faultlessly. He kept his position for four years and remarked in his notebooks, not without irony: '. . . only in the year 1830 did it come to pass that at one and the same time the King of France lost his throne and I my censor's post'. However this may have been, S. N. Glinka, the censor *sans peur et sans reproche* (as posterity has rightly named him), proved that given chivalrous personal relationships one can rely on the operation of self-censorship—nothing more is needed to

[1] Sergei Mikhalkov, children's poet, playwright, one of the leaders of the Writers' Union.

maintain order in the literary world. In Soviet conditions there is no longer any chivalry, and we no longer see censors *sans peur et sans reproche*, but self-censorship still fulfils its disastrous role; it has become a sort of servile instinct. In any case it is not so much a question of censorship as of the lack of freedom of choice, the Party and state monopoly on publishing. Until recently things were better in the field of journals—so long as there was Tvardovsky's *Novy Mir*; but afterwards there remained only the choice between different degrees of reactionary ideology, from the Russophile to the Stalinist.

Lack of choice is the most complete form of unfreedom. Choice is tiring, it is hard work. It is hard to choose between scores of world-views, each with a doctrine that is attractive in its own way; hard to decide which paper to read when you are tempted by a host of mutually exclusive headlines; hard to choose which party to vote for at the elections, when they are all offering you heaven on earth, hard even to choose between hundreds of makes of car. Each act of choice is tiring, but it is a good fatigue; in using your free-will you become a human being. In the Soviet Union life is so much simpler, and above all so much more irresponsible! Your world-view is laid down in advance and you cannot choose another, not only because that would be dangerous but because you haven't the necessary sources. As for newspapers, there is really only one, which is printed under different names and with slight superficial variations; *Komsomol Pravda* is distinguished from *Pravda* proper by certain liberties of style and the attempt to be more entertaining. When it comes to choosing a party, there is no great difficulty. And as for deciding *who* is to govern us. . . . The people have taken no part in this decision since the time of Boris Godunov's election:

The people (kneeling. Wailing and tears):
        Take pity on us father! Govern us!
        Be tsar and father to us!

First commoner (in a whisper):
        Why these tears?

Second commoner:
        How can we tell? The nobles know such things,
        But not the likes of us.

People coming to the West from the Soviet Union, after a brief period of envy, are inclined to curse the material and spiritual richness of choice: what do they need all that for? Choice is exhausting. They would rather not tire themselves. It's so simple when everything is laid down in advance. Unfreedom is easier than freedom. You have no responsibility to yourself, let alone to your neighbours.

But now let us speak seriously, without irony. Lack of choice is a form of slavery. But life is simpler for the slave than for the free man. This desire for an easy life is one of the explanations for the submissiveness of many of our contemporaries to Party ideology, a submissiveness that amazes anyone who is born free and regards all slavery as a curse. He, the free man, puts the highest value not on the ease of ready-made decisions but on the proud dignity of independence. How often I have heard, or even read, that the absence of choice is true freedom, because choice (including elections) clutters our lives with unnecessary worries and our heads with superfluous thoughts, stirring up an absurd turmoil of feelings and distracting us from the real business, the unswerving purpose which enables us to create a healthy collective life. Choice favours the development of bourgeois individualism and the erosion of social or national community spirit, whereas the absence of choice favours the construction of communist society.

The Soviet man of letters who has not dedicated his pen to decisions imposed on him from above finds himself relentlessly squeezed out by the hordes of uncomplaining yes-men. Nor does this occur only when his political opinions fail to coincide with those in the current issue of *Pravda*. The specialist is mistaken if he thinks he understands the problems of, say, linguistics better than the secretary of the District Committee. The secretary always knows best. In Khrushchev's halcyon days of freedom the writer E. Katerli said as much in a speech to the Leningrad Writers' Union, and she quoted the Eastern saying: 'If we know and can, we do. If we know but cannot, we teach.'

A friend of mine, a famous philologist, was expelled from the Party at the beginning of the 70s partly because in the 30s and 40s he had expressed his disagreement with Academician Marr. It is well known that for several decades N. Y. Marr was regarded as the one and only exponent of Marxist linguistics and his opponents were branded as opponents of dialectical materialism. Then in 1949 Stalin suddenly dethroned Marr and it was his opponents who became the true Marxists. However, at the beginning of the 70s our linguist was expelled from the Party, partly on the grounds that in the 40s he had spoken against Marr. 'But why?' asked the linguist in amazement. 'I was right, wasn't I? Didn't the Party subsequently adopt my views?'

And then he was told (at a meeting of the Party committee): 'Do you mean you are cleverer than the Party and were right when the Party was wrong? Are you boasting that you did not share in its mistakes and that it came over to your side after you had fought against it? Yes, you fought against it, you set yourself against it. There's no place for you in the Party.'

And he was expelled. He tried to argue, but it was no use. The Party is always right. And if this is the case, then it was not mistaken in excluding from its number a linguist[1] who anticipated and contradicted it in expressing his disagreement with Marr.

The essence of slavery is the absence of freedom of choice.

So there in front of me was yet another report with the intimidating name of 'control report'; its 'control' function was to check that everything was legal and above board, that the previous reports had not been written by the author's close friends or in exchange for a bottle of cognac, and that the author had not just cribbed the whole thing from the man next door. In short, it was a 'control' report emanating from the governmental circles of the State Committee for Publications. I began to read this extraordinary document. I glanced at the end—the signature had been cut off. No doubt that's normal, all in the name of impartiality. All right then, I'll read it without knowing who wrote it. I'll try and construct a mental image of him.

The report began with a few lines of introduction:

It would have been normal practice in the world of serious literary publishing for this huge scissors and paste manuscript to be accompanied by a reasoned document from the editorial board (it does not matter

[1] Now I can name this linguist; he is Viktor Levin, currently a professor at the University of Tel Aviv. [E.E., 1976.]

whether we call it a decision or a conclusion) explaining not only the reasons for publication (the first edition was published in 1970), but the necessity or indispensability of republishing this work in 'Children's Literature', that is of republishing a book which would naturally be directed above all at young people who come across poetry at school or in life.

The proposal of the editorial board is not accompanied by any such document. As a result, whether intentionally or not, anyone reading the manuscript which it is proposed to republish is put in the position of having both to argue the publishers' case for republication and, if this case is unconvincing (and it is nowhere made by the editorial board), to refute it. To put it mildly, this is unethical behaviour on the part of the publishers towards both authors and readers. But unethical behaviour on one side always leads to complications for the other side.

In the present case, however, we cannot evade these complications since we are concerned with a social rather than a personal act, the desirability of republishing a book.

And as soon as we touch on the social function of publishing practice we meet with a host of problems and difficulties.

Even if I hadn't known where the report came from, I could have guessed it was from high up; whoever wrote it is giving the publishers a good telling off for not arguing the case for republication: this is unserious and unethical. The writer is such a big-wig, and so superior to the publishers, that he can afford to be illogical and even illiterate. It is a turgid piece of writing, but one thing emerges clearly: this is a serious matter of national importance. The critic is a man of consequence, he is discussing not mere trifles but the 'social function of publishing practice'. But let us go on:

To read E. Etkind's book is a difficult business, or to be frank a boring business. It was possible to write about the subjects discussed by E. Etkind in a much shorter, more interesting and more persuasive way; it was also possible to write about them at even greater length and less persuasively. E. Etkind stands on the second road.

No, the reader will not reproach him with ignorance about poetry or lack of erudition. The author knows many poems, possibly from memory, possibly with the help of a library as he worked on his manuscript. But that is only a detail.

What, however, is the main point? The main point is that Etkind's book has an amazing, nay an irresistible, power to frighten the young reader away from poetry. It does not help him to breathe the capacious

air of its true function, but it dismembers it in a pathological or anatomi-
cal way into concepts of a limited scope which fail to define its true
mission. It does something which would seem very awkward; standing
over the dismembered body of a former human being, it speaks enthusiastically and at length about the great destiny of Man and Humanity.

It is always unpleasant to be slated. On reading these lines I was
not so much offended as amazed. Who could have written this
stuff? Did he understand what he was saying? Did he realize that
his report was a parody? 'It was possible to write . . . in a much
shorter, more interesting and more persuasive way; it was also
possible to write . . . at . . . greater length and less persuasively. E.
Etkind stands on the second road.' Of course you can always write
at greater or lesser length—was this worth saying? But what road is
Etkind standing on? Does he write 'at even greater length and less
persuasively' than he himself wrote? 'Etkind's book . . . does not
help' the reader. . . . What's he talking about? I read it carefully,
several times, but still I couldn't understand it: 'to breathe the
capacious air of its true function'. But one thing was certain: my
adversary was in a furious rage and this had carried him away.
Then came a literary illustration; I cannot omit it, as it shows the
level of my opponent's argument:

A good contemporary Russian prose-writer Evgeny Nosov has a story
called *My Dzhomolungma*, which contains a splendid idea; a man who
has been crippled and left *legless* by the war but who has remained
vigorous and manly, is talking to his friend:
'I too like you once studied man in school—he said with a wry laugh.—
We had to swot up all sorts of vertebrae and intestines. We took man apart
bone by bone. There was a mock skeleton with all the parts, the tibia,
the fibula. . . . To hell with it! Is that what man is made of? No, brother,
he's something else besides.
'Ivan sat in front of me like a bird, clutching the sides of his chair
with his wiry hands, and I, reflecting on what he had said, was struck by
the truth of it; he had no tibia or fibula now, but he was still a man.'
The reader will not find this Man—Poetry—in Etkind's book, all he
will see will be the tibias and fibulas. . . .

It's a curious comparison with *My Dzhomolungma*; it is quite
true that man is more than tibias and fibulas, but anatomy has
never pretended to replace, say, psychology. Does the undoubted
fact that man is more than the sum of his bones really make
anatomy a non-science or a pernicious formalist science? Why on

earth didn't the author of the report think about this? What was he after? And in any case my book does not confine itself to the 'tibias and fibulas'—metre and rhythm for instance; it gives analyses of poems as a whole. But this 'wholeness' is impossible without anatomy. . . .

We have quite a lot of books about poetry. E. Etkind does give some bibliographic references. But it is striking that nowhere does he mention the genuinely serious works in the field of the theory of verse by such a poet as Aleksandr Kovalenkov, in spite of the fact that the students— the creative students of the Gorky Literary Institute—based their studies on his works for two decades. There is not a word about the profound and truly magnificent reflections on poetry of such poets as Mikhail Lukonin, Vasily Fyodorov, S. Narovchatov, S. Vasiliev, and K. Vanshenkin, who have published interesting books on this subject in the last few years.

How can the erudite author not be aware of this? Perhaps he does not know these books? But more likely it is because each of the authors relates the meaning of poetry to its artistic and social function. Obviously this is not a question of absent-mindedness. Here we have a different aim: to talk about poetry in isolation from the main thing, from the content of the poet's work and its social function. Etkind does not analyse poetry as a living organism. He reconstitutes a sort of model of poetry for the dissection that Nosov's story talks about. It is a strange thing: the declared aim is to encourage love for living and immortal poetry, but what we are given is the anatomy of a dummy.

Terminological depression [*sic*] and the misuse of concepts which are specific to the poet's craft—this is the major content of E. Etkind's book.

This time my nameless but exalted critic is right. I did not say a word about the books by the authors he names. But I will say something—here and now. What sort of people are they?

Digression concerning Cannibals

> We shall name them all by name
> Who raised a hand against you.
>
> ALEKSANDR GALICH, 'To the Memory of
> Boris Pasternak'

Aleksandr Kovalenkov. For many years he taught young writers in the Literary Institute, wrote poetry himself, and published a few works about poetry, works which were both vulgar and openly reactionary. I mentioned them in my book *Poetry and Translation*, which came out in 1963; I was on the point of starting a debate with Kovalenkov, but realized that his 'works' were not worth arguing with and contented myself with a few ironical paragraphs. What the 'creative' students learned from him can be imagined from this report whose author clearly owes a lot to Kovalenkov's 'serious works in the field of the theory of verse'. I should add that I knew Kovalenkov himself during the war; he was serving as 'poet' on the Karelian front-line paper *Into Battle for the Fatherland* where he was distinguished only by his fantastic memory and his political denunciations, one of which caused the arrest (and nearly the death) of my old friend, the late critic Fyodor Markovich Levin. Kovalenkov wrote to the 'special branch' at the front accusing Levin of 'defeatist talk', of lack of faith in victory, and of slander against the Soviet armed forces. As the times went, Levin might easily have been sentenced to be shot by a military tribunal, but he had a fabulous piece of luck: the investigator in charge of his case turned out to be a decent man who had more sympathy with Levin, an old-time communist (since 1917), than with the informer, so he rescued the apparently doomed prisoner. After spending about a year in a military prison and putting in a spell on the White Sea Canal (in the town of Belomorsk, on lock number 19), Fyodor Levin returned to *Into Battle for the Fatherland* rehabilitated, and Kovalenkov had to ask to be moved to a different unit. Not out of conscience, but because he was scared of his comrades.

This is the man who 'for two decades' taught our future writers and the man I did not refer to in my book. The musicians of every land swore not to play Salieri's music, regarding him not as a composer, but as Mozart's murderer. Should we literary people be any more magnanimous?

Mikhail Lukonin. Poet, author of several collections of verse and of a book about his own poetry. I won't describe him in detail, but simply quote a few lines from his 'Problems of Soviet Poetry—1948', published in the journal *Zvezda* in the year 1949 of happy memory (No. 3):

'Pasternak was pleased and satisfied only with the praise of degenerate foreign trash. . . . All his life he has lived like a pig under the oak-tree[1] of our poetry. The bourgeois aesthetes and rootless cosmopolitans have sung the praises of Pasternak's false and idiotic verse in every key, simply because he titillated their anti-patriotic feelings and dripped holy oil on their West-worshipping souls. It is not by chance that the cult of Akhmatova thrives so vigorously among the formalists and aesthetes; Akhmatova is like a magnet attracting all the rusty filings and scrap metal among us' (p. 185).

And about Zabolotsky: 'He is possessed by a sort of inner panic. . . . False and affected rejection of human conversation, phoney meaningfulness. . . . No one has any need of this icon-painter's skill, these discussions about elements, crowds, the universe and suchlike symbols. We need Soviet man, standing his full height, intelligent and proud. . . . etc.' (p. 189).

Isn't it obvious why my book contains 'not a word about the profound and truly magnificent reflections on poetry of such poets as Mikhail Lukonin . . .'?

Sergei Vasiliev. This 'satirist' (like the two preceding writers) died not long ago, and as we all know, 'aut bene . . .'. No, S. Vasiliev (like the two preceding writers) does not even deserve the respect due to death. He is a rare example of the avowed Jew-baiter. In his day, in 1949, S. Vasiliev permitted himself —sure of impunity—to read in the Writers' Union a long anti-Semitic poem with the revealing title 'Who can we do without in Russia?'[2] In this so-called poem the author ('almost like a Nekrasov') writes how:

> In guess which year and century,
> In guess which land and continent,
> There met on the broad thoroughfare
> Of our own Soviet criticism
> A slander-speaking company
> Of twelve malicious heads.

These 'heads' are the cosmopolitans, or Jews to put it bluntly, and they argue about which Russian writers should be the first to be eliminated and which of them, the Jews, should be the leader:

[1] A reference to the fable 'The Pig under the Oak-Tree' of Ivan Krylov. The pig eats the acorns, then uproots the tree. [Tr.]
[2] In its title as in its form this poem parodies the long poem *Who is Happy in Russia* by the nineteenth-century poet Nekrasov. [Tr.]

> The rootless cosmopolitans,
> Bull-like, from early infancy,
> Get one thought in their minds.
> It sticks so fast that pick-axes
> Can't dig it out; they're obstinate
> And none of them will budge!
> They made such pandemonium
> That all the passing citizens,
> The Soviet readers, thought:
> You'd think those cosmopolitans
> Were sharing out some stolen goods;
> They're arguing and racketing,
> And with quotations bludgeoning—
> When will it ever stop!

The cosmopolitans are hatching a loathsome plot 'to help our foreign enemies, And spite old Russia's friends'. To seal this devilish pact they obviously have to have food and drink. And so:

> For vodka one goes running off,
> Another to the grocery
> For herring, and impatiently
> For garlic goes a third.

It has to be garlic of course. A Jew would be lost without it! You can always tell them a mile off from the smell of garlic. Having eaten and drunk, the cosmopolitans work out an anti-Soviet literary programme:

> What do we want with lucid prose,
> Or poetry that's readable,
> Or topical theatricals
> On subjects such as work?

It's all useless, let's destroy it, smash it to pieces! Liquidate it! And instead of comprehensible, healthy, socialist literature about work—

> Let's have Céline the decadent,
> Let's have James Joyce and Kipling too,
> Let's have Madame Akhmatova
> And let's have Pasternak!

And the cosmopolitans rush off and wade into Soviet literature, crushing and breaking everything in their path; there are a lot of them, these wreckers, these Jewish terrorists, these Finkelsteins:

> There's Gurevich and Sutyrin,
> There's Berstein and there's Finkelstein,
> There's Chernyak and Goffenshefer,
> And B. Kedrov and Selektor,
> And M. Gelfand and B. Runin,
> And Holtsman and Munblit.
> They made such a hullaballoo,
> Let themselves go so brazenly,
> Behaved so free-and-easily
> They overstepped the mark.

These villains overstepped the mark by so much, they grew so fat on money stolen from the State, and they cooked up so many 'poisonous' books, articles, and reviews that they forgot the terrible people's court:

> Spitting and boasting crazily
> And even daring openly
> To scoff at Pushkin's name,
> In all their shameless hue-and-cry,
> Their vile pernicious chattering—
> Like regiments of mice—
> The Yids, the sneering Israelites
> In their delirium failed to see
> How our great Soviet people's court
> Had seized them by the scruff of the neck
> In its majestic hand.
> It seized them by the scruff of the neck,
> By the gesticulating arms
> By the eyes dimmed with jealousy
> And fiercely spoke the truth.

This is not the end of the 'poem', which with good reason came to be called the 'Pogrom Encyclopedia', but it's too nasty to quote any more. It can be read in full in Grigory Svirsky's very interesting book, *Hostages: the Personal Testimony of a Soviet Jew* (tr. Gordon Clough, New York, 1976). Never before, I think, had Russian verse and Russian literary language served for such unbridled racialist obscenity. But what was the outcome? Was

Sergei Vasiliev condemned as a fascist hooligan? He was not even reprimanded or ostracized, he was elected on to executive bodies and printed in *Pravda*. And when he snuffed it, many respectable organizations hastened to express their grief. In *Moscow Pravda* for 4 July 1975 there appeared a solemn obituary notice as follows:

The Secretariat of the Executive of the Writers' Union of the USSR
The Secretariat of the Executive of the Writers' Union of the RSFSR
The Secretariat of the Executive and the Party Committee of the Moscow Writers' Organization
announce with deep regret the death of
Sergei Aleksandrovich Vasiliev
Member of the CPSU
Member of the Writers' Union of the USSR
Laureate of the RSFSR State Prize
and well-known poet
and express their sympathy to his family and friends

Thus all these secretariats of all these executives proclaimed their solidarity with the man-eating laureate who wrote the 'Pogrom Encyclopedia'! But what could you expect? They have no sense of history. They had doubtless forgotten the notice with which they honoured the memory of a truly great poet:

The Executive of the Literary Fund of the USSR
announces the death of the member of the Literary Fund
Boris Leonidovich Pasternak
which took place on May 30th of this year, at the age of 70, after a serious and prolonged illness, and expresses its sympathy to his family.

The juxtaposition of these notices is revealing. They are separated by just fifteen years. Has anything changed between

1960 and 1975? Pasternak died a member of the Literary Fund,[1] and Vasiliev a State laureate. They still write of Pasternak that his poetry is remote from the people and that he provoked the indignation of the public by the treacherous foreign publication of his novel and the award of a Nobel Prize. It is different with Vasiliev; he is the embodiment of national and party spirit. His death in 1975 is announced by all the secretariats with a 'deep regret' which they did not experience fifteen years earlier, when Boris Pasternak's death was bewailed in Anna Akhmatova's unforgettable poem—and even so, she was forced to put a false date on it (1957 for 1960) so they would not guess who it was about:

> A voice unparalleled fell silent yesterday,
> The trees' companion has deserted us.
> He is transformed into the life-giving grain
> Or into the fine rain that fills his verse.
> And all the flowers that live in the world
> Spread out their petals to greet this death,
> But all at once a silence has covered the globe
> That bears the humble name of Earth.

Clearly the old cannibal was right in juxtaposing these two poets:

> Let's have Madame Akhmatova
> And let's have Pasternak!

But none of his cheap jibes can cast the slightest shadow on the luminous memory of Pasternak. As for Sergei Vasiliev, if his name survives in the history of Russian literature, it will be as the instigator of a shameful pogrom.

After all, why not quote Sergei Vasiliev alongside Pasternak, Akhmatova, and Zabolotsky? As I have said, the author of the report was undoubtedly a pupil of Kovalenkov and the rest of them (apart from K. Vanshenkin, who has got in here by mistake)—this is why he writes so well, like Vasiliev and Lukonin: 'Terminological depression [?!] . . . this is the major content of E. Etkind's book.' And a few lines further on:

---

[1] Having been expelled from the Writers' Union, Pasternak remained a member of the Literary Fund.

Other terminological concepts are introduced—thus, the 'ladder of meanings'. It is done in detail, too—'to go up the ladder of meanings', and we even get it rung by rung, 'first step', 'second step', 'third step', 'fourth step'. . . . He is writing about Fet's poetry. Forgive me, but you really get more pleasure from reading a 20-line poem of Fet's, 'The bonfire's bright sun flares in the wood', than from all the commentator's climbing 'up the ladder', which only takes the soul out of poetry and leaves simply the 'ladder of meanings', which is, in the author's words, 'directly connected with the principle of indeterminacy'.

It would be astonishing if our young people were greedily waiting for just this sort of 'scholarly commentary' on the profound poetic work of many centuries by the most talented sons of the nation (p. 41).

As if I claimed that my commentary should give the reader 'more pleasure' than Fet's poetry! The writer's irony is as over-whelmingly convincing as his eloquence. I shall only say one or two words about the rest of his report; the absurdity of his arguments is obvious even to those who are not particularly familiar with the question. Everything that he says about the meaning of words for a poet, the notion of 'context' and 'time' in poetry, and particularly in Mayakovsky, is of the most primitive incompetence. No one could have invented such a document. Everything in it is typical: the seething anger which finds an outlet in the somewhat illiterate exclamations and vitriolic political insinuations, the crude conversational turns of phrase which are deliberately set against what philistines call egg-head language, the mocking quotation of self-evident remarks with ribald comments, the condemnation of any attempt to explain, analyse, or even understand, the shameless political or ideological *sous-entendus* intended to discredit and enrage the author:

'That's just the trouble, that you can't read Etkind as you read Belinsky, Dobrolyubov and Pisarev. . . .'

' "Vadim Shefner is a master of verse", "Yakov Kozlovsky is a poetic virtuoso". . . . Most probably the authors themselves would have felt awkward reading this about themselves.' (Here he is misled by the foreign or Jewish-sounding names of the poets; it just happens by chance that the Russian poet V. Shefner has a non-Russian name.)

Later I discovered who wrote this report: Vladimir Pavlovich Turkin. I discovered that he was an important official in the Committee for Publications. And, what's more, that he was himself a versifier of the school of Sergei Vasiliev and Vasily Fyodorov. The *Literary Encyclopedia* tells us that V. P. Turkin worked for a long time, from 1947 to 1953, in China (where he clearly learnt the methods of the 'cultural revolution') and subsequently as the chief editor of the Russophile publishing house 'Soviet Russia' (from 1965 to 1972); that he has published several volumes of verse, the first of which, entitled *Moscow–Pekin* (1951), celebrates the friendship of Mao and Stalin; that he was glowingly reviewed by people as pathologically reactionary as himself: V. Dementiev, V. Tsybin, D. Kovalov. I have had a look at his poems, but I will not quote them here. The reader can get some idea of Turkin the poet by reading Turkin the critic; the one is worthy of the other. Even so, two lines of his perhaps deserve to stay in our memory, so well do they characterize their author:

> More and more often anxiety visits me
> For those who are afflicted with charity.

So once again I was faced with the question: submit or resist? In such cases one can appeal to the Committee for Publications, but Turkin *is* that committee. What's more, he represents both committees at the same time, the RSFSR committee where he is chief editor, and the USSR committee where he is deputy chief. I say *both* committees, but I don't think I would be wrong to talk of *three* committees. The third is the Committee of all committees, the Committee of State Security. It is not for nothing that Turkin was given the job of slating my book just before its publication; his report is dated February, immediately after the expulsion of Solzhenitsyn.

D-Day was approaching.

It is the end of March. I am given Turkin's report, which is the last in a long line of events: the appearance in the West and the beginning of lengthy readings of *The Gulag Archipelago* on various radio stations; the witch-hunt against its author in the Soviet press; his expulsion from the USSR in the middle of February 1974; and in the same month of February, after the extremely high-level decision to expel Solzhenitsyn, the decision to crush his 'Leningrad plenipotentiary'—this evidently is why Turkin had demolished *Talking about Poetry* in February. Then comes April:

1 April. Mikhail Heifets's apartment is searched. They find my notes in the margin of his article about Brodsky and my letter giving my opinion of this article.

10 April. I am summoned to be questioned by the KGB in connection with Case No. 15 (Heifets and Maramzin) and also about my relations with Solzhenitsyn.

12 April. I write an answer to Turkin and send it to various addresses.

23 April. I am summoned by the Rector of the Herzen Institute and warned of my impending expulsion from the Institute.

25 April. Meeting of the Academic Council—dismissal and removal of academic title. Secretariat of the Writers' Union—expulsion.

This is the context (if Turkin will forgive me this word) for the report which the reader has just seen. In the light of subsequent events one can say with certainty that it was not an accident that it was written and released precisely at that time. Before expelling a writer from the Writers' Union and depriving him of his job and his title of professor, it was necessary to discredit and crush him as a man of letters and close the publishers' doors to him.

I did not know what was going to happen two weeks later and, as before, I rushed into the fray; I wrote a strongly-worded and (I hoped) irrefutable answer to the report. I still thought that a struggle might bring me victory. Indeed I was glad that the report was so feeble, bad-tempered, and (I thought) powerless; all this strengthened my position. For greater respectability I signed with all my titles, not knowing that I would only have them for another two weeks and that this was my last chance to flourish them. I typed out Turkin's report in a large number of copies, just as I had done for Timofeev's piece on *The Material of Verse*, and sent it off to a number of addresses. I have kept copies of three covering letters which I sent with these texts to the Writers' Union of the RSFSR and the USSR and, on this occasion, to the Central Committee of the CPSU.

These letters were to be my last attempts to fight for my books in 'the other life'. They received no answer. Everything was suddenly interrupted. After 25 April I had another struggle to wage, other letters to write and other answers to expect.

6

The Noose Tightens
(10 April and 25 June 1974)

On the morning of 10 April there was a ring at the door; it was a young man in mufti with a summons to the KGB headquarters at 6 Liteiny Prospect. Until then I had had no dealings with the KGB —unless one counts the spies and narks who had been trailing me for the last few months. I set off for the Big House, which I had quite often walked past with a glance at its solid, tightly closed gates. It is a huge brown building towering menacingly opposite the Mayakovsky Writers' House as a constant reminder of the 'avenging sword of the Revolution'—on public holidays this sword (made out of harmless plywood it is true) adorns the impressive façade on Liteiny Prospect. I could still remember the façade of the Big House in 1937, when they were facing it with granite tombstones on which you could read the faded pre-Revolutionary inscriptions: 'General of Infantry . . .', 'Councillor of State . . .'. They were being put up with the inscriptions facing inward. This made a lasting and eerie impression on me. I remembered too the story of how the architect Noi Trotsky had planned the Big House while imprisoned in the Shpalernaya prison, which was eventually included in the Big House, forming an 'inner prison'. By then, however, Noi Trotsky was no more; he had died a victim of his unfortunate surname (and also of course of the fact that he had designed the Big House and therefore knew the topography of the place inside out). What a name—Trotsky! It is true that *the* Trotsky was really Lev Bronstein, but no one worried about that. Another Trotsky, Iosif Moiseevich, was removed from Homer's *Iliad*, to which he had written a preface; his seditious surname was obliterated from the title page and poor Iosif Moiseevich, who was already (in the 1930s) a well-known classical scholar, had to change his name to Tronsky (and in the next three and a half decades he managed to make this pseudonym famous too). This story is not

just a piece of nonsense; it is a tragi-comic expression of the terror
inspired by the magical power of the word. This terror is tied up
with the essential nature of the regime. Just recently one of the
readers of *Soviet Culture*, I think it was, traced the name Solzhenitsyn without a shadow of humour back to its supposed roots:
solzhets, a liar (to the imperialists), and *nits*, flat on his face (in front
of them); a man with a name like that is obviously predestined and
deserves to be exterminated.

All this—and much more besides—was going through my mind
as I approached the Big House and made my way up its staircases
and through its long corridors. A few doors were half open and
over each writing desk in each identical room hung the same eternal
Lenin; at the end of each many-doored corridor, with its back to
the window, stood the same gilded plaster bust. Major Ryabchuk
turned out to be a fairly young man in horn-rimmed spectacles,
with a parting in his hair and a round, womanish, impenetrable face.
He looked more like a teacher than what he really was, an investigator of top priority cases. Our conversation was a long one.
Ryabchuk asked full-length official questions (from a long list lying
ready prepared in front of him) and wrote down my answers which
were generally short, if not monosyllabic.

'I have summoned you as a witness in connection with Case No.
15 in which M. R. Heifets is accused of keeping in his possession
and distributing slanderous material. What statements can you
make in connection with this case?'

'None. I don't know what you mean by slanderous material. I
don't know what Heifets is accused of.'

'Let me put the question another way. What do you know in
general about the distribution of slanderous anti-Soviet material?'

'Do you mean Samizdat?'

'I mean slanderous anti-Soviet material, which is sometimes
familiarly known as Samizdat.'

'I haven't come across any Samizdat recently. Clearly the KGB
has acted energetically and stopped its distribution.'

'And what have you seen in the past?'

'Various things, but nothing answering to the description you
have given. They were neither anti-Soviet nor slanderous.'

'What material do you mean?'

'I mean, for instance, the transcripts of legal proceedings, of
the trials of Brodsky, of Sinyavsky and Daniel, of Ginzburg and

Galanskov, the final speeches of the accused, the speeches of the lawyers. I do not consider these as anti-Soviet documents because they are genuine records of open sessions which have taken place in Leningrad or Moscow under Soviet authority. For the same reason I do not consider them slanderous.'

'You have seen no other material?'

'No.'

'Are you acquainted with Mikhail Ruvimovich Heifets?'

'Yes, but not closely. He lives in the same block as my daughter and I have met him two or three times in the entrance hall or on the landing.'

'Did M. R. Heifets give you for your perusal his article "Iosif Brodsky and our generation"?'

'Yes, he asked me to read the manuscript, I agreed to do so and read it.'

'Did he hand you the manuscript personally or by way of a third party?'

'He handed it to me personally, having met me on the stairs.'

'Why did he give his article to you to read?'

'I work on the theory of verse and am a specialist in that field; also Heifets knew that I had been on friendly terms with Brodsky for many years.'

Suddenly Ryabchuk changes his tempo. Until now the interrogation has been slow, even leisurely, with pauses for note-taking. Now he thrusts some sheets of paper fastened with a paper-clip rapidly in my direction (clearly expecting to shake me with this sudden revelation):

'Is this your handwriting?'

I see my review of Heifets's article and, speaking slowly and deliberately, I reply:

'Yes, of course. It is a letter I wrote to Heifets about his article.'

'And this?'

He pushes towards me Heifets's article, typed on a small typewriter, with many corrections, and points to my pencilled comments.

'I wrote that too.'

'Do you realize the anti-Soviet character of Heifets's article?'

'It is a discussion of poetry and has no connection with politics.'

'It is an anti-Soviet article and your marginal notes confirm this and strengthen it.'

(Am I still a witness or am I now in the dock? I cannot remember what I scribbled in the margins, but I certainly didn't write it with a view to a discussion in the Big House.)

'That's your imagination. My remarks simply concern the presentation.'

'Like this one, for instance?'

He points with his finger, and I read, scribbled in small letters, the words: 'Why semi?' I look across at the typed text; the question refers to Heifets's remark: 'Since the occupation of Czechoslovakia the Soviet Union has become a semi-colonial power.' Yes indeed, why 'semi'? But I smile and say:

'That is a stylistic comment. In Russian you can talk of a "colonial power" or a "semi-colony", but there's no such thing as a "semi-colonial power". I was drawing the author's attention to a point of style.'

Ryabchuk looks at me with a mocking air of reproach:

'It's quite clear what you had in mind. And here, in your review, is this a stylistic point too?'

He points to a passage underlined by someone where I am arguing against Heifets. Heifets considers that Brodsky and his contemporaries were shaken by the events in Prague in 1968, whereas I, basing myself on Brodsky's own words and my knowledge of his generation, argue that it was not the 1968 events that had a decisive impact on these boys, but the suppression of the Hungarian revolution of 1956. These are the words that had been underlined: 'Just think, there had been the 20th Congress, the truth had been told, everyone's eyes had been opened on their own past and even on the true nature of our victories, and then suddenly it was bombs and ropes on the other side and tanks and machine-guns on this. Budapest awakened a disgust for imperialism, but also a feeling of hopelessness. After the 20th Congress it came as an immense shock. Iosif Brodsky is right to refer to it. But 1968? Everything that had been said at the 20th and 22nd Congresses had already been forgotten, the fateful affair of Kirov had already been consigned to the dustbin, and the good-hearted tyrant N.K. had long ago been put in his place. In a context like this you couldn't really be surprised by the tanks in Prague.'

'Who do you mean by N.K.?'

'The same person as you: Nikita Khrushchev.'

'Efim Grigorievich, do you admit writing that anti-Soviet sentence about Soviet imperialism?'

'Not at all. I wrote: "Budapest awakened a disgust for imperialism, but also a feeling of hopelessness." Not "Soviet imperialism". It could just as well be American or West German imperialism. Have a look at my letter, I don't give an idealized picture of the Hungarian rebels; look: "it was bombs and ropes on the other side", that means the Hungarian side, "and tanks and machine-guns on this", that is the Soviet side. I emphasize that Brodsky's generation saw the world situation as hopeless, and Brodsky's poetry is tragic poetry. . . .'

Ryabchuk wrote it all down, occasionally glancing ironically at me. Then he asked me to sit at a little table like a chess table and to write out the same text with 'different markers', a pencil, a ball-point pen, a fountain-pen, a felt-tip. 'Anything you like', he said, and took out of his briefcase the latest number of the journal *Foreign Literature*; 'this will do, just ten lines or so.'

I began to copy it out, but then stopped and said to Ryabchuk, who was writing his report:

'No, I'm not going to write this. Afterwards you'll accuse me of intending to spread pernicious views among the KGB.'

It was an article by a Japanese writer about the relations between literature and the State. I couldn't deny myself the little pleasure of pointing this out to the investigator and at the same time reminding him of their way of cooking up a case against someone.

I spent a long time executing samples of my handwriting in 'different markers', but Ryabchuk kept writing even longer. I had finished long ago and was walking up and down in the office to stretch my legs, looking at the wall-map of Leningrad with a tiny newspaper cutting pasted along the river Neva saying: 'Words are not birds. . . .' Was this really how the solemn Ryabchuk amused himself? And who was this wise advice addressed to? To those who were already being interrogated? Or perhaps to those who were still strolling out there, on the banks of the Neva?

'Sign every sheet separately.'

I read it and sign. The interrogation is finished. Ryabchuk leans back in his chair, waiting.

'Give me your pass, I'll sign it to let you out.'

He had already lifted his hand to sign when he suddenly checked himself:

'Let me ask you one more question—quite apart from our conversation.'

Now he returned to the method of stunning me with sudden and unexpected questions:

'Do you know Aleksandr Isaevich Solzhenitsyn?'

'I do.'

'Since when?'

'Since 1963.'

'Did you meet frequently?'

'No, infrequently.'

'When was the last time?'

'In March 1972.'

'Where?'

'In Leningrad.'

'Was he on a visit?'

'Yes.'

'Have you seen him since then?'

'We were in touch through his family. When he got divorced we stopped seeing one another.'

'What do you know of Solzhenitsyn's manuscript *The Gulag Archipelago*?'

'Nothing.'

'What do you mean, nothing?'

'Nothing.'

Slowly and meaningfully:

'Efim Grigorievich, it will be very awkward for you when we prove the opposite.'

'It's you it will be awkward for. You have conducted this interview very properly so far, but now you are threatening me and alluding to non-existent proofs.'

'Do you persist in denying it?'

'I do.'

'I shall write that down.'

'Go ahead.'

He writes. I follow his movements and realize that the real point of the whole interrogation lies in this final and apparently unpremeditated section.

My pass is signed. I ask permission to put one or two questions:

'You have used the expression "slanderous documents" several times. Is that now the official name for Samizdat?'

'Yes, it is the term, the precise designation.'

'Do you consider that it applies to Brodsky's poetry?'

'Well, he probably also wrote purely lyrical poems to which the definition would not apply.'

'I know Brodsky's poetry well and I ask you this question because he has not written a single political poem, let alone an anti-Soviet one.'

'I have not studied Brodsky's poetry. Up to now I have only had to look carefully at the work of two other poets.'

'Who were they?'

'You want to know too much.'

'You say you have not studied Brodsky's poetry. And yet you are dealing with a case which is closely bound up with it.'

'We are not interested in the poems, but in the interpretation put on them.'

'Can you deal with an interpretation if you don't know the original subject?'

'Are you trying to interrogate me?'

'Sorry, I didn't mean to. One last question. I have in my possession the manuscript of several quite harmless poems of Brodsky, given me by the author. Is that a criminal offence?'

The investigator smiles:

'It all depends on the poems. In any case, if you don't distribute them, it is your own affair. We don't consider it criminal to have something in one's possession.'

And as a parting shot one final insignificant question:

'You summoned me here on a Wednesday when I have no lectures. Was this an accident or was it deliberate, so that they wouldn't know in the Institute?'

'An accident. We work from our timetable, not yours. But they don't know about it in the Institute, rest assured.' (Oh yes, I could rest assured, and just two weeks later this assurance was confirmed in the most singular manner—Ryabchuk was a man of his word!)

The interrogation was over. On coming out of the Big House I immediately rang home from the nearest call-box. I'll be home soon. They've let me go. I'm free.

When I left him, Major Ryabchuk had seemed quite affable. This was on 10 April. Eleven days later, on 21 April, Heifets was arrested. Another four days later, on 25 April, came my civic execution.

I was to have another meeting with Ryabchuk two and a half months later, on 25 June. On the morning of that day a note came summoning my daughter Masha to the KGB. Having accompanied her to the office in the Big House where passes were delivered, I came home and sat down by the telephone, waiting with bated breath for it to ring. There was no ring for one hour, two, three. Then came a ring at the door; it was another note telling me to appear immediately. I knew that I might not be returning. I wrote a note to my wife, who was at the *dacha*. I rang a friend from the public call-box, saying that first my daughter and then I had been summoned to the KGB. If we didn't come back, they would know where we were. I was prepared for anything and even put on shoes without laces—in gaol they take away your laces.

This time I was shown into a dusty waiting-room with soft arm-chairs, where I had to wait forty minutes. Finally Ryabchuk appeared and apologized for keeping me waiting; it wasn't his fault, the confrontation of witnesses had dragged on a long time. —What confrontation?—Between your daughter Maria and Heifets. Come with me.

We sat opposite one another as we had two and a half months before. He was the same well-fed, well-groomed Major Ryabchuk, but I was no longer a professor, a doctor of philology, or a writer. Who was I then? A witness in Case No. 15? Or the accused? How-ever, I felt more sure of myself than in April; the Western press had given world-wide publicity to my case and already universities in France, Austria, Switzerland, and Germany had come to my defence, and the International PEN Club, the Austrian Literary Society, the Darmstadt Academy, and the French Association of Translators had declared their solidarity. . . .

I was getting very little by post except for telegrams—but quite a lot of them. Every day, however, I was getting telephone calls from Geneva, Paris, Basel, Vienna telling me of invitations, letters, and protests. I knew that all my mail was being held, but then Ryabchuk would have read it. . . . So the two interlocutors were the same, but the relations between them had changed. On 10 April it had been an investigator talking to a witness, now it was the execu-tioner and his victim. Nevertheless, the one who in the first con-versation had seemed defenceless in spite of his various ranks and titles, now wore the protective armour of world publicity, even though he was a 'nobody'. In April he had been obscure and easy to get at, but now he was in the full glare of press and radio and it had become dangerous to touch him.

'Where is my daughter? What did you want with her?'

'Your daughter was called as a witness. She kept making false statements, which you had obviously cooked up together. We had to have a confrontation with Heifets. Now she has changed her statements and is telling the truth. Here, read the written statement of the accused Heifets.'

Heifets recounted in detail how he had written his article about Brodsky's poetry and taken it to the next-door flat, to my daughter, asking her to pass it on to me. Ryabchuk waited until I had read it and then said:

'On 10 April you claimed that he handed you the article directly. Heifets asserts that he gave it you by way of your daughter. Now Maria Efimovna Etkind has agreed to Heifets's statement. There remains a contradiction with your statement.'

I say nothing.

'We have to hand this case over to the courts. Heifets has been sincere and so far he has not lied to us. If you insist on sticking to your version, that will complicate matters. Admit that you got the article by way of your daughter and we'll close the investigation.'

'I have no intention of changing my statement.'

'We shall have to confront you with your daughter.'

'That is illegal. You cannot confront a father and his daughter.'

'We know the law. We need to have the truth. In a moment you will see Maria Etkind's statement.'

A second investigator appeared, the one who had questioned Masha. I read his report: at first Masha had repeated that Heifets had not handed her the article, but after the confrontation she had declared: 'If that's what he says, that's how it was. I didn't want to say so because I was afraid of being held responsible.' This was not true. She was not afraid of being held responsible, but she did not want to contradict what I had said. But I stuck to my guns, since I did not want to increase Heifets's guilt; if his manuscript had passed through a third party's hands he could easily be got for 'distribution'.

'You are a father and you are frightened for your daughter', said Ryabchuk. 'I give you my word of honour as a communist that she will be quite safe.'

'What guarantees have I?'

'Guarantees? I have given you my word of honour as a communist. If you are obstinate, the investigation will drag on,

Heifets will be sitting in prison, and we shall keep on with the confrontations and interrogations until we clear up the contradiction between the statements.'

I knew well enough that their motives were quite different; they didn't want to close the investigation but to convict Heifets of 'distribution' too. But I gave in; if Heifets had not stuck to our original agreement and had named Masha for some reason, and if Masha after a confrontation had for some reason confirmed Heifets's version, it was silly for me to dig my heels in. I signed a report saying that I had changed my statements and that the previous ones were to be explained by my fear for my daughter. (Masha had acted under direct pressure from Heifets, who claimed that the initiative came not from him but from them—clearly on the basis of bugged conversations.)

I knew that now I could leave the building, perhaps not for long, but I could leave it nonetheless, together with Masha who was sure to be waiting downstairs for me in fear and trembling. But all the time I spent in the investigator's office I was looking at the proceedings from the angle of 'We are born to make Kafka come true'. What a crazy nightmare! A young author gives an article to an expert to read—that was the sum of his crime. A whole day goes on answering the question: who handed it over? Did the daughter give it to her father? And in any case the manuscript contained absolutely nothing criminal in the eyes of a sane person. Perhaps Kafka did in fact foresee better than anyone else our present insane society?

Nor was that the end of the affair—it was only the beginning. Before we left, Masha was given another summons, for the following morning—put out your finger and they'll chop off your arm! The next day she was questioned for several hours. How long did she have Heifets's manuscript? All day, until evening? Who came to see her that day? She can't remember? How about Vladimir Zagreba? Possibly? So it's not ruled out that he came to see her? And where was the manuscript? She can't remember? On the desk? Surely it's not impossible that it was on the desk? Did she leave the room, to feed her child for instance? She did? So while she was out of the room a visitor could have read the manuscript? No? But surely it's not ruled out. . . .

Here Masha cried out: 'Yes, it is ruled out. He's a decent person and doesn't go reading other people's papers when his hostess has left the room.'

'Where does he usually sit? Near the table? The file was marked "Iosif Brodsky and our generation", wasn't it? And Vladimir Zagreba is a friend of Brodsky's and belongs to the same generation? Could he restrain himself from reading an article about his friend and himself? Don't you agree?'

But Masha did not agree. They tormented her for two days, then let her go.

This was how they put together a case against Heifets for 'distribution'.

'Well, that's all turned out all right for you then', said Ryabchuk as he signed my pass. 'You'll have nothing to worry about now.'

'Nothing to worry about? After what you have done to me?'

'It's not us. We have nothing to do with the decisions of society. The decisions don't come from us.'

This pharisaical remark was the last thing he said to me. We did not meet again. But I often think about it. I wonder if he will read these reflections of mine. He could profit from them.

Major Ryabchuk was conducting an investigation into a 'top priority' case, which in reality was not worth serious consideration, as he knew full well. He also knew of the courageous statement made by Vladimir Maramzin on 30 May in the Western press. I will quote only the beginning of it:

I have a nagging feeling of guilt which probably springs from our inveterate lack of legal sense. My friend, the Leningrad writer and historian Mikhail Heifets, has been in investigatory custody for more than a month. According to the rumours that have reached us, he was arrested in connection with the publication in Samizdat of a five-volume edition of Iosif Brodsky and his article about Brodsky's poetry. The investigator knows quite well that Samizdat is not a publishing house and that Heifets is not responsible for collecting Brodsky's poems. Everyone knows that I spent three years collecting these poems, because Brodsky, like all great poets, never kept his poems and gave them away freely. I wanted to collect them in order to preserve for Russian culture the work of this great poet. The same people who have taken part in the persecution of Brodsky will be proud of him even during his lifetime. I have taken one further step to preserve the texts which I assembled with such difficulty—I have sent them abroad, where their author is now living. Perhaps this will not please some people, but my sole motive was my concern for Russian culture.

V. Maramzin was not being hypocritical in talking of his concern for Russian culture. Otherwise why should he have spent three whole years collecting the poems of an exiled poet? For money? For fame? For the sake of his career? The same applies to Heifets; why should he have written an article attempting to show the significance of these poems? Mikhail Heifets, historian and writer, was also concerned for his country's culture; it was his passion and his life. But what was in the minds of the investigators of this 'top priority' case? Did they really believe that a case concerning a collection of metaphysical poems remote from politics was 'top priority'?

Digression on the Theme: 'For Whose Benefit?'

> Who could these men be? What were they talking about? What authority could they represent? K. lived in a country with a legal constitution, there was universal peace, all the laws were in force; who dared seize him in his own dwelling?
>
> KAFKA, *The Trial*, tr. W. and E. Muir, p. 11
>
> For whose benefit?
>
> VIKTOR NEKRASOV, press statement, February 1974

The same investigator of top priority cases was in charge of Case No. 15, on the basis of which Heifets and Maramzin were tried and I was subjected to civic execution. As he prepared his dossier on Heifets he cannot have failed to realize that there were no grounds for a trial; he was dealing with a young historian who had no political programme and belonged to no 'anti-Soviet' group. Mikhail Heifets is a quiet, modest man who leads a respectable family life with a young wife who is a musician and has two little daughters; however hard you looked, you could find nothing against him. He has written stories about the revolutionary movement in Russia in the second half of the nineteenth century, the last one being devoted to Lenin's elder brother, Aleksandr Ulyanov, who was hanged for his attempt on the Tsar's life. Heifets was interested in Brodsky's poetry and had even tried to write an article about it, but he never completed it and it remained in a rough draft which was read by only two people: his close friend, the well-known science-fiction writer B. Strugatsky, and me, a specialist in the theory of verse. His flat was searched and they discovered several typewritten texts, by Solzhenitsyn and Amalrik it seems, but no proof that he had distributed these texts in order to work for the overthrow of Soviet power or some such nonsense. In short, if the investigator had been an honest man and had any thought for the government which paid him his salary and the system he was supposed to be protecting, he would have thought differently. Something along these lines:

Heifets can do valuable work as a gifted writer and historian, in one way or another his activities will enrich Russian culture, and his books are useful or even necessary to their readers. He presents no threat to the authorities. It is true that among friends he condemns certain Government actions, such as the occupation of Czechoslovakia. But these things are condemned by all intellectuals both in Russia and abroad, communists and non-Party members alike. A KGB officer could not fail to know that the 1968 occupation was only welcomed by consistent anti-communists and by Stalinists. The Stalinists were afraid in the first place that the Czech experiment might succeed, with the result that 'socialism with a human face' might attract vast numbers of people who were hostile to any form of socialism, and in the second place that there might be a growth of left-wing forces in the West, who might then start looking more closely at the Soviet Union. The crushing of Dubcek's Czechoslovakia put paid for good to the dangerously attractive version of socialism and helped to discredit all the regimes of Eastern Europe, not to speak of the Soviet Union. The Stalinists were understandably jubilant. And equally understandably all those who favoured democracy and socialism were downcast. Heifets was possibly one of them. But you can't send everyone off to the camps who did not approve of 21 August 1968. Lenin Prize winner Aleksandr Tvardovsky wrote the unforgettable quatrain I quoted in the prologue, but the investigator of top priority cases did not interrogate 'Jupiter' Tvardovsky. Nor indeed was this the charge against Heifets, 'the bull'.[1] He was tried above all for his article about Brodsky's poetry.

But Brodsky's poems themselves contain nothing criminal.

---

[1] 'Quod licet Jovi, non licet bovi.'

Brodsky is a 'metaphysical' poet, who remains aloof from political squabbles. When they organized his trial back in 1964, the KGB made a serious mistake. Of course Brodsky wasn't like other people, but was that grounds for a trial? And the trial itself was hypocritical; they had one thing in mind, but they tried him for something else. They had got it into their heads that Brodsky was a danger to the Soviet regime, but they tried him for parasitism. This trial of a poet was enough to breed criticism and discontent. Brodsky was sent off to a Northern village to do forced labour like an incorrigible drunkard, and then allowed back to Leningrad. By this time he was world-famous; mere poems, even his marvellous poems, would not have brought him such fame in the crazy sensation-hungry world as this idiotic trial. His poems were translated into many languages, and not by obscurantists but mainly by left-wing poets. They then banished Iosif Brodsky to the West, putting on a show to the effect that he himself wanted to emigrate to Israel. Now he teaches in American universities, writes poems as before, not about politics or the Soviet system (neither for nor against), is translated into all the major languages, speaks at conferences. . . . Readers in many lands think highly of him; he has the reputation of being one of the best contemporary poets. So who gained from his trial and the unbelievably stupid sentence? Who gained from the world-wide publicity and from his banishment? Isn't it obvious who gained? And isn't it obvious that if there had been saboteurs in the Soviet Union, they would have been the ones to cook up this 'Brodsky affair'? This is even more obvious today, now that the originator of the whole business, Lerner, the secret collaborator of the KGB, has been given six years in the camps for speculation in second-hand cars and other criminal offences.

Stage two. V. Maramzin collected Brodsky's poems, M. Heifets wrote the rough draft of an introductory article to this unpublished collection of poems. Is that a crime? Possibly, if the poems were counter-revolutionary, but not if they are unpolitical. Heifets is given four years in the camps plus two years in exile—and all on account of this same Brodsky. This virtually means that the judicial error of 1964 is not recognized as such and still operates ten years later. If someone had had the intention of compromising Soviet justice and the KGB into the

bargain, he could not have thought of anything better than
these two trials of 1964 and 1974. Do our majors really not
understand this? Of course they understand. But what do they
care for Soviet justice or even for the organization they work
in? So long as they can make a career for themselves! Or perhaps they are powerless to resist the orders of someone higher
up?

And then there is the case of Viktor Nekrasov. A well-known
Soviet writer, a veteran of the last war, the author of one of the
best war books—*Front-Line Stalingrad*—which has been translated into dozens of languages. Year after year he was harassed,
he was noisily and unpleasantly expelled from Moscow, his flat
was searched, he was expelled from the Party. Then he was
forced to emigrate. Nekrasov has written a letter with the
accurate title: 'For whose benefit?' For whose indeed? The only
ones to benefit are the enemies of the Soviet regime.

In 1970 I asked the same question in a speech at the funeral
of a brilliant scholar, one of the best historians of Russian
literature, Yulian Grigorievich Oksman. He had put in many
years as a bath-house attendant in one of the camps and after his
return had only been able to publish under a pseudonym; then
he died, but his name was still banned and this ban had now
been renewed. What did he do when he came back from the
camp rehabilitated? Organize a plot against the regime? Throw
bombs? Write pamphlets? Nothing of the kind. There is a
famous line in Boileau's first Satire: 'J'appelle un chat un chat
et Rolet un fripon'. Oksman's crime was that he called a spade a
spade and Lesyuchevsky a swine. And so in my funeral speech I
asked: 'For whose benefit did Yulian Grigorievich Oksman die
without writing all the books he should have written, all the
books he had in him? For whose benefit was Russian culture
deprived of all it had the right to expect from Oksman? Today
we are burying his great knowledge, his fine artistic taste and
his dozens of unwritten books. For whose benefit?' And I said
also that if you could build power-stations on the intellectual
energy we allowed to run into the sands, we could have built
thousands of fraternal hydro-electric plants. Who benefits from
this monstrous waste?

Who indeed? Perhaps one day someone will make a rough
calculation of all we have wasted. Apparently there has been a

count of our physical losses, of the people who died and died for nothing. But how much energy, intelligence, and talent has been thrown to the winds! The great Shostakovich died in 1975 before reaching the age of 70. Who knows how long he would have lived if it hadn't been for that stupid and disgusting article 'Cacophony in place of music', which removed him and Prokofiev and other remarkable musicians from the scene for several years. Who can tell what books were lost with the writers who gave up writing and then died before their time: Zoshchenko, Bulgakov, Pasternak, Bely, Eikhenbaum, Orbeli?

I remember how the intelligent and honest writer Mikhail Slonimsky once told me that the ninety-third bee-sting is fatal. According to something he had read, the bee's poison gradually builds up in the human organism, so that at the ninety-third sting you die. 'That', he added, 'was how my best friend Mikhail Zoshchenko died. He read a note in the newspaper where he was not mentioned in a list of writers, although by rights he should have been. Just as if there wasn't and had never been any such writer as Zoshchenko. It wasn't such a bad sting, but it was the ninety-third. Can we know which sting is lying in wait for each of us today or tomorrow? And they sting us unceasingly and mercilessly, without thinking of the consequences.'

In the USSR people who think about these things are punished. And the punishment just prolongs the same criminal waste; Mstislav Rostropovich and Viktor Nekrasov, Andrei Volkonsky and Iosif Brodsky are all forced to emigrate. Someone ought to be punished—the wasters. The enemies of enlightenment. The persecutors of talent. It is those who grieve over the fate of their culture who are the true patriots. Are such elementary truths really beyond the comprehension of the stage managers of our Punch-and-Judy show trials, which have become simply grotesque in recent years? The trial of Mikhail Heifets, who got four years' camp and two years' exile for the draft of an article about Brodsky, and the trial of his accomplice Vladimir Maramzin who for some reason was merely banished to the West for more serious crimes, are astounding in their very absurdity—the difference between the two sentences shows quite clearly that legality has given way to utter capriciousness. For whose benefit?

'For some reason', I just wrote about the different sentence given to Maramzin. But in fact the reason is quite clear: Heifets's case remained in silence and darkness, whereas Maramzin's, thanks to the article by Brodsky published in many Western newspapers, was given the full glare of world publicity. Our people don't like strangling in broad daylight. One law for the dark, another for the light. What an apotheosis of legality!

7

Struggle for Life (June–October 1974)

1. *At Home*

I have said that after 25 April I had 'another struggle to wage'.
That is both true and untrue. Another struggle abroad, yes. But I
also thought that something could still be done at home, particularly with the Writers' Union; after all, this was a public organization, in which I had long been well known both in Leningrad and
Moscow, and moreover the decision taken by the Leningrad
Secretariat was blatantly illegal. I still hoped that there was some
point in appealing to the Writers' Union of the USSR in Moscow
and that they might be indignant at 'local' injustice. I did not
know that there was already in existence a document which
officially confirmed my expulsion—a decision of the Secretariat
of the Writers' Union of the RSFSR dated 5 May. The most
astonishing thing is the date; the Secretariat met infrequently, the
Leningrad meeting had been on 25 April, there had been public
holidays on 1 and 2 May, so the RSFSR Secretariat had met
straight away on one of the days immediately following the holidays, in order to finish off the operation as quickly as possible. No
one, however, was in a hurry to send me the document. It was only
at the beginning of July that I was invited to the Writers' House
and handed a paper containing the words: '. . . expelled from the
ranks of the Writers' Union of the USSR on account of his
hostile, anti-Soviet activity'.

Later I was told that the Leningrad decree was differently
worded ('. . . on account of his anti-social activity'), that the
Moscow people had apparently given Kholopov a dressing-down
for his 'liberalism', and that the RSFSR Secretariat, who knew
nothing about either me or my accusers, had insisted on the
strongest possible wording: '. . . on account of his hostile, anti-
Soviet activity'.

On getting this paper I concluded that my case was either completely hopeless or very hopeful.

Hopeful, because the wording was so inappropriate and so obviously vindictive; why the tautological pair of adjectives to describe my 'activity'? If it was really anti-Soviet, why bother to call it 'hostile' as well? The two are synonymous; can you be anti-Soviet without being hostile? My dossier did not justify either the noun 'activity' or the two adjectives. So I had what you might call juridical grounds for continuing the struggle. I still naïvely believed—or wanted to believe—in certain juridical standards. We intellectuals have an incurable faith in the eventual triumph of justice and right.

Hopeless, because wording such as this meant not just expulsion from the Writers' Union but a seven-year spell in the camps. Just think: 'hostile anti-Soviet activity'! People are arrested for less. The Writers' Union had apparently issued an official decree to the effect that my guilt was proved and that I ought to be condemned in a criminal court in accordance with Article 70 of the Criminal Code.

However, being an optimist, I decided to act on the hopeful interpretation and continue the fight which had begun much earlier with a letter to Brezhnev—sent on the insistence of all my friends. I had sent a copy of this letter for information to the Writers' Union of the USSR and the Rectorate of the University, and had then sat back and waited. There was no reply for exactly a month. On 8 June I was invited to the Smolny[1] to see Z. M. Kruglova, the Second Secretary of the Provincial Committee of the Party. Two days later I went to her office and wrote down an account of our conversation on returning home the same evening.

But before giving this account, I should like to introduce Zinaida Mikhailovna Kruglova, Second Secretary of the Leningrad Provincial Committee, and at that time in charge of 'propaganda', i.e. the press, books, museums, education—all our cultural life in fact. I had first set eyes on her four years earlier, when she appeared on the rostrum of the historic great hall of the Smolny. There I saw a middle-aged woman whom I did not know (I had arrived late) and who looked like a cross between a fish-wife and a Mother Superior.

---

[1] The former Smolny Institute for Young Gentlewomen, since the October Revolution the home of the Leningrad Provincial Committee and City Committee of the Communist Party.

She was reeling off in a toneless voice from a piece of paper in front of her all the stock phrases about the flourishing of Soviet culture and its future prospects; she spoke in a lifeless, desperately boring and rather illiterate way, and stared blankly in front of her; on her bony impassive face there was not the flicker of a smile, no emotion, no embarrassment, nothing human at all. Having got to the end of her speech she returned to the presidium and it was then that I realized that she was not a fish-wife but the mistress of this hall, of this meeting, and of my life (if she wanted to, she could get rid of me just like that!). She was famous for her Jesuitical logic and for an open cynicism unusual in her circles and showing her to have extremely powerful connections. Not that she needed connections to attain such heights; she had the ideal combination of qualities for this sort of career: shamelessness and determination, complete lack of opinions combined with lack of talent, striking mastery of Soviet phraseology, suitable appearance. Here is a true story that sums her up. The world-famous scholar N. was elected to an honorary doctorate in one of the Western universities, but our authorities would not allow him to attend the ceremony; he tried every possible step at all levels, and in the end he applied to Kruglova. She told him: 'We cannot let you go to the West; they may not care about their scholars there, but we value our top people and look after them properly.' 'But Zinaida Mikhailovna, I am going to be given a doctorate, not blown up by a bomb.' 'You never know,' answered Kruglova, 'we cannot be sure that they won't provoke you into saying something quite different from what you really think.' 'Are you serious? Can I repeat what you have told me?'

Kruglova made it clear to him once again that he would have to do without travels and doctor's robes and that her point of view was entirely justified.

And now for the account of our talk.

Conversation in the Smolny with Zinaida Mikhailovna Kruglova, Second Secretary of the Regional Committee. 10 June 1974.

Entering the large office I saw not only Kruglova, but two young men. She introduced them rapidly—'workers in our departments' —and mentioned the name of Nikolaev for one of them, I think. We sat down at the desk; I was opposite Kruglova and the young men were opposite one another, one to my right, the other to her left. Why were they there? I don't know. Where were they from? I don't know that either. They remained silent almost all the time, and looked at me with fixedly hostile eyes. Nor did their hostess appear very lively; in the hour our 'chat' lasted, not a muscle moved in her expressionless face.

'You have written a letter to the Central Committee of the Party, to L. I. Brezhnev,' began Kruglova, 'and I am empowered by the Provincial Committee to explain to you our attitude to this affair and to your letter. At the same time we shall be able to clarify your position. I have known about you since 1968, when I had to speak at the Bureau of the Provincial Committee concerning your preface to the two-volume *Masters of Russian Verse Translation*. In that preface you put forward a pernicious line, presenting literature as opposed to the Party. You wrote that poets, not being free in their own creative writing, took refuge in translation so as to be able to express themselves to the full. . . .'

I tried to object at this point and later in the conversation; I quoted my 'sentence' and repeated once again how absurd it was to think that I was saying that poets worked on translations out of the desire to express anti-Soviet ideas—in Shakespeare's sonnets or Goethe's songs and poems! I recalled Mayakovsky's words: 'Lyric poetry we've attacked more than once with bayonets fixed', and reminded her that in the period in question lyric poetry was out of favour even with the poets themselves. Kruglova listened, but heard nothing and kept to the same refrain, adding: 'That's what you say, because it suits you to say so. We all know how to read and everyone sees the meaning of your sentence; it is blatantly anti-Soviet.'

I could see straight away that I had been wrong to hope for anything from this conversation. There was no dialogue, nor could there be. Kruglova had summoned me in order to expound her views, not to hear my arguments. In what followed I occasionally tried to get an answer in, but in vain; she took no notice and simply replied: 'You're evading the issue' or 'trying to wriggle out of it' or 'hiding something', or else 'it suits you to say that' . . . etc.

'Now about your letter to L. I. Brezhnev. The first thing is that it gives an inaccurate account of the charges against you; you keep quiet about the most important thing, your review of Heifets's preface to the five-volume Brodsky. In this review you approved of the malicious and violently anti-Soviet position of Heifets, who, as you know, has now been arrested for his activities. You did your best to improve and correct this anti-Soviet text of Heifets, making it even more anti-Soviet in character. Where Heifets wrote about the semi-colonial nature of our country after the events in Czechoslovakia, you wrote in the margin: "Why semi? Our country is an imperialist and fully colonial power" . . . .'

'As far as I remember I wrote only: "Why semi?" in the margin, and that can be read in various ways. . . .'

'You think you are dealing with idiots who don't understand anything. We understand perfectly well what "Why semi?" means —it is an assertion that our country is a colonialist and imperialist power. In another place, where Heifets was writing about Brodsky's Roman poems, you wrote in the margin: "The authorities won't read this, and if they do, they won't understand." So that is what you think of the Soviet Party leadership, but we have read it and we do understand it.'

'To understand this remark of mine, you probably need to see it in a wider context; the word "authorities" must be repeated from Heifets's text. . . .'

'I have given you a wide enough context. And this is how you, a teacher, a professor, teach our young people, this is how you fulfil your role as an educator! Heifets is young enough to be your son, and this is the sort of advice you give him! You are a double dealer; naturally you didn't say things like that in your lectures, you saved them up for your underground activity.

'It's the same with your relations with Solzhenitsyn. You try to present them as domestic and family ties, as if you met in one another's homes and went on jolly outings together. But in fact your relations were those of accomplices. You used your literary talents to help Solzhenitsyn. We know that you edited his books, particularly *The Gulag Archipelago*, an anti-Soviet book for which Solzhenitsyn has been banished from the Soviet Union—the most severe form of punishment provided by the Code of 1925. You share Solzhenitsyn's views and collaborated with him.'

'Let me answer the second charge first. I did not edit Solzhenitsyn's works and had nothing to do with *The Gulag Archipelago*. Anyhow, how could I have edited Solzhenitsyn? His Russian is much better than mine and I could never have corrected his style— he would not have let me. It is a very personal style and the author would not have allowed it to be polished. I couldn't have edited it for the facts either, since the author knows them much better than I do. So how could I have performed the task of editor? As for his opinions, you are wrong in stating that I completely share them. Particularly from his most recent declarations you know the role that Solzhenitsyn attributes to the Orthodox Church and Russia's Slavonic roots—it's not hard to guess that those ideas leave me cold. Even the story *Matryona's House*, which made a strong impression on me by its artistic qualities, did not entirely convince me intellectually—I argued against Solzhenitsyn when he put forward such an archaic ideal as the patriarchal Russian peasantry, and our arguments were extremely fierce.'

'I can accept that—I daresay you did not agree with those ideas. But I was thinking of other views of his which you fully shared with him.'

'Are you thinking of his attitude to the Stalinist camps or to Soviet power?'

'Yes, precisely; you followed Solzhenitsyn in adopting a negative attitude towards our regime.'

'What grounds have you for such a categorical statement?'

'The fact that you edited *The Gulag Archipelago*. You adduce subtle legal points to the effect that Voronyanskaya, who made statements concerning this matter, has died and cannot confirm her statements. Yes, she has died, and unfortunately she cannot confirm anything. But we have two of her letters to Solzhenitsyn, in which she writes about it [she points to a file lying on the table in front of her].'

'That is impossible. She could not have written anything of the kind.'

'On the contrary, she did write it and letters are irrefutable legal documents.'

'I repeat that I had nothing to do with *The Gulag Archipelago* and did not even read the manuscript.'

'You read it, we know you did, and you not only read it, but corrected the author's style. There is no doubt in our minds about this. You know how to edit a manuscript, you have the necessary qualifications, as can be seen from your editing and review of Heifets's article.'

'You are wrong to apply the word "review" to rough notes which I jotted down as I read and never wrote out in a fair copy; they are not even typed out. I did not intend them for general distribution, they are just notes I made of various ideas that occurred to me.'

'Yes, I know they are rough notes, but they reveal your true thoughts, which you kept carefully concealed. For instance Heifets writes about the 1968 events in Czechoslovakia in an anti-Soviet spirit, and you want to go still further: not just 1968 but 1956, not just Czechoslovakia but Hungary too.'

'You are misrepresenting what I wrote. What I wrote was that for Brodsky and many young people of his generation it was not Czechoslovakia but Hungary that was crucial. These were tragic events, when two armed forces clashed, and the situation seemed hopeless to young people of his generation. I know very well how young people experienced this tragedy at the time, and there is nothing anti-Soviet in noting this fact.'

'True Young Communists drew other conclusions from these events; their communist world-view emerged all the stronger. What you are writing about is the anti-Soviet reaction to the Hungarian affair. Do you think that is how a Soviet teacher ought to regard these events? And your claim that this is a private letter is simply not worth discussing—you were helping Heifets concoct an anti-Soviet document for Samizdat. This is no more a private letter than your "Appeal to Jews about to emigrate to Israel".'

'It seems to me unhelpful even to mention this letter. It was written for my former son-in-law and was an attempt to dissuade him from emigrating, which I considered and still do consider a disastrous course of action.'

At this point the young man called Nikolaev suddenly interrupted: 'You mean harmful or incorrect as a means of struggling against our system?'

'No, I mean disastrous for the person who has decided to emigrate. I wrote that he cuts himself off from his culture without acquiring any other culture of his own. . . .'

Kruglova: 'Your main idea is different. You argue that one should fight for freedom and a multi-party system here, in one's own country. Here is a sentence from this document: "One independent word spoken at home is worth more than big demonstrations outside the Soviet Embassy in Washington." '

'I am sure that is so—one should fight for justice in one's own country—and I can't see anything criminal in that.'

'Here's something else you wrote: "What do you want with

foreign freedom? What good will it do if you are able to shout slogans outside the Capitol? If you want to, you can go and demand Angela Davis's freedom on Red Square now. The fact that you are enjoying foreign freedom will not make them free Pavel Litvinov from his camp or set up a multi-party system . . .".'

'But that doesn't mean that I am demanding a multi-party system, I am just dealing with objections my reader might make.'

'No, those are your views and your demands. And this letter is not in the least private; you knew that your daughter was showing it to many of her friends.'

'I did not know that, and I believe that if anyone showed my letter around, it was not my daughter but her ex-husband.'

'You did not know, but we know. And in any case you knew full well, but it doesn't suit you to admit it. You knew—and you even encouraged it. You gave a copy of that same letter to Kopelev, who spread it around Moscow—yes, Kopelev. Your daughter passed it around in Leningrad and Kopelev in Moscow.'

'It is true that I did give Kopelev one copy of the letter; at that period he shared my fears—his daughter was thinking of emigrating —and he asked me for the letter so that he could show it to her. He was hoping that my arguments would help him to persuade his daughter of the disastrous effects of emigration. I did not authorize him to disseminate a personal letter of mine.'

'I have no doubt that this was exactly what you wanted. The sentences which I have quoted are not the only anti-Soviet things in your letter. Here, for instance, you write near the beginning: "I shall call myself a Jew as long as discrimination exists." Have you suffered from discrimination, then? You, who were [this was the only point where Kruglova's manner became lively, even excited] a professor of the Institute, a member of the Writers' Union, widely published by various publishing houses? This shows your hostile, anti-Soviet position.' [I tried to make her understand that it wasn't just a question of discrimination against me personally, but that if there was persecution of the Jews in some corner of the globe, I, even though I did not consider myself a Jew in the cultural sense, did not have the right to renounce my Jewishness—to do so would be an act of base cowardice. I quoted the words of the Polish poet Julian Tuwim, which Ehrenburg liked to repeat: 'There is the blood that flows through the veins and there is the blood that flows out of the veins. It is in the second sense that I am of Jewish blood.'

As long as there is blood flowing out of the veins of Jews, I shall be a Jew. That was what I meant when I wrote: 'I shall call myself a Jew as long as discrimination exists.'

But all these words of mine simply bounced off her like water off a duck's back; her job was not to listen but to give me the point of view of the Provincial Committee.] Kruglova went on:

'Your anti-Soviet position was shown by the speed with which the anti-Soviet radio stations picked up your case—it was reported on such reactionary stations as Radio Liberty, Deutsche Welle, and Radio Canada. We know that you have numerous connections with foreigners, and naturally you had your own channels for getting news abroad. You sent a letter to Brodsky by way of a foreigner, from whom it was confiscated at the airport customs at Sheremetevo.'

'That is correct, I did once send a letter to Brodsky in that way. But as it was confiscated you ought to know that it didn't contain a line about politics—it was entirely personal.'

'It's not the contents that interest us, but the fact that it was sent by illegal means. You have been deliberately carrying on anti-Soviet activity for many years.'

Second young man: 'There were methodological errors even in your Candidate's thesis, as long ago as 1949.'

E.E. 'It seems to me indecent to talk now about errors committed in 1949. Do you remember what was going on in 1949?'

Young man: 'In 1949 there was a Party line, and you were already going against it.'

Kruglova: 'We had socialism in 1949 too. Your trouble is that you have never been a Marxist. In other books too you looked at literature from an aesthete's point of view; this showed itself in 1949, when you also spoke against Marxism.'

E.E. 'Can you really, twenty-five years later, defend what went on in 1949? The persecutions, the *prorabotkas*, the arrests of the best representatives of our intelligentsia? 1949 was the year of the campaign against the cosmopolitans. And you reproach me now with ideological errors committed in 1949? With aestheticism? I know quite well that I was still very immature, but at that time my weakness lay more in excessive sociologism than in aestheticism. . . .'

Kruglova: 'You had one weakness then and another one later on. You have always deviated from the Party line, you have never had a correct, Marxist view of things. That's your trouble, and that's why you reacted as you did to Solzhenitsyn's writings and ideas.'

'Solzhenitsyn's writings and his ideas are two different things. Let me remind you that Balzac, who had such importance for world literature as a revolutionary writer, was a monarchist and a pro-Catholic in his ideas. Lenin wrote about Tolstoi in 1908 that he was a great writer, but a reactionary thinker. Solzhenitsyn's literary works I regard as remarkable—*One Day in the Life of Ivan Denisovich*, *An Incident at Krechetovka Station*, *Matryona's House*. But, as I have already told you, I was far from sharing all his opinions.'

'You mention only works published here, but in fact you are thinking of others you have read, including *The Gulag Archipelago*.'

'*The Gulag Archipelago*, to the best of my knowledge, is more of a historical or political work than a literary one. So it has nothing to do with what I was saying.'

'Why? Of course it has something to do with it. It is subtitled "A Novel". So the author obviously thinks differently from you.'

At the end of our conversation I showed her the proofs of the second volume of *French Poetry Translated by Russian Poets*, together with the first volume which had already been published, and told her that the type had been broken up and the book would not appear, although it was awaited both in France and in the Soviet Union, where it had been given advance publicity.

Kruglova (pointing to Volume 1): 'Is that the book which you sent to the French president?'

'Yes, only that was a copy of the first edition, and this is the second edition.'

'We know that you sent the book to France by illegal means, through a private individual. The second volume will not be published now of course—your name can no longer appear in print. It's your own fault, you got many of your own colleagues into trouble, what do you expect?'

When I asked what there was left for me to do, if my name could not be published and I was not allowed to teach, I was told: 'Naturally there can be no question of teaching or publishing. But you must work. In our society it is essential to work.'

'I think we have reached a dead end. Let me sum up. It seems to me that all your charges are based on two private letters and, what's more, on isolated and ambiguous sentences in those letters.'

'They are not private letters, they are political documents. And you are forgetting your collaboration with Solzhenitsyn and all the rest.'

'You can't prove collaboration. All you can reasonably talk about is acquaintance.'

'We know what we know, and you only say what suits your case. And N. I. Grudinina was telling us that you are a real Russian scholar. . . . Anyhow, you must look for work. There are other kinds of work apart from what you are used to. Leningrad is a big city, it's not the provinces, there are archives and libraries and all sorts of research institutes of a different kind.'

'I am not young, I am 56; it is too late for me to start a new life, and I can't afford to lose several years for my work.'

'It can't be helped, you'll have to look for work. You're a clever man with a lot of friends and acquaintances, you find something and we'll help if necessary. But I repeat that it must have nothing to do with teaching or publishing. Your fate is in your own hands.'

Such was the reply I received to my letter to Brezhnev. This conversation with Kruglova was a great strain for me; I could not be completely sincere, but had to make use of my legal rights. She for her part kept repeating that she knew my hidden secrets, although she could only make use of sentences taken from letters—my letter to Heifets and my letter about the danger of emigration for young Jews. Kruglova did not want to understand my objections; she steam-rollered her way through the conversation, hinting at information received from sources unknown to me.

Digression concerning the Revolutionary Sense of Justice

> The Revolutionary Court is sitting,
>   The righteous court.
> And 'Little Apple'[1] sings the guard.
>
>   MIKHAIL GOLODNY, 'A Judge of the
>   Revolutionary Tribunal', 1932

Pravosoznanie (sense of justice), n. (Spec.) Sum of legal views of people expressing a judgement on existing law, society, or state

[1] The most famous popular song during the Civil War. [Tr.]

organization, lawfulness or unlawfulness of behaviour of citizens. 'In Europe unemployment is constantly increasing, as is the revolutionary sense of justice of the proletariat' (M. Gorky, *Where do you stand, masters of culture?*).

Dictionary of Contemporary Russian Literary Language, 1961, vol. 2, p. 35

In the early years of the Revolution we had the concept of the 'revolutionary sense of justice'. This 'sense of justice' completely replaced the law; a tribunal could condemn anyone to death without bothering with proofs—class intuition was enough: 'I sense an enemy in him.' How could you answer intuition? There's no rational way of refuting it. This was what Sholokhov had in mind in one of his most shameful speeches—from the platform of the 23rd Party Congress (1971), when he said of the Sinyavsky-Daniel affair: 'If these evil-minded people had been caught in the twenties, when they tried people without worrying too much about the criminal code and relied on their revolutionary sense of justice (applause), you can imagine what would have happened to them, the werewolves (applause). And to think there are people who make a fuss about the severity of the sentences!' These sentences were no laughing matter, however—seven years and five years in labour camps.

This 'revolutionary sense of justice' is sheer mysticism. It was this belief in class intuition which gave rise to the monstrous illegalities of 1937–8 and more recent years. 'I am a genuine revolutionary and a proletarian, I possess infallible class feeling, and if I sense an enemy in him, that proves he is an enemy. Enemies must be destroyed.' When Kruglova says: 'We know', that always means: 'We feel'. The only documents she referred to were two letters said to have been intercepted, from E. D. Voronyanskaya to Solzhenitsyn. I assume she was lying, since she never showed me these two letters. But even if they did exist, could they be used as a basis for penalizing me without their being put before my judges and inspected by experts and lawyers (if only to ascertain their genuineness)? The theory of the revolutionary (or class) sense of justice is constantly at work in our so-called political trials. During Brodsky's trial the prosecution witnesses affirmed as one man: 'I do not know Brodsky, I am unacquainted (or only slightly

acquainted) with his poems, but what he does disgusts me.'
Pipe-layer Denisov knows of Brodsky only that he is a 'parasite'. This is what the papers say and he believes the papers,
because that is what his class intuition tells him. He believes the
papers and makes his damning speech on the basis of newspaper articles, and then the papers believe him and print even
more damning articles on the basis of his speech. It's a vicious
circle: the papers—Denisov—the papers again—the sentence.
In this same Brodsky trial the public prosecutor Sorokin said:
'The article in *Vecherny Leningrad* aroused a considerable
response. There was a particularly large number of letters from
young people, who strongly condemned Brodsky's behaviour.
[Reads letters.] The young people consider that he has no place
in Leningrad, that he must be severely punished.' Once again:
a newspaper article—letters from young people based on the
article—publication of these letters in the newspaper—condemnation on the basis of the demands contained in these
letters. But what if the article was telling lies? This was indeed
the case on that occasion; the article quoted poems which were
quite unconnected with Brodsky. But 'the young people' *believe*
the papers, and then the papers *believe* the young people.
'Revolutionary' and 'class' sense of justice is nothing but faith.
Faith instead of proof.

Is not this same principle of intuition or faith at the root of
the newspaper campaigns against writers? Not one of the
'toilers' who in 1958 threw mud at Boris Pasternak had read
Doctor Zhivago. In 1974 the Soviet press harried Solzhenitsyn
for his *Gulag Archipelago*, and before that for *August 1914*;
there were personal statements from steel-workers, writers,
physicists, actors, pipe-layers—and all on the strength of what
they had read in the papers. The same charmed circle: the
newspaper as a source of information—the anger of the readers
of this newspaper—the same newspaper as mirror of the readers'
anger. It is a variant of the old theory of the 'revolutionary sense
of justice'.

This theory did sterling service in my case. No one had read
anything, neither Solzhenitsyn's writings, which I had supposedly kept in my possession and even edited (even Kruglova
had not set eyes on *The Gulag Archipelago*, or she would not
have said it had the subtitle 'A Novel'), nor Heifets's article, nor

my review of it, nor my letter to the Jews—not a thing! Kruglova too, who was apparently my chief judge (as Second Secretary of the Provincial Committee), like all the rest, relied on class intuition, on her 'revolutionary sense of justice'.

My talk with Kruglova might have told me that struggle 'from within' was useless. But my friends insisted, and I still believed, that I could continue to work in Russia. So I went on sending out letters. Not that I had any great hopes. But I thought all the time that some letter of mine might find its way to a reasonable person who would read it in astonishment—and then everything would start moving in the opposite direction with the same stunning suddenness and unexpected twists and turns, and common sense would come into its own. As the reader will remember, the Writers' Union had not yet officially confirmed my expulsion, and it seemed possible to me that the Union too might have second thoughts. My responsible friends went to see various Union leaders, Georgy Markov, Yury Bondarev and others, and spoke warmly of Etkind's cultural usefulness and of the pernicious nature of this obviously set-up case; they had to listen to vaguely sympathetic answers, sometimes even including offers of financial help, but that was all. As I have said, at the beginning of July I was summoned to the Leningrad Writers' Union to see the so-called 'Working Secretary' (i.e. a non-writing official) G. N. Popov; he had been given the job of showing me the minutes of the Secretariat meeting of over two months ago (why the delay? Popov did not tell me) and giving me a copy of the Moscow decision concerning my 'hostile, anti-Soviet activity'. For the first time I read what appears in Chapter 2 of this book, and as I read I could not refrain from exclamations of amazement and anger. I shouted at Popov: 'How dare Dudin talk about nationalism, Zionism, and fascism? Was he drunk, or mad? Or had they shown him something else instead?' The peace-loving and highly embarrassed Popov kept protesting: 'It's not my doing, I am simply empowered to inform you, they are not my words.'

But I raged at him: 'No one would see me at the Writers' Union. I did all I could to see Kholopov, but he evaded me for a few days and then went off on holiday. The others all kept out of my way. You are the first person I have been able to see since 25 April. There's no one else for me to ask. You were at the meeting; that means that you are responsible too. How could you keep silent when Dudin was slandering me and talking obvious nonsense and Chepurov was trotting out his irresponsible fantasies and Orlov was lying and backbiting to settle old scores? How could you say nothing?'

Popov tried to calm me down—he was a little man, only a technical worker, the writers knew best, everything would sort itself out in the end. As I was leaving he came out from behind his desk and announced: 'You put your name down for a new car and I want to tell you that you are still on my list and the cars will be here soon.'

'For Heaven's sake, Gennady Nikolaevich, what have cars to do with it? I have other things to worry about.'

What he had said was so stupid that it wasn't worth answering. But I was touched; perhaps after all Popov wanted to show me that he had remained a human being, to speak the only words of oblique sympathy of which he was capable?

Lyrical Digression: Mayakovsky Writers' House

Garden, Garden, where the look of a beast means more than heaps
  of books.
Garden . . .
Where wolves express willingness and devotion . . .
Where marvellous possibilities perish in the beasts, like the Lay of
  Igor's Campaign inscribed in a Book of Hours.

VELEMIR KHLEBNIKOV, 'The Menagerie,' 1909

I went away crushed; I had set foot for the last time in the Writers' House, the old Sheremetiev palace, with which my life was so bound up. At the age of 13 (still in short trousers) I had been brought here by my then protector, Vera Semyonovna Valdman, the translator of French and German authors. She brought me to the literary translation workshop, which was run at the time by Professor Aleksandr Smirnov. And from 1931 on I was constantly coming there, not less than once a week (with a break for the war). At first I took part in translation workshops directed by A. Smirnov, I. Mandelstam, A. Fyodorov, and A. Kulisher; later on, I was for many years the director of such workshops, a participant in innumerable writers' meetings, one of the leaders of the translators' section, and organizer of the poetry readings 'For the First Time in Russian'. More than forty years of my life had gone by within these walls—here I had studied and taught, indignant at what some people said (what dishonourable things we had to listen to!), but overjoyed at discovering others (what gifted people!); here I had seen and heard Anna Akhmatova, Mikhail Zoshchenko, Nikolai Zabolotsky, Boris Eikhenbaum, Viktor Shklovsky, Vera Panova, Aleksei Panteleev, Samuil Marshak, Lidia Ginzburg, Viktor Zhirmunsky, Grigory Gukovsky, Aleksandr Smirnov, Mikhail Lezinsky . . . the whole splendid company of literary people whose contemporary I was fortunate enough to be.

One of many first impressions of this House is of the long, dark room with carved oak panelling, the 'Gothic Room', with its long and massive table around which, on chairs with high carved backs, sat unknown old men and women (they may have been all of thirty or forty), and in their midst a gorgeous ageing beauty who later turned out to be Tatyana Lvovna Shchepkina-Kupernik—since my childhood I had adored her translations of Edmond Rostand's *L'Aiglon* and *Cyrano de Bergerac*. In a cheerful lilting voice she read her translation of some comedy of Tirso de Molina, *Pious Martha* I think. She was followed by an elegant giant with a large, heavy, and very kind face, who boomed out in a deep bass voice, with humorous solemnity and passion, a play by Lope de Vega, *The Dog in the Manger*, which he claimed just to have finished. From the voice of Mikhail Lozinsky I learned a lesson for life—how to try to fall out of love:

> You only need to recollect
> The sight of some disgusting object,
> The thought of something really nasty
> Will spoil your appetite for days.
> So try and try again to set
> Your mind on your beloved's defects,
> You'll pacify your throbbing heart-ache
> And love will quickly flit away.

At this black gothic table every word was weighed on apothecary's scales in the attempt to find something as accurate, full-bodied, and sonorous as possible—together we translated Maupassant and Villiers de l'Isle-Adam. And in another workshop, run by the still very youthful Andrei Benediktovich

Fyodorov, they worked on the prose of Tieck and Kleist. The walls of the House have become associated in my mind with this selfless, noble, and passionate love for the word—Russian and French, Russian and German. And later on, remembering as I often did these long arguments about shades of meaning and style, this atmosphere of total devotion to literature, I realized that it had been a feast in time of plague. At the time I did not understand that those who disappeared from our company had not just stopped coming to the workshop because they were too busy, but had gone for good. This youthful love for the word and for the House where it was cradled and nurtured, could not even be wiped out by everything which later degraded the House. Within these walls—in the cosy rococo hall—Zoshchenko was crucified, my masters the Formalists were put through their *prorabotkas*, and Pasternak was trampled underfoot (in his absence). I shall never forget how Sergei Mikhalkov shouted stutteringly from the rostrum: 'Let everyone ask himself how many of these Pasternaks there are all round him!', and everyone listened in silence, not daring to raise their eyes. In the same rococo hall were the annual writers' meetings at which a prepared list of names for the executive was put forward in the name of the Party Bureau, and at which Vera Panova invariably disrupted the pre-established order by going up to the presidium and proposing five or six, or even ten, extra candidates; they didn't dare stop her, but the moment she had finished some specially delegated communist jumped up and demanded that 'the line be drawn', i.e. that the list be closed with no further nominations, since if we weren't careful these might wreck the Party Bureau's list. 'Draw the line!' repeated the chorus of dozens of law-abiding voices. On one such occasion Aleksei Panteleev came slowly up to the platform at the critical moment and, looking over his dark glasses at the hall, said in a quiet, firm voice that it was too soon to draw the line, that not everyone had made their nominations, and that if we went on this way we should be drawing the line through democracy. That is how things were not long ago—resistance still seemed possible. Subsequently many people lost hope and simply stopped going to meetings. But we all remembered the euphoria of the late fifties and early sixties; those were the days when freedom-loving speeches thundered from the rostrum, the lost art of oratory began to revive and we breathed freely. Alas,

> Young witnesses of yesterday's defeat,
> Our heroes are perplexed to find their feet.
> Gath'ring late fruits of harsh experience,
> They rush to balance income with expence . . .

(PUSHKIN, 'To a Noble Lord')

The ebb and flow of freedom was nowhere more apparent than in the Writers' House. At times the same speakers who the day before had inveighed against the tyranny of the personality cult, now used the same tone of incorruptible honesty to lash the lackeys of imperialism, the revisionists and the unorthodox.

Even physically the House was an allegory of double-think. From the front windows there were unequalled views of the mighty Neva and the magnificence of Petersburg, but the other windows looked out to the north-east, towards the looming granite pile of the Big House. The same duplicity was to be seen in everything, constantly. Here they humiliated, insulted, and trampled into the mud Anna Akhmatova, Boris Eikhenbaum, and Mikhail Zoshchenko. But here too, some years later, they draped sheets over the mirrors and hundreds of people gathered round a dead body to listen to impassioned speeches about the victims of the ideological pogrom. By some miracle the erstwhile criminals were transfigured after death; from being anti-social aesthetes, scandalmongers, and saboteurs, they became models of moral greatness and the pride of Soviet literature.

But even so:

> O House, House!
> Where wolves express willingness and devotion.
> Where marvellous possibilities perish in the beasts.
> Where fear overcomes reason, conscience and honour.
> Where memories live.
> And where hover immortal shades of the departed.

Have I succeeded in communicating to the distant reader even a spark of the emotion I feel when I think of this particular homeland? Have I explained at all adequately my attachment to this one old Petersburg house, to the Neva as seen from its windows, to the shades of the departed, to the joys and emotions I experienced there?

And can the Western reader understand how indissolubly I am bound to that life? I was a thread woven into the whole fabric, only a thread perhaps, but still a part of the fabric. Pull out the thread and it no longer belongs to the fabric, it loses its usefulness and its beauty.

Is it surprising then that a thread possessing a mind and a will, or at least the illusion of a will, should cling with all its might to the fabric that gives meaning to its existence?

And so I tried to speak, to persuade, and to write. No sooner had I received the decision of the RSFSR Writers' Union than I wrote to protest to the Leningrad section, arguing that it was illegal to expel me in my absence and that in any case the charges against me were absurd and lacked all legal force. I demanded that my case be discussed by the Executive, that is at an open public meeting with many people present.[1] There were more than fifty writers on the Executive and most of them were decent people who valued their good name and had learnt wisdom from their experience of life and literature. A discussion by the Executive seemed desirable to me if only because it might give me the chance to say everything that I was thinking but had so far kept to myself.

Ten days later, on 15 July, my protest was returned to me by post and G. N. Popov rang up to explain that I had not gone through the proper channels; apparently one did not have the right to appeal to the executive of one's own organization, but only to the congress of the Writers' Union. They saved themselves the trouble of a written reply, obviously having decided that the correspondence with this expelled saboteur should be closed. So he thinks the decision of the Secretariat is illegal? He thinks the charges against him are unproven and absurd? Let him think to his heart's content. What matters to us is that the authorities should be satisfied, the Provincial Committee, the Central Committee, the Big House, the Secretariat of the Writers' Union. . . . They are? Thank Heaven for that. The writers aren't likely to rebel, whether they are on the Executive or not. They've put up with it so far. They'll get used to it. And indeed they did not rebel. They got used to it.

[1] See Appendix II.

Digression concerning State Security

Scorn ripens into anger . . .

BLOK, *Iambics*

No, I do not intend to talk about the Committee for State Security, but security with a small 's'. Does it need unusual wisdom to understand that it is no good stirring up discontent or even alarm among the population in the name of internal peace and quiet? It is unwise to provoke any social group; once one of them has got out of the habit of obedience, it can become dangerous. It is not a question of open revolt, but of the gradual ripening of various latent moods. Of course it is possible that the Committee stands to gain by these moods; they justify its activity, its terrorist actions or intentions. The writers did not rebel, but they can hardly have been calmly indifferent to what was going on. They were not asked for their opinion, nothing was explained to them, they were not even properly informed about anything—they were simply intimidated. They were accustomed to fear. All right. But was it worth bringing them nearer to breaking point? The students too were accustomed to everything, but even so these usually peaceable and unassertive boys and girls started doing what in the West led so naturally to the events of May 1968, and what seems so unnatural in our silent land.

On the benches in the garden of the Herzen Institute appeared painted slogans. They blossomed by night on the walls of the Institute, the lecture-room blackboards, and even the walls of the nearby streets. And they weren't the usual indecent graffiti, but the demand: 'Bring back our professor.' The administration had to go around with buckets and brushes painting over them. You may be able to paint over slogans, but can you paint over discontent, mistrust, and indignation? It turned out to be more long-lasting than one might have thought. At the end of April 1975, on the anniversary of these events, the same (or different?) students of the Herzen Institute organized a strike and distributed leaflets. Things of that sort did not happen in the Soviet Union—it needed a great effort to provoke them. I was told that on the day after the leaflets were discovered several students disappeared without trace from the Institute.

My students in the Institute had been responsible for getting together a collection of articles under the title *Stylistic Problems of French Literature*. It had been widely advertised and about four thousand orders had been placed by various institutions and bookshops throughout the country. Four thousand copies had already been printed. The book contained an introduction by me and nearly all of the twenty or so authors referred to my writings; this is understandable, since they were my students and were following my line of research. On 25 April, the day I was thrown out of the Institute, a decision was taken to destroy the whole printing. To burn all four thousand volumes! And then to publish the book on a new footing—without mentioning the wicked name which was henceforward to be banned from print and consigned to oblivion. And that indeed is how the book was published. My book without my name. Quotations from my works, without any reference to me. What an unbelievably cynical idea (even the cover was designed by my daughter)! Isn't the destruction of a printing of four thousand copies and the issuing of a fraudulent publication an incitement to disaffection, even if this remains deep down in people's minds?

The 'Progress' publishing house had prepared the second volume of a bilingual anthology, *French Poetry Translated by Russian Poets*, in which I was publishing the work of many young poet-translators whom I intended to introduce to the reader side by side with well-known masters. The book had not yet been printed, but it had gone through the proof stage. This book too was suppressed and the type broken up. Perhaps it too will one day appear without my name and in some new shape? But dozens of writers still know who conceived the book, edited it, and wrote the introduction and notes to it. Isn't the suppression of such a book an act of provocation?

The stylistics of French literature. Classical and contemporary Russian translations of French poetry. What have these to do with politics and subversion of the State? It was in these things that I saw my purpose in living and working. But it was all destroyed, suppressed, and mutilated. Dozens of authors suffered. And hundreds of students, if not more. Now my pupil is lecturing to them, but I know only too well that he has not yet had time to finish his own studies.

And today, a year later, not only is my name banned from

print (together with those of Y. G. Oksman and V. S. Grossman), but all the works signed by these accursed names have been burnt by every library in the land. Works on the theory of verse and the theory of translation, the history of French, German, and Russian literature, stylistics and poetics.

'Today I have been a fascist', said an old librarian to a friend of mine, returning from work in tears. 'I have been burning Etkind's books.' As she was throwing the volumes into the flames, she cast her eye over them. And she could not begin to understand why she was burning them. How had these literary studies proved dangerous to a mighty nuclear power? Nothing had been explained to her, just as previously, a year ago, nothing had been explained to the writers or the students. The latter were simply told: 'Professor Etkind was engaged in illegal activity and will not be teaching here any longer.'

'But who will examine us?' asked the dumbfounded students. They were examined by a colleague of mine, a specialist in a different field, as the students knew full well when they answered his questions. From time to time one of them came to see me, bringing flowers or tears, and passed on to me the fanciful student accounts of what had happened. Etkind was co-author of *The Gulag Archipelago* with Solzhenitsyn, or at best had edited the book for him. He had given a typist Solzhenitsyn's manuscript to type, and she, working 'blind', had not known what she was typing until she reached the end, read it through and hanged herself in horror at what she had done. Etkind had had an affair with the typist who was typing the *Archipelago* and concurrently living with Solzhenitsyn, and this intimacy had been her ruin. Etkind's flat had been searched, and they had discovered forty copies of *The Gulag Archipelago*, whereas you are only allowed (?) to keep ten copies at home. . . .

Occasionally the 'phone rang. I picked up the receiver but after a few moments the caller would hang up; it was someone wanting to make sure I had not been arrested, as was rumoured. Everyone was saying my flat had been searched several times— even fairly close acquaintances. In all probability this last rumour had been put out by the KGB; it was necessary as a sort of justification or explanation of their actions. The stories became more and more fantastic and absurd, as is always the case when imagination takes the place of information.

My incitement to disaffection, if such it was, cannot be remotely compared with the actions of my persecutors. Who then is the threat to State security?

Certain fearless well-wishers of mine were far more active than I myself; that champion of justice, the well-known poet Natalia Grudinina, who ten years before had worked with me in defence of Brodsky, now threw herself into the fray. She was constantly in and out of the Writers' Union, in Leningrad and most of all in Moscow; she was tireless in telling my story, which she genuinely believed to be a provocation engineered by mysterious conspirators; she forced her way in to see officials of the Party, the Government, and the KGB, and she returned home in a glow of optimistic euphoria—everyone had listened patiently and sympathetically to what she had to say and had said that it was impossible, and that she ought to write detailed reports and explanations. She wrote them, and sent them off or delivered the eloquent documents by hand, and they all disappeared into the maw of bureaucratic indifference. Her mind was full of fantastic villains and sinister underground workers, who were deliberately organizing this anti-Soviet sabotage—she thought I was a victim of these dark forces. But gradually she too came to recognize that no one had any intention of taking up the fight against this 'underground', and her warm-hearted energy faded away.

2. *Abroad*

While I myself and a few active well-wishers were trying to carry on the struggle at home and meeting with well-intentioned impotence, hypocritical sympathy, and genuine indifference, public opinion in the West was stirring and growing. On the evening of that dramatic day, 25 April, I had written a letter to the Rector of the University of Amsterdam, from whom I had recently received an invitation to give a series of lectures. Apologizing to the Rector for my involuntary refusal, I gave him a brief account of what had just happened:

Dear Colleague,
I am sincerely grateful to you, and through you to the University of Amsterdam, for the offer to give a series of lectures on the theory of translation, and problems of comparative literature, stylistics and poetics.

I should esteem it a great honour to lecture in the ancient university which you represent. Even in normal circumstances, however, it is unlikely that I would be able to take up your kind invitation. During the last few years I have received a number of invitations from universities, institutes, and writers' organizations in European countries, but I have never yet been able to go to any of them.

This was my situation until this morning. But today everything has become hopeless. During this one day I have been deprived without warning of all my rights as a scholar and man of letters, deprived of my post and the possibility of publishing my work, deprived of all means of support.

On the morning of 25 April there was an extraordinary meeting of the Academic Council of the Herzen Pedagogical Institute in Leningrad; it took the decision to dismiss me from the Institute and strip me of the academic title of professor. The same afternoon a meeting was called of the leaders of the Writers' Union, and I was expelled from the Union. I was ill and did not attend this meeting, nor did I even have the possibility of defending myself. On the other hand, both meetings were attended by representatives of the KGB. I was accused of meeting A. Solzhenitsyn and I. Brodsky, and of writing a letter—a review of a manuscript article by a certain young critic on Brodsky's poetry; two sentences were also held against me, both from private letters not intended for distribution and in no way implying any judgement on the present political course of the USSR.

These ridiculous charges were enough for the Institute, where I had worked for twenty-three years, and the Writers' Union, of which I had been a member for about twenty years, to throw me out. This morning I was still a professor of the Institute and a fully recognized man of letters. This evening I am left stripped of everything. Both publishing and teaching are now closed to me. The publishing houses are already receiving orders not to print my works, or even my name. The most terrible fate that can befall a scholar and a writer now awaits me— silence, which is a kind of civic death. As I write I listen for the step on the stairs and hasten to finish this letter before I am prevented from doing so. After losing my work, my titles, and the right to publish, I may at any time lose my freedom, which is all I have left.

25 April 1974

The following day this letter flew to the West with one of my devoted pupils and friends, and on 30 April it was published in the Danish newspaper *Politiken* with an article by I. B. Holmgaard entitled: 'The day when everything became hopeless', and in another Danish newspaper, *Information*. I had taken a risk in sending it. However, the experience of the last few years has shown that salvation lies in the widest possible world publicity. Between the day 'when everything became hopeless' and the day when the West learned what had happened in Leningrad, four days had passed. Our witch-hunters hardly expected such a rapid counter-attack, although Solzhenitsyn should already have taught them that today you can no longer kill people in darkness and universal silence. The letter was reprinted from *Politiken* in the major Western newspapers. There was a news item on 4 May in the *Frankfurter Allgemeine Zeitung*, and the same newspaper published the full text on 6 May. The same number of the *Frankfurter Allgemeine*, and the *Neue Zurcher Zeitung* and other papers reported a statement which had already been issued by the International PEN Club.

This was only the beginning. Heinrich Böll returned to the attack at the end of May, when he made a speech to the congress of the International PEN Club in Ohrid in Yugoslavia. The *Frankfurter Allgemeine* reported this on 27 May in an article by Andreas Razumovsky entitled 'PEN and the frontiers':

> . . . Heinrich Böll spoke pessimistically in Ohrid of the future possibility of realizing the concrete political aims of the PEN Club. In his view the position of the creative intelligentsia in the Soviet Union was growing visibly worse and the creation of a Soviet PEN Centre was at present inconceivable to him, 'if we see in the charter of the PEN Club a minimum of moral obligation'.
>
> Böll sees a particularly blatant case in the persecution and 'cashiering' (as in the army) of the Leningrad professor Etkind. He knows Etkind well personally and knows him to be a totally apolitical person. Now Etkind has been deprived of the means of existence merely because of his friendly relations with Solzhenitsyn and Brodsky. The practice of the Soviet Writers' Union has nothing in common with the most elementary assumptions of the PEN Club or other Western literary associations which exist in order to defend their members from persecution and harassment. 'The sinister side of the Soviet Writers' Union is that it immediately expels its members once they find themselves in a difficult situation.'

This speech was made before he knew the full details of the affair. It was not just that the Union of Soviet Writers had expelled me when I was in a difficult situation; the Union leaders had actively contributed to making this situation 'difficult', or rather, impossible. They had not simply expelled me in compliance with some previous decision made higher up; they had put on the comedy of a political trial and, without any proper knowledge of the charges against me, had consented to play the part of a tribunal of the Inquisition.

Meanwhile the news spread. On 19 May the *Washington Post* published the full text of the meeting of the Academic Council of the Herzen Institute, together with my 'Declaration to the Press', dated 3 May and passed on to the foreign correspondents on that day.[1]

On 25 April the Academic Council of the Herzen Pedagogical Institute in Leningrad relieved me of my duties in the Institute, where I had taught for twenty-three years, and stripped me of my academic title of professor. On the same day there was a meeting of the Leningrad Secretariat of the Writers' Union, and I was expelled from the Union, of which I have been a member for about twenty years. All this took place in my absence—I was unwell. On the other hand representatives of the KGB took part in both meetings. At the Academic Council a document entitled 'Report' was read out, which listed my 'crimes' against the Soviet state. This is a list of totally unfounded allegations and isolated sentences taken out of context and interpreted in a quite arbitrary way; it contains for instance a reference to my 'methodological errors' of 1949, a time when in the Soviet Union cybernetics and the theory of relativity were declared to be ideological nonsense and T. D. Lysenko and his disciples were recommending us to develop oak trees out of elms.

The 'Report' refers to the fact that in 1964 I spoke as a defence witness in the case of Iosif Brodsky and was unrepentant about this. There is also a vague statement to the effect that I had in my possession a manuscript of A. Solzhenitsyn's *Gulag Archipelago*—this charge is based on the ambiguous testimony of the typist E. D. Voronyanskaya. As is now widely known, this seventy-year-old woman took her own life after several interrogations in August 1973. The other charges are equally unfounded; they are supported for instance by reference to a former Vlasovite, who is not known to me, and who was allegedly told something about me by the same Voronyanskaya. In the end all these charges boil down to one thing, that I was personally acquainted with Iosif Brodsky and Aleksandr Solzhenitsyn and even, as the 'Report' says, 'aided and abetted them'. This was enough to justify the conclusion formulated in this same 'Report': 'Over a long period Etkind has

[1] The declaration to the press is given in my own translation rather than the version which appeared in the *Washington Post*. [*Translator's note.*]

been deliberately engaging in ideologically harmful and hostile activities. He has acted like a political double-dealer.' And this conclusion was enough for the professors of the Institute who are members of the Council and the Secretaries of the Writers' Union to subject me to this civic execution. Not one of them showed the slightest interest in my real biography, which bears no resemblance to the list of felonies contained in the 'Report'. I have done other things besides making 'ideological mistakes'—for instance I fought in the war for four years. Such things are not taken into account during the ritual of civic execution. And what are the consequences of this execution? They are as follows:

Having been dismissed from the Institute, I am deprived of the possibility of teaching; having been expelled from the Writers' Union, I have no chance of publishing my work. This ban even extends to my name. On the strength of a series of empty charges the academic and literary work of many years is simply wiped out and I and my family are to all intents and purposes deprived of the means of existence.

Yes, I do know Solzhenitsyn. Yes, I did speak as a witness in the case of Iosif Brodsky and did what was in my power to help this young poet to publish translations which brought him a sort of livelihood. Yes, I have written articles and books in which I have tried to express my own opinions about French literature, Russian verse, and German theatre. I have done all this in the firm belief that I was furthering the growth of the national culture for which I live. In concerning myself with the theory and history of literary translation I was firmly convinced that I was furthering the cause of friendship between the peoples who speak Russian, French, and German.

In the 'Report' all my writings are described as 'harmful' or 'hostile'. However, dozens of critics and hundreds of readers have expressed their approval and gratitude for such books of mine as *Poetry and Translation* (1963), *The Art of Reading* (1964), *Seminar on French Stylistics* (1965), *French Poetry Translated by Russian Poets* (1969 and 1973), *Talking about Poetry* (1970), *Bertolt Brecht* (1971), *Russian Poet-Translators from Trediakovsky to Pushkin* (1973).

And now two or three sentences from private letters and notes, sentences which were never made public, have been sufficient to cancel out all the books I have written and the other books I may write in the future, and to deprive a scholar and writer of the chance to talk to students and readers, condemning him to silence and civic death.

My generation well remembers the meetings of 1949; that was the time when the best professors, our teachers, were being hounded out of the universities and the best writers driven out of the literary world. I am not comparing myself with them. But people of my generation will remember until their dying day the bloodthirsty unanimity with which the speakers at these meetings pilloried Zhirmunsky, Eikhenbaum,

Azadovsky, Gukovsky, and demanded their immediate removal from the University of Leningrad. Exactly a quarter of a century has gone by. Truth has won the day. There are constantly new editions of the books of these true scholars who were once persecuted and even physically destroyed, and meanwhile the writings of their persecutors are consigned to oblivion, and their names covered with scorn. It would seem that a return to 1949 is impossible. . . .

Alas, it is not only possible, it is simple. The professors, the writers, and the poets have known their colleague for many years, but they have been told that their colleague is a state criminal and they make haste to believe it. Anyone who does not believe it is himself a criminal. They are told that he committed 'methodological errors' in 1949 and they do not reflect on the absurdity of this statement; they do not hear the date 1949 but only the familiar and intimidating words about errors, and they agree to punish him. They are told that their colleague 'used his position in society in order to drag into his works ideas opposed to the Soviet system' (a quotation from the 'Report'), and they forget that every book has to pass through a complicated control system with editors and readers, censors and committees for publication, they forget all that and they agree to punish him. And the execution is carried out unanimously. Unanimity was an indispensable procedural condition in those far-off days as well. And yet you would have thought that in a quarter of a century a new public spirit would have grown up and people would have achieved a measure of civic consciousness. Can it be so easy to put the clock back twenty-five years?

Is it possible that people have learned nothing from history? That even *Novy Mir* has taught them nothing? That they have forgotten the poems of Tvardovsky, the repentant articles of Simonov, the suicide of Fadeev, the resurrection of Bulgakov, Mandelstam, Babel, Akhmatova and so many others? Is it possible today, in 1974, to resort to the arguments of the bad old days, and to meet with general approval in referring to 1949?

No, I believe in progress, in the new public spirit, in the growth of civic consciousness. I believe that no one will succeed in putting our country back twenty-five years. And finally I believe in the democratic forces of the modern world.

E. Etkind   6, Aleksandr Nevsky Street, Flat 17,
Leningrad.
3 May 1974.

This optimistic ending was only justified in part. Neither 'the new public spirit' nor 'the growth of civic consciousness' showed themselves in this affair; they were not even strong enough for questions to be put to the authorities. And did anyone 'succeed in putting our country back twenty-five years'? No, of course not, this was not their intention. But as a trial run it was successful; it showed that if they needed to put the clock back they would perhaps be able to do so. Perhaps. In spite of everything, arbitrary power does not hold unlimited sway in our country; it is limited not by a parliament or by internal public opinion, but by international public opinion. So it was not in vain that I believed in 'the democratic forces of the modern world'. These forces operated. Publishing the transcript of the Academic Council meeting and my press declaration, the Moscow correspondent of the *Washington Post*, Robert Kayser, wrote: 'These documents are self-explanatory. They reveal how the KGB—the political police—influence what Westerners would regard as purely academic matters, how friendship with notorious dissidents is a liability in today's Soviet Union, and how a man who falls foul of the authorities can be treated by his colleagues' (*Washington Post*, 19 May 1974).

The European press joined the fight with energy and understanding; nor was it only the right-wing dailies and weeklies—as they like to remark in such cases in the Soviet Union—but newspapers of all tendencies. The authors of the articles were not 'professional anti-communists', but eminent writers, well-known experts in Slavonic studies, theoreticians of literature, essayists, historians.

It was a real broadside. I realize perfectly well that they gave a highly exaggerated account of my achievements, sometimes in the interests of journalistic sensationalism, sometimes for tactical considerations. Even so it was a powerful broadside. I was unable to read it, I only knew about the texts which were broadcast on the radio, the BBC, the Voice of America, Deutsche Welle, and Radio Liberty, and what I was told on the telephone. I remember with gratitude the regular calls I had from Alfred Blatter of Radio Basel; these were a great moral support to me and kept me in touch with what was going on abroad. I was grateful also for telephone calls from the representatives of the Austrian Literary Society, from Heinrich Böll, and from Michel Gordey of the French weekly *L'Express*, who in June interviewed me by telephone and gave me the chance to state publicly my attitude to the problem of emigration. 'Do you intend to emigrate?' asked Gordey, and in reply I asked him to record the following declaration of principles:

'A writer and scholar who has close ties with his mother tongue and works for the development of culture and the arts, cannot of his own free will leave his native land; emigration is not only difficult for him, it is unthinkable. If, as was recently announced in the Provincial Committee of the Party, I am deprived of the possibility of working—teaching and publishing—that will mean that I am being materially and morally stifled. In this case my departure from the Soviet Union should not be thought of as voluntary emigration, but as forced exile.'

Digression concerning Emigration

> Immer fand ich den Namen falsch, den man uns gab: Emigranten.
> Das heisst doch Auswanderer. Aber wir
> Wanderten doch nicht aus, nach freiem Entschluss,
> Wählend ein anderes Land. Wanderten wir doch auch nicht
> Ein in ein Land, dort zu bleiben, womöglich für immer.
> Sondern wir flohen. Vertriebene sind wir, Verbannte,
> Und kein Heim, ein Exil soll das Land sein, das uns aufnahm.
>
> BERTOLT BRECHT, 'Uber die Bezeichnung Emigranten'

> I always found the name false that they gave us: Emigrants.
> That means those who leave their country. But we
> Did not leave, of our own free will
> Choosing another land. Nor did we enter
> Into a land, to stay there, if possible for ever.
> Merely, we fled. We are driven out, banned.
> Not a home, but an exile, shall the land be that took us in.
>
> BRECHT, 'Concerning the label Emigrant', tr. S. Spender

In recent years more and more of the creators of Russian culture have been leaving the country—writers, mathematicians, biologists, musicians, artists, dancers, linguists, historians, art experts, physicists. They leave in different ways, as best they can; some make use of the relatively favoured conditions open to Jews, some remain abroad when they are on holiday, and some ask for political asylum when they are on a mission to the West. For several years I had been watching with growing concern this tragic exodus, which incidentally is by no means limited to Jews—it is enough to mention such non-Jewish émigrés as the cellist Mstislav Rostropovich, the singer Galina

Vishnevskaya, the composer Andrei Volkonsky, the artist Mikhail Shemyakin, the poet and translator Vasily Betaki, the writers Viktor Nekrasov, Vladimir Maksimov, Andrei Sinyavsky, the linguists Vitaly Shevoroshkin and Sebastian Shaumian, the theologian Levitin-Krasnov, the musicologist Genrikh Orlov, the chess-player Mikhail Korshnoi and many others. In any case it is ridiculous to divide people into Jews and non-Jews; it is the creators of Russian culture who are leaving, whatever it may say on their passports. Naum Korzhavin is a Russian poet, although in the years of the struggle against cosmopolitanism he would doubtless have been reminded that his real name is Mandel. Iosif Brodsky is a poet of the Russian language and belongs to the literature created—independently of passport information—by Anna Akhmatova, Marina Tsvetaeva, Osip Mandelstam, Boris Pasternak. The author of these pages is a Jew by blood, but neither his language, his culture nor his way of thinking divide him from the Russia of Pushkin and Tolstoi, Blok and Mandelstam.

We, who were brought up on the progressive ideas of our century, will not stoop to the zoological racialism which stained the consciences, alas, of many of our compatriots, including even people as gifted as V. V. Rozanov. 'The Jew endeavours to wipe from himself a sort of universal uncleanness or antediluvian sweat. . . . The achievements of the Jews are like nails in my hands. The gentleness of the Jews burns me like fire. For in making use of these achievements my people will perish. . . . The strength of the Jews lies in their viscosity. Their fingers are like glue. . . . All our literature is [now] "taken over" by the Jews. Our purse was not enough for them; they have come "for our Russian soul".' (*Fallen Leaves*, 1st and 2nd gatherings, 1912–1915.) It was sixty years ago that these words of hatred and persecution were written.

And yet at the same time there was another Russian writer and journalist, Vladimir Korolenko, who initiated a different world view; clearly the hate inspired by Rozanov has proved stronger than Korolenko's noble attitude. Today, in the middle of the 1970s, they are again trying to persuade our countrymen that Russia's Jews are distinct from the 'true' population by virtue of their blood with its 'universal uncleanness' and 'viscosity'. But we have witnessed Oswiecim and the case of the

'murderers in white coats' and we want no repetition of such
affairs. For we know how easy the transition is from 'fallen
leaves' to Babii Yar, the gas chamber, and the crematorium.

And now we see the turbid floods of anti-Semitism spreading
once again through our land. This anti-Semitism goes hand in
hand with an ever-increasing Russian nationalism, as indeed it
does in the other camp—we see this among dissidents inside the
Soviet Union, and also in the West, in certain émigré circles
which flaunt their tolerance. All the time in articles, journals,
newspapers, and books one catches glimpses of implicit, or
sometimes quite explicit, ideas such as these: What do the Jews
care for the Russian nation? Jews are by nature internationalists
(i.e. communists). The Jews are to blame for the Russian Revolution and the camps, they imposed on Russia an alien and
inorganic Marxism. . . . Here are a few lines from a story
published in 1975: 'How much more natural it is for a Jew to
exert pressure from above, and for a Russian to sneer his
grievances from below. . . . Here we have Chekhov's fastidious
but brilliant prediction: Solomon is the forerunner of the future
commissars [this concerns Solomon Moiseevich in Chekhov's
story 'The Steppe', who longed to have ten millions so that his
master Varlanov would become his lackey. E.E.] Now I can
trace the line of descent and establish the genealogy, the black
genealogy of the sons of Israel in our times. Yes, here it is:
Solomon begat the commissars, and the commissars laughed at
his spiritual nakedness and naïve simplicity, and shut him up in
a mad house. The commissars begat the people's commissars,
who stood the commissars up against a wall or sent them off to
the camps. The people's commissars begat . . . who? Why, him
of course, Bolotin—who else! Here he is, the last pathetic off-
shoot, the final extinction of the line. What next?' (A. Sukonik,
'My Consultant Bolotin', *Kontinent*, No. 3.) Chekhov is a red
herring; he wrote 'Rothschild's Violins' as well as 'The Steppe'.
But as for Sukonik . . . Well, Sukonik is no Chekhov. When I
read these lines (in 1975!), for all my uncompromising internationalism I declare with pride: I am a Jew. And the more the
Sukoniks snarl, the greater the pride I shall derive from the
consciousness of being a Jew. What does it matter whether it is
by one's blood (which the Nazis want to shed) or by the shape of
one's nose (which they hate) or by one's internationalism

(which contradicts their ideas of racial enmity)? Incidentally Aleksandr Sukonik is apparently of Jewish blood too, so he is not a true son of the Black Hundred. But my ideal remains Ariadna Skryabina, daughter of the great composer and a member of the Russian nobility, who during the Nazi occupation took the name of Sarah and met her death.

Among those who are leaving there are the Jews—those who consider themselves Jews and see their life's work in the building of the state of Israel. There are the non-Jews—those who are non-Russian according to their passports, but rank themselves among the descendants of Pushkin ('Ugly descendant of the Negro race, brought up in wild simplicity'). And finally there are those who have no connection with the Jews except—sometimes—moral solidarity. It is the intelligentsia who are leaving.

Previously it was different. The so-called first emigration was a class phenomenon: the clergy, the nobility, the officers, the bourgeoisie, and the literary and artistic circles connected with all these groups. All those who did not accept the socialist revolution and were afraid of it (even if they had no clear idea of what it would bring to Russia) made haste to leave their country. The Revolution was directed against them; no wonder they flocked into exile.

The second wave was caused by the war: 'displaced persons', prisoners of war and refugees who chose to remain in the West. They were mainly the so-called 'non-returners' and they were motivated not so much by a conscious political choice as by the desire to avoid the Stalinist terror which awaited all those who had been taken prisoner or for some other reason had been on the other side of the Curtain.

And now it is the third wave. Not a class wave like the first and often not caused by external circumstance like the second. These are people who have for the most part decided for themselves to leave their own country and go to live in another one beyond a closely sealed frontier, with no hope of return. Among them there are some self-seekers and philistines, who are attracted by the material affluence of the West, the erotic or pornographic films, the smart cars, the night clubs, the long-legged nymphs of Pigalle. I need not dwell on this group; the nation will be all the better for their departure. Then there is an

intermediate category of people who are morally superior to the
philistines, those who left because life in the West was better,
freer and less difficult, and allowed you to travel in different
countries, read the newspapers of different parties, and exist
without fear of spies, informers, hidden microphones, and
night visitors. . . . One can understand these people and sym-
pathize with them; the Soviet Union has done a great deal to
make them lose even the semblance of patriotic feeling. There
are also, as I have said, the committed Zionists or German
nationalists, who leave in order to create a future for their children where no one will say that their fingers are 'like glue' or
call them Hans Wursts. And yet even quite recently, as I well
remember, they used to call themselves Russians—or at any
rate Soviet citizens. But they have had explained to them at
length that try as he may, a foreigner remains a foreigner,
whatever he does to help the 'true-blooded'. It's no good; all
your efforts will not make the 'true-blooded' grateful—at best
the fate of the great general Barclay de Tolly awaits you. In
1812 the Russian army was saved from destruction by Barclay,
but even Prince Andrei, discussing his achievement, said to
Pierre Bezukhov: 'Your father may have a German servant, and
an excellent servant, who can minister to all his needs better
than you could; but if your father is at death's door, you will
send his servant away and begin to nurse your father with your
own untrained and clumsy hands, and you will be more of a
comfort to him than a skilful stranger. This is how it was with
Barclay. As long as Russia was healthy, a foreigner could serve
her and do an excellent job as a minister, but once she is in
danger, she needs one of her own sons.' Tolstoi was fully answered (a quarter of a century before *War and Peace*, it is true)
by Pushkin, who addressed these lines to Barclay:

> Unhappy warrior, bitter was your fate.
> Offering your life's work to an alien state,
> Uncomprehended by the untaught rabble
> You walked alone with your great thoughts, untroubled.
>
> But spurred to anger by a foreign name,
> Pursuing you with shouts, the people came,
> And, rescued by your modest bravery,
> They covered your grey head with mockery. . . .

Here we have the hidden motive of all anti-Semitism, even when it appears to be as intellectual as Rozanov's—'spurred to anger by a foreign name'. Anything can be forgiven but the alien-sounding name. How can a Russian poet be allowed to bear the name of Küchelbecker or Mandelstam, an artist that of Levitan or a philosopher that of Gershenzon?

High-minded people have been able to remain above vindictiveness and forgive the 'untaught rabble' its prejudices. Barclay de Tolly remained a Russian patriot and gave his life for Russia. Mandelstam remained a Russian poet and in spite of everything dreamed of 'wrapping Russia's senseless plains in the warm folds of his greatcoat'.

There are others who emigrate: those who have faith in their spiritual potential and know that this will never be able to develop in their native land. Personnel departments will not give them work. They are not taken on as research students, even when it is patently obvious that they are natural research workers. They are not allowed to attend congresses. Their books are kept out of print whenever possible, lest a 'foreign name' appear on the cover!

Travelling with me on the plane out of Leningrad was the violinist Yakov Milkis, a leading member of the Leningrad Philharmonic Orchestra, one of the best orchestras in the world. For several years in succession this orchestra had toured various countries in Europe and the East, but he had not been allowed to go. Why? No one told him. One day someone said it was because he had an aunt in Canada. Milkis was flabbergasted; what had his aunt to do with it, especially when apparently he did not even know her? The orchestra continued to travel round the capitals of the world, and Milkis continued to sit at home. No one doubted that he was a first-class musician. But he was, in Prince Andrei's words, a 'German servant', and although Russia was not at death's door as in 1812, it was still better to leave Milkis at home. The Jews are 'like glue', they are all Zionists at heart, you can't trust them. And so Milkis, a Russian musician, whose Jewishness consisted simply in what was to Russian ears an unfamiliar 'foreign name', emigrated. He went to join his aunt in Canada. And there he was able to join an orchestra, and his children to enter a conservatoire.

It is a sad and alarming business. The creators of Russian

culture are being scattered throughout the countries of the West, our culture is distintegrating. A poet works with language, and when all about him he hears a foreign tongue, he gradually grows dumb, his linguistic sense is blunted and words fail him. If a scholar, trained in a certain school, in which he has his allies and his opponents, finds himself all alone in a foreign environment, he often loses momentum; without teachers and pupils, opponents and readers, he no longer has the sense of travelling along a road with a definite end in view. A 'stateless' person, without a home, he runs the risk of contenting himself with a mere day-to-day existence—this happens sometimes, but luckily not always. Wise Pushkin wrote:

> Two feelings feed our hearts
> And bind us to our homes—
> Love for our native hearth,
> Love for our fathers' tombs.

> The independent soul
> That makes us truly great
> Is founded by God's will
> On this eternal base.

Subsequently Pushkin changed the second stanza in manuscript for another, even more solemn and unequivocal:

> Life-giving sanctuary!
> Earth without you is dead,
> A hopeless wilderness,
> An altar with no God.

So for Pushkin the essential meaning of the life and dignity of a truly free and independent person, and indeed the vital spirit of earthly life itself, were all founded on the feeling of being indissolubly linked with one's past and on the inseparability of existence in space and in time. The severing of these ties is like death:

> Earth without you is dead.

When the thread is torn from the fabric, the thread loses its meaning, and at the same time the fabric is ruined and falls apart. You have to emigrate when the noose is round your neck, so that to stay at home would be suicidal and useless, when they have already pulled the thread out of the fabric and will not weave it back in again. But as long as it has not been pulled out, as long as you are still there, on your home ground, and the irreparable has not yet happened, stand fast, hold on with all your might.

3. *Coda*

This is what I told myself as I tried to work out my future and think about the present. I longed to go to the West; all my life I had studied French literature, and I had never been allowed to visit France, not even as a tourist. For many years I had been translating German poetry, from Hans Sachs to Bertolt Brecht and Erich Kästner, but I had never seen Germany and had given up hope of setting foot on German soil. I had studied the work of Maeterlinck and Verhaeren and written a lot about them, but a visit to Belgium seemed out of the question.

My close friend Vladimir Shor, who had a deep knowledge of French literature and the French language, liked to walk in an imaginary Paris; he knew every Parisian street by heart and played at walking as a grand master plays chess without looking at the board. He had repeatedly applied to visit the beloved country, but in vain—'spurred to anger by a foreign name', they refused to let him go, either as a private visitor, or as a tourist, or to work. He died at the age of fifty-four with his dream still unrealized—he had only seen Paris in his imagination, and in films. His example was constantly in my mind. I desperately wanted to see Aix-en-Provence, Paris, Ferney, Lübeck, Geneva, Bruges—and the island of Réunion.

But the exile is not a tourist. Is it worth seeing the world at the cost of losing one's native air, one's friends, one's readers, one's language, one's surroundings, one's pupils? This seemed monstrous to me. Inconceivable. I was ready to struggle, if there was any possibility of struggling. And this in spite of my lack of civil rights as a Jew, the omnipotence of the Big House, and the numbing fear which paralysed even my well-wishers.

Only too soon, however, it became clear that the struggle was impossible.

At the beginning of June I assembled a number of invitations from universities—some of those which had reached me through the postal blockade—and attached them to a letter to the President of the Presidium of the Supreme Soviet of the USSR, N. V. Podgorny, in which I asked permission for a two-year stay in France with my family. A month later I was summoned to the Visa and Registration Department. I was received in a large office by an official in civilian clothes, who turned out to be General Smirnov (by his side I could see the revolving spools of a tape-recorder, perhaps to intimidate his visitor, or else to make sure that he himself did not say the wrong thing). He announced that my request to President Podgorny could not be granted. 'We do not allow visits of this sort.' I tried to refer to some of my predecessors—had not M. Rostropovich, V. Maksimov, and V. Nekrasov left the USSR on two-year visits? But General Smirnov gave me to understand quite clearly that this path was closed to me. 'For you', he emphasized, 'it is not possible.' I understood: those whom I considered as my predecessors were all 'true nationals'; they were Russians, whereas I was a Jew and was expected to emigrate to Israel, and the sooner the better. But emigration to Israel entails immediate and irreversible loss of citizenship; as he receives his Israeli visa the émigré hands in (and loses for ever) his Soviet passport. What is more, according to the regulations he has to pay 500 roubles (about £300) for his repudiation of Soviet citizenship. There was no point in arguing: banishment was presented as voluntary emigration, and the loss of citizenship as 'repudiation'.

Even so I held on for another three months in the hope that something might turn up. But nothing did. With every passing day I could feel the clouds growing thicker and the KGB more active, so that I and particularly my daughter were directly threatened. In the end one of my friends, who has been close to me and my family for several decades, said to me: 'You must go, and not wait a day longer than you have to. You are meeting people and this could ruin them. Young people come to see you, trying to help you and openly showing their sympathy for you. They are defenceless— they won't get invitations from Western universities or be written about in the Western press. As long as you are here they are in serious danger. Any of them might be given the sack any day. Surely you realize your responsibility towards them and all of us. Even the older ones among us are in danger of losing our jobs or at best of being retired early. You must go.'

This conversation has remained in my memory as one of the bitterest experiences of my final months in the Soviet Union. Even this close friend avoided me like a leper. Solidarity had finally given way to fear. Of course he was right; being under constant observation by the KGB, I involuntarily drew their attention to anyone who came to see me or even shook hands with me in the street. I had no right to ask even of my friends that they should behave like heroes. More and more often I recalled Brecht's words: 'Unhappy the land that needs heroes.'

At the end of September we applied to the Visa and Registration Department for an exit visa for Israel. The experience of others suggested that I would get an answer in a couple of months at the earliest; I needed this time to send off my library, put my papers in order, deal with my property, and say goodbye to my friends. We thought we had plenty of time and had nothing to worry about on this score. But even this turned out to be a false sense of security; the answer came in four days. The decision to expel me had been taken long before and they had frequently tried to tell me as much, but I had refused to understand. On 16 October we flew to Vienna and on 25 October arrived in Paris.

I have quoted some words of Brecht. When in the fifties I translated his poems about emigration and later on his 'Conversations of Refugees' I never thought that Brecht's words would become so vitally relevant to me. The poem 'Concerning the label Emigrant', written by Brecht in 1937 and translated by me just twenty years ago, in 1955, ends with some lines with which I would like to end this book:

Restlessly we wait thus, as near as we can to the frontier
Awaiting the day of return, every smallest alteration
Observing beyond the boundary, zealously asking
Every arrival, forgetting nothing and giving up nothing
And also not forgiving anything which happened, forgiving nothing.
Ah, the silence of the Sound does not deceive us! We hear the shrieks
From their camps even here. Yes, we ourselves
Are almost like rumours of crimes, which escaped
Over the frontier. Every one of us
Who with torn shoes walks through the crowd
Bears witness to the shame which now defiles our land.
But none of us
Will stay here. The final word
Is yet unspoken.

Esery—Suresnes. August–September 1975.

Appendix 1

Second Hearing of the Case against I. Brodsky
Hall of the Builders' Club, 22, Fontanka. 13 March 1964.

Psychiatric evidence indicates that psychopathic traits are present, but Brodsky is capable of work. Measures of an administrative nature can therefore be taken.

Those entering the courtroom are greeted by a notice: 'Trial of the Parasite Brodsky.' *The large hall of the Club is full of people.*
'Be upstanding. The court.'
Judge Savelieva asks Brodsky if he has any requests to the court. It is revealed that he was not informed of the case against him before either the first or the second hearing. The judge declares an intermission. Brodsky is taken out to be informed of the case. A short time later he is brought in and declares that the poems on pages 141, 143, 155, 200, and 234 (he names them) are not by him. He further asks that the diary kept by him in 1956, when he was 16, should not be included in the case. Defending counsel supports this request.
Judge: Concerning his so-called poems the request is granted; concerning his private notebook there is no reason not to include it. Citizen Brodsky, since 1956 you have changed your place of work thirteen times. You worked for a year in a factory, then did not work for six months. One summer you took part in geological field-work, then you did not work for four months . . . (*lists places of work and periods without work*). Can you explain to the court why you did not work in these intervals and led a parasitic life.
Brodsky: I did work in the intervals. I did what I do now: I wrote poems.
Judge: So you wrote your so-called poems? What good did you do by changing jobs so often?
Brodsky: I began work at the age of 15. Everything interested me. I changed jobs because I wanted to know as much as possible about life and people.
Judge: And what have you done that is of value to the fatherland?

Brodsky: I have written poems. That is my work. I am convinced . . . I believe that what I have written will be of service to people not only now but in generations to come.

Voice from the hall: Go on! you're kidding yourself.

Another voice: He's a poet. He's bound to think that way.

Judge: So you think your so-called poetry is of service to people?

Brodsky: Why do you say 'so-called poetry'?

Judge: We call your poetry 'so-called' because we have no other conception of it.

Sorokin (Public Prosecutor): You say that your curiosity was highly developed. Why did you not want to serve in the Soviet Army?

Brodsky: I am not going to answer such questions.

Sorokin: Answer!

Brodsky: I was exempted from military service. It was not that I did not want to serve, I was exempted. Those are two different things. I was exempted on two occasions. First because my father was ill, and then because of my own illness.

Sorokin: Is it possible to live on the sums you earned?

Brodsky: Yes. When I was in prison I was always signing papers to the effect that 40 kopecks a day had been spent on me. I used to earn more than 40 kopecks a day.

Sorokin: But you had to buy shoes and clothes.

Brodsky: I have one suit, an old one, but it's wearable. I don't need another one.

Counsel: Have your poems been assessed by specialists?

Brodsky: Yes. Chukovsky and Marshak spoke very highly of my translations. Better than I deserved.

Counsel: Had you any relations with the translators' section of the Writers' Union?

Brodsky: Yes, I took part in the regular poetry readings called 'For the First Time in Russian' and read translations from the Polish.

Judge (to Counsel): You should ask him about useful work, not about public appearances.

Counsel: His translations *are* his useful work.

Judge: Brodsky, it would be better if you explained to the court why you did not work during the intervals between jobs.

Brodsky: I did work. I wrote poetry.

Judge: But that didn't have to stop you working.

Brodsky: But I did work. I wrote poetry.

Judge: But there are people who manage to work in a factory and still write poetry. Why didn't you do that?

Brodsky: But people aren't made the same way. Even the colour of their hair and their facial expressions are different.

Judge: We don't need you to tell us that. You'd do better to explain to

us how we should assess your contribution to the great onward march
to communism.

Brodsky: The building of communism is not just a question of working
at a lathe or ploughing the fields. It involves intellectual work too,
and . . .

Judge: Don't give us your high-flown phrases! We'd rather hear how
you intend to organize your working life in future.

Brodsky: I wanted to write poetry and do translations. But if that is
against some social norms, I'll take a regular job and continue writing
poetry.

Assessor Tyagly: Everyone works in our society. How could you spend
so long doing nothing?

Brodsky: You don't consider my work as work. I wrote poetry and I
consider that to be work.

Judge: Did you draw your conclusions from the statement in the press?

Brodsky: Lerner's article was full of lies. That is the only conclusion I
drew.

Judge: So you drew no other conclusions?

Brodsky: No. I do not consider myself a person who leads a parasitic
life.

Counsel: You have said that the article entitled 'A Drone of Literature'
in *Vecherny Leningrad* was untrue. In what respects?

Brodsky: Only my name is correct. Even my age is wrong. Even the
poems are not by me. The article describes people as my friends
whom I hardly know or don't know at all. How can I consider this
article correct and draw conclusions from it?

Counsel: You consider your work useful. Can the witnesses I have
called confirm this?

Judge (to Counsel, ironically): Is that all you called them for?

Sorokin (to Brodsky): How could you translate independently from the
Serbian, without using the work of others?

Brodsky: That is an ignorant question. A translator's contract sometimes specifies the use of plain prose versions. I know Polish, I don't
know Serbian so well, but they are related languages and I was able
to make my translation with the help of a plain prose version.

Judge: Witness Grudinina.

Grudinina: I have been supervising the work of young poets for over
eleven years. For seven years I have been a member of the committee
for work with young authors. At present I am supervising the poetry of
senior pupils in the Palace of Pioneers and am in charge of the young
writers' circle in the Svetlana factory. At the request of publishers I
have compiled and edited four collections of the work of young poets,
including over 200 new names. In this way I am acquainted with the
work of almost all the young poets in the city.

I knew Brodsky's early work from his poems of 1959 and 1960. They were still far from perfect, but they contained some striking passages and images. I did not include them in my anthologies, but I considered the author talented. I did not meet Brodsky personally until the autumn of 1963. After the publication of the article entitled 'A Drone of Literature' in *Vecherny Leningrad* I asked Brodsky to come and talk to me, since the young people kept asking me to intervene on behalf of a man who was being slandered. When I asked Brodsky what he was working on, he replied that he had been learning languages and working on literary translations for the last eighteen months or so. He gave me some of his translations in manuscript so that I could see what his work was like.

As a professional poet and trained literary critic, I can state that Brodsky's translations are of a high professional standard. He possesses the specific and rare talent of literary verse translation. He has shown me 368 lines of verse and I have read another 120 lines of his verse translations which were published in Moscow.

From personal experience as a literary translator I know that such a volume of work calls for not less than six months' full-time work, not counting the time taken arranging for publication and consulting specialists. Even at the lowest rates, those translations by Brodsky which I have actually seen are worth at least 350 roubles and the question is merely when all that he has done will be published.

Apart from contracts for translations, Brodsky showed me contracts for radio and television, the work for which is already completed, but which have not yet been fully paid for.

From conversations with Brodsky and some of his acquaintances, I know that he lives very modestly, denying himself new clothes and entertainment and spending most of his time at his desk. The money he receives for his work he hands over to his family.

Counsel: For literary translation is it necessary to have a full knowledge of the author one is working on?

Grudinina: Yes, for good translations such as Brodsky's you need to know the author's works and be familiar with his voice.

Counsel: Is payment for translation reduced when a plain prose version is used?

Grudinina: Yes. When I translated Hungarian poets in this way, I received ten kopecks per line less.

Counsel: Is the use of plain prose versions normal practice among translators?

Grudinina: Yes, it is very common. One of the most eminent Leningrad translators, A. Gitovich, translates in this way from the classical Chinese.

Assessor Lebedeva: Can you learn a foreign language by yourself?

Grudinina: I have learned two languages by myself in addition to those I studied at the university.

Counsel: If Brodsky does not know Serbian, can he still do good translations?

Grudinina: Naturally.

Counsel: But don't you think that the use of plain prose versions is an exploitation of the work of others?

Grudinina: Heaven forbid!

Assessor Lebedeva: Take this book. It only contains two little pieces by Brodsky.

Grudinina: I should like to say a few words about the specific nature of literary work. The point is . . .

Judge: That is not necessary. So what is your opinion of Brodsky's poems?

Grudinina: My opinion is that he is a very talented poet and head and shoulders above many of those who are considered professional poets.

Judge: But why does he work by himself and not attend the meetings of literary groups?

Grudinina: In 1958 he asked to join my literary group. But I had heard him spoken of as a hysterical young man and personally rejected him. That was a mistake, and I greatly regret it. At present I will gladly accept him and work with him if that is what he wants.

Assessor Tyagly: Did you personally see him working on poems himself, or did he use the work of others?

Grudinina: I have never seen Brodsky sitting and writing. But neither have I seen Sholokhov sitting at his desk and writing. This doesn't mean that . . .

Judge: You can't compare Brodsky with Sholokhov. Surely you must have explained to the young people that the government wants them to study? And Brodsky only had seven years' schooling.

Grudinina: He is extremely knowledgeable. I could see that from reading his translations.

Sorokin: Have you read his nasty pornographic poetry?

Grudinina: No, never.

Counsel: Here is another question, witness. Brodsky's work for the year 1963 was as follows: poems in the anthology *Dawn over Cuba*, translations from Galczyński (still unpublished, it is true), poems in the anthology *Poets of Yugoslavia*, gaucho songs, and publications in *Kostyor*. Can this be regarded as serious work?

Grudinina: Certainly. That is a full year's work. It may not bring in money immediately, but only in several years' time. It is wrong to determine the work of a young poet by his total earnings at a given moment. A young author may be unfortunate and may be obliged to start again on a long-term project. There is a joke to the effect that the difference between a parasite and a young poet is that the parasite eats and does no work, whereas the young poet works but does not always eat.

Judge: We do not like that statement. In our country everyone is paid for the work he does and it is impossible for anyone to work a lot and receive only a little. In our country, where such great care is devoted to young poets, you say that they are starving. Why did you say that young poets do not eat?

Grudinina: I did not say that. I mentioned that there is a joke which contains a grain of truth. The payment received by young poets is very uneven.

Judge: Well, that's their business. It's not up to us to sort that out. All right, you have explained that it was a joke. We accept your explanation.

A new witness is called: Efim Grigorievich Etkind.

Judge: Let me see your passport. I didn't catch your surname. (*Takes the passport.*) Etkind . . . Efim Gershevich. . . . Go ahead.

Etkind (member of the Writers' Union, teacher at the Herzen Institute): The nature of my social and literary work, which is connected with the training of young translators, means that I often have to read or listen to translations by young writers. About a year ago I came across certain writings of Iosif Brodsky. These were translations of poems by the great Polish poet Galczyński, whose poems have so far been little translated into Russian. I was strongly impressed by the clarity of poetic expression, and the musicality and passionate energy of the verse. I was struck also by the fact that Brodsky had learned Polish by himself, with no outside help. He read Galczyński's poems in Polish as enthusiastically as he read his Russian translations. I realized that here was a person of rare gifts and—what is equally important— a conscientious and assiduous worker. The translations which I subsequently had occasion to read confirmed me in this opinion. These included translations from the Cuban poet Fernandez, published in the anthology *Dawn over Cuba*, and translations from contemporary Yugoslav poets printed in the anthology published by the State Literary Publishing House. I have had many conversations with Brodsky and have been amazed at his knowledge of American, English, and Polish poetry.

Verse translation is extremely difficult work, calling for devotion, knowledge, and poetic talent. In this field writers must expect to meet with many failures, and their material rewards are reserved for the distant future. It is possible to translate poetry for several years without earning a single rouble. Such labour calls for an unselfish love of poetry and of work itself. The study of the languages, history, and culture of a working people takes a great deal of time. Everything that I know about Brodsky's poetry convinces me that he has a great future as a poet-translator. This is not merely my opinion. The Bureau of the translators' section, learning that the publishers had broken off their contracts with Brodsky, passed a unanimous resolution requesting the director of the publishing house to give Brodsky work and renew their contract with him.

I know for a fact that this opinion is shared by eminent specialists in the field of verse translation; Marshak and Chukovsky . . .

Judge: Speak for yourself, not other people.

Etkind: Brodsky must be given the chance to work as a poet-translator, and this would be very difficult, if not impossible, far from a big city with its books and literary environment. It is my deep conviction that he has a great future in this field. I must say also that I was very surprised to see a notice saying 'Trial of the Parasite Brodsky'.

Judge: You are familiar with this description, though.

Etkind: Yes indeed. But I never thought that such a description would be adopted by a court. With his technical skill it would have been possible for him to churn out pot-boilers, he could have translated hundreds of lines if he had taken the easy way out. The fact that he earned so little money does not mean that he was work-shy.

Judge: But why doesn't he belong to a collective?

Etkind: He used to come to our translation seminars . . .

Judge: Oh, seminars . . .

Etkind: He belongs to the seminar in this sense . . .

Judge: Or nonsense? (*Laughter in court.*) I mean, why didn't he belong to any official group?

Etkind: We don't have membership, so I can't say that he 'belonged' to the seminar. But he came and read his translations to us.

Judge (to Etkind): Have you had problems at work and in your personal life?

Etkind (surprised): No. But I have not been to the Institute for two days. Perhaps something has happened there. (*The question remains incomprehensible to the public and apparently to the witness as well.*)

Judge: Why, when you speak of Brodsky's knowledge of literature, do you insist so much on foreign literature? Why don't you say anything about our own native literature?

Etkind: I spoke with him as a translator and was therefore interested in his knowledge in the field of American, English, and Polish literature. His reading is wide, varied, and not superficial.

Smirnov (witness for the prosecution, director of the House of Defence): I do not know Brodsky personally, but I should like to say that if every citizen had Brodsky's attitude to the accumulation of material wealth, we should be a very long time building communism. Reason is a dangerous weapon for its possessor. Everyone has said that he is clever, wellnigh a genius. But no one has said what sort of a person he is. He was brought up in an intellectual family but he only had seven years' schooling. Ask the people here if they would want a son who had only done seven years? He didn't go into the army because he was the family's only breadwinner. But what sort of breadwinner was he? They have been saying he is a talented translator, but why has no one said that his head is full of mixed-up ideas? And what about his anti-Soviet verse?

Brodsky: That's not true.

Smirnov: He needs to change a lot of his ideas. I don't trust the certificate given to Brodsky by the psychiatric clinic concerning his psychiatric illness. His influential friends will have raised a hue-and-cry to save the poor young man. What he needs is forced labour treatment, with no one to help him, no influential friends. I don't know him personally. I know of him from the press. I have seen these certificates. I don't trust the medical certificate which exempted him from military service. I am not a medical man, but I don't trust it.

Brodsky: When I was given exemption as the only breadwinner, my father was ill, he had had a coronary, whereas I was working and earning money. Then I fell ill. How do you know enough about me to speak in that way about me?

Smirnov: I have seen your private diary.

Brodsky: Who gave you the right?

Judge: That question is out of order.

Smirnov: I have read his poems.

Counsel: We have seen that there are poems in his dossier which Brodsky did not write. How do you know that the poems you read were really by him? After all, you are talking about unpublished poems.

Smirnov: I have read the lot.

Judge: Witness Logunov.

Logunov (Deputy Economic Administrator of the Hermitage Museum): I do not know Brodsky personally. This is my first meeting with him. He can't carry on living as he has been. I should not envy parents with a son like him. I have worked with writers and moved in their circles. Compare Brodsky with Oleg Shestinsky; Oleg worked with an Agitprop team, he completed courses at Leningrad State University and Sofia University, and what's more he has worked in the mines. I wanted to speak to the effect that one should work and transmit cultural habits. In that case Brodsky's poems would have been real poems. Brodsky must begin a new life.

Counsel: Witnesses should really stick to the facts and not . . .

Judge: You can give your assessment of the witnesses' statements later on. Witness Denisov.

Denisov (pipe-layer, UNR-20): I do not know Brodsky personally. I only know him from what has been written in the press. I am speaking as a citizen and a representative of public opinion. After what the newspapers have written, I am indignant at Brodsky's work. I wanted to see what his books were like. I went to the library, and they didn't have his books. I asked my acquaintances if they had heard of him. They hadn't. I am a worker. I've only changed jobs twice in my life. But what about Brodsky? I am not satisfied with Brodsky's statement that he has many specialities. You can't learn any speciality in such a short time. They say that Brodsky is some sort of poet. Then why wasn't he a member of some organization? Doesn't he agree with dialectical materialism? Engels says that man has been created by labour. But Brodsky is not satisfied with that statement. He thinks differently. He may be very talented, but why can't he find a place in our literature? Why doesn't he work? I want to express the view that as a worker I am not satisfied by Brodsky's activities.

Judge: Witness Nikolaev.

Nikolaev (a pensioner): I do not know Brodsky personally. I want to say that I have known about him for three years through the corrupting influence he exerts on his contemporaries. I am a father. I have discovered from my own experience that it is hard to have a son who does not work. I have seen Brodsky's poems in my son's hands more than once. There was a poem in 42 parts and various shorter poems. I know Brodsky through the Umansky case. There is a proverb: birds of a feather . . . I knew Umansky personally. He is an inveterate anti-Soviet. Listening to Brodsky, I recognized my own son. My son also said that he considered himself a genius. He too doesn't want to work, just like Brodsky. People like Brodsky and Umansky exert a corrupting influence on their contemporaries. I am surprised at Brodsky's parents. They obviously humoured him and kept in tune with him. From the verse form it is obvious that Brodsky can write poetry. But his poems have done nothing but harm. Brodsky is not merely a parasite. He is a militant parasite. People like Brodsky need to be treated without mercy. (*Applause.*)

Assessor Tyagly: You consider that your son was affected by Brodsky's poems?

Nikolaev: Yes.

Judge: Adversely affected?

Nikolaev: Yes.

Counsel: How do you know that Brodsky's poems were to blame?

Nikolaev: He had a file marked 'Iosif Brodsky'.

Counsel: Your son was acquainted with Umansky?

Nikolaev: Yes.

Counsel: Then why do you think that it was Brodsky and not Umansky who had a corrupting influence on your son?

Nikolaev: It was the pair of them. Brodsky's poems are disgusting and anti-Soviet.

Brodsky: Give the names of my anti-Soviet poems. Quote just one line from them.

Judge: I will not allow any quotations.

Brodsky: But I want to know what poems he is talking about. They may not be by me.

Nikolaev: If I had known I was going to speak in court, I would have brought photocopies of them.

Judge: Witness Romashova.

Romashova (teacher of Marxism-Leninism at the Mukhina school): I do not know Brodsky personally. But I am acquainted with his so-called activity. Pushkin said that talent is first and foremost work. What about Brodsky? Does he work? Does he labour to make his poems intelligible to the people? I am amazed that my colleagues create such a halo round him. It is only in the Soviet Union that a court could speak so indulgently to a poet and advise him in such a comradely way to study. As secretary of the Party organization at the Mukhina school I can say that he has a bad influence on young people.

Counsel: Have you ever seen Brodsky before?

Romashova: Never. But I can judge him from his so-called activity.

Judge: Can you give the court any facts?

Romashova: As a teacher of young people, I know their reaction to Brodsky's poetry.

Counsel: But do you know Brodsky's poetry yourself?

Romashova: I do. It is *shocking*. I can't bring myself to repeat it. *Shocking!*

Judge: Witness Admoni. Your passport please, since you have an unusual surname.

Admoni (professor at the Herzen Institute, linguist, literary scholar, translator): When I learned that Iosif Brodsky was being tried for parasitism, I considered it my duty to declare my opinion to the court. I think that I have the right to do so, because I have worked with young people for thirty years in institutes of higher education, and because I have been a translator for many years.

I hardly know Iosif Brodsky. We greet each other, but I doubt if we have ever exchanged as much as two sentences. However, in the last year or so I have been following his work as a translator closely, both in his appearances at translators' evenings and in his publications. This is because his translations are talented and striking. And on the basis of these translations from Galczyński, Fernandez, and others, I can say without hesitation that they called for exceptionally hard work from their author. They bear witness to the great culture and skill of the translator. Miracles don't happen. Neither skill nor culture come of their own accord. They call for constant and unflagging work. Even if a translator works from a plain prose version, in order for the translation to be really successful, he has to gain some idea of the language from which he is translating, feel the structure of this language, get to know the life and culture of the people and so on. And Iosif Brodsky not only did this, but learned languages as well. This makes it clear to me that he works with perseverance and determination. And when I discovered today for the first time that he only had seven years' schooling, I realized that he must have done an enormous amount of work to acquire the skill and culture he possesses. Mayakovsky's words about the work of the poet apply equally to the poet-translator: 'For the sake of a single word you extract thousands of tons of verbal ore.'

The decree under which Brodsky is charged is directed against those who do not work much, not against those who do not earn much. Parasites are people who do not do much work. So it is absurd to charge Brodsky with parasitism. You can't bring such a charge against someone who works as hard and perseveringly as Iosif Brodsky, someone who works without thought for large earnings and is prepared to limit himself to the bare necessities so that he can concentrate on perfecting his art and creating truly valuable artistic works.

Judge: What did you say about not trying those who do not earn much?

Admoni: I said that the essence of the decree is to try those who do not do much work and not those who do not earn much.

Judge: What do you mean by that? Have you read the decree of 4 May? Communism can only be created by the labour of millions.

Admoni: All labour that is useful to society should be honoured.

Assessor Tyagly: Where did Brodsky read his translations, and in what foreign languages did he read them?

Admoni (smiling): He read in Russian. He translates from foreign languages into Russian.

Judge: If an ordinary person asks you a question, you should answer him and not smile.

Admoni: I am explaining that he translates from Polish and Serbian into Russian.

Judge: Speak to the court, not the public.

Admoni: I am sorry. It's an old teacher's habit to speak to the audience.

Jusge: Witness Voevodin. Did you know Brodsky personally?

Voevodin (member of the Writers' Union): No. I have only been working in the Union for six months. I did not know him personally. He does not come to the Union often, only for translators' evenings. Apparently he realized how people would react to his poetry and avoided going to other meetings. I have read his epigrams. You would blush to read them, comrade judges. People have been talking about Brodsky's talent. The only measure of talent is popular esteem. He does not possess that and never could possess it.

A sheaf of poems by Brodsky were sent to the Writers' Union. They contain three themes: isolation, pornography, and dislike for fatherland and people—Brodsky speaks of an alien fatherland. Just a moment, let me remember . . . 'Monotonous is the Russian crowd'. May these disgraceful lines remain on his conscience! As a poet Brodsky is non-existent. He may be a translator, he is not a poet. I entirely support the opinion of the comrade who spoke of Brodsky's pernicious influence on his son. Brodsky lures young people away from life and work in the world. That is his great anti-social role.

Judge: Have you discussed Brodsky's talent in your committee?

Voevodin: There was one brief meeting when Brodsky was discussed. But it did not amount to a full-scale discussion. I repeat that Brodsky wrote nothing but semi-obscene epigrams and rarely went to the Union. My friend, the poet Kuklin, once declared in public his indignation at Brodsky's poetry.

Counsel: Does the report which you wrote on Brodsky represent the views of the whole committee?

Voevodin: We did not get the report approved by Etkind, who has a different opinion.

Counsel: But the other members of the committee are acquainted with the contents of your report?

Voevodin: No, not all of them.

Brodsky: But how did you get hold of my poems and my diary?

Judge: I disallow that question. Citizen Brodsky, you have not worked regularly. Why not?

Brodsky: I have already said that I worked all the time. First in an official job, then writing poems. (*In desperation.*) Writing poems *is* work.

Judge: But your earnings are very small. You say that you earn 250 roubles a year, but militia reports give the figure as 100 roubles.

Counsel: At the previous hearing it was decided that the militia should check the reports on Brodsky's earnings, but this has not been done.

Judge: Your file contains a contract which the publishers have sent us. But it's only a piece of paper without a signature.

(*A note is passed up from the public to the effect that contracts are signed first by the author and then by the directors of the publishing house.*)

Judge: Please do not send me any more notes.

Sorokin (Public Prosecutor): Our great people is building communism. A splendid quality is developing in Soviet man, the joy in socially useful work. Only those societies can flourish in which there is no idleness. Brodsky is far removed from patriotism. He has forgotten the essential principle—he who does not work shall not eat. For many years

Brodsky has been leading the life of a parasite. In 1956 he gave up
school and went to work in a factory. He was 15 at the time. The same
year he was dismissed. (*Repeats Brodsky's work record and once again
explains the gaps between official jobs by idleness. Just as if there had been
no explanations from witnesses that literary work is a form of labour too.*)
We have ascertained that for one piece of work Brodsky received only
37 roubles, whereas he says 150 roubles.

Brodsky: That was just an advance. It was only a part of the total payment.

Judge: Be quiet, Brodsky.

Sorokin: In the places where Brodsky worked he shocked everyone by
his undisciplined and work-shy manner. The article in *Vecherny
Leningrad* aroused a considerable response. There was a particularly
large number of letters from young people, who strongly condemned
Brodsky's behaviour. (*Reads letters.*) The young people consider that
he has no place in Leningrad, that he must be severely punished. He
is completely lacking in a sense of conscience and duty. Everyone
regards themselves as fortunate to serve in the army. But he wriggled
out of it. Brodsky's father sent his son to the clinic for a check-up and
they gave him a medical certificate which was accepted by the credulous military commission. Even before he was summoned to the
military commission, he wrote to his friend Shakhmatov, who has
since been condemned: 'I have a date with the Defence Committee.
Your desk will be a secure hiding-place for my iambics.'

He belonged to a set of people who greeted the word 'labour' with
satanic laughter and listened respectfully to their Führer Umansky.
Brodsky is united with him by his hate for work and Soviet literature.
This gang particularly favoured pornographic words and ideas. Brodsky used to call Shakhmatov 'Sir'. That was the word he used.
Shakhmatov has been condemned. And this was the stinking hole that
Brodsky came out of. They talk about Brodsky's talent. But who are
they? People like Brodsky and Shakhmatov.

Exclamation in the hall: What? Chukovsky and Marshak like Shakhmatov?
(*Members of the volunteer militia lead away the protester.*)

Sorokin: Brodsky is defended by swindlers and parasites, lice and cockroaches. Brodsky is not a poet, but a person who tries to scribble
verse. He has forgotten that in our country everyone is obliged to
work and create things of value: machines and bread as well as poetry.
Brodsky must be forced to work. He must be expelled from the herocity. He is a parasite, an oaf, a ruffian, an ideologically filthy individual.
Brodsky's admirers drool over him. But Nekrasov wrote:

> You do not need to be a poet,
> But you must be a citizen.

Today we are trying a parasite, not a poet. Why have people been defending a man who hates his fatherland? We ought to scrutinize the moral character of his defenders. He wrote in his poems: 'I love a foreign land.' In his diary there is a note saying: 'I have been thinking for a long time about crossing the red line. Constructive ideas are maturing in my ginger head.' He also wrote: 'The Stockholm town-hall inspires more respect in me than the Prague Kremlin.' And he calls Marx 'the old glutton, framed in a wreath of pine-cones'. In one letter he writes: 'I wanted to spit on Moscow.'

That is what Brodsky and his defenders are worth.

(*Then he quotes from a letter by a young girl who writes disrespectfully of Lenin. We cannot see what possible connection this letter has with Brodsky. It is not written by him or addressed to him. At this point the judge turns to me and says:* Stop taking notes!)

F.V.: Comrade judge, I request permission to take notes.

Judge: No.

F.V.: I am a journalist and a member of the Writers' Union, I write about the education of young people and I request permission to take notes.

Judge: I don't know what you are writing. Stop it.

Voice from the hall: She's still writing.

(*Sorokin goes on with his speech, then the defending counsel speaks; since I was not allowed to take notes, I can only give a summary.*)

Summary of defending counsel's speech:

The public prosecutor has used material which was not in the dossier and came up for the first time during the hearing. Brodsky was not questioned on this material and was not able to give any explanations.

We have not been able to check the authenticity of the material taken from the special hearing held in 1961, and we cannot verify the public prosecutor's citations. As far as Brodsky's diary is concerned, it dates from 1956. It is the diary of an adolescent. The public prosecutor cites readers' letters to *Vecherny Leningrad* as evidence of public opinion. The authors of these letters do not know Brodsky, they have not read his poems, and they are judging by a tendentious and largely inaccurate newspaper article. The public prosecutor insults not only Brodsky ('oaf', 'parasite', 'anti-Soviet element'), but also those who have spoken in his favour, respected witnesses such as Marshak and Chukovsky. Conclusion: not having any objective proofs, the public prosecutor uses improper tactics.

What is there against Brodsky?

(a) A report on his working activity from 1956 to 1962. In 1956 Brodsky was 16, he could have carried on studying and lived quite legally at his parents' expense until the age of 18. His frequent changes of jobs are the result of psychopathic character traits and the inability to find his place in life straight away. The intervals between jobs are to be explained in particular by the seasonal nature of geological field-work. Up to 1962 there is no case for calling Brodsky work-shy.

(Counsel expresses her respect for the assessors, but regrets that they do not include anyone competent in questions of literary work. When a minor is charged, there is always an educational expert among the assessors, and when it is a doctor, they include a doctor. Why then is this just and reasonable custom neglected when it is a question of literature?)

(b) Brodsky has not had an official job since 1962. But there is evidence of his creative work in the publishers' contracts submitted to the court and dated November 1962 and October 1963, the report from the TV studio, the report from the journal *Kostyor*, and the published book of translations of Yugoslav poetry. There is a report signed by E. Voevodin, an extremely hostile report containing inadmissible charges of anti-Soviet activity, a report which recalls the worst periods of the personality cult. It has emerged that this report was not discussed by the committee or seen by members of the committee and is the personal opinion of Voevodin. There are opinions from such people as Marshak and Chukovsky, well-known experts and eminent translators. Witnesses such as V. Admoni—an eminent scholar, linguist, and translator—and E. Etkind—an expert on literary translation, a member of the translators' section of the Writers' Union, and a member of the Committee for Work with Young Writers—all think highly of Brodsky's work and speak of the great amount of labour demanded by his publications during the year 1963. Conclusion: Voevodin's report cannot be held to refute the opinions of these witnesses.

(c) Not one of the prosecution witnesses knows Brodsky, or has read his poems; the prosecution witnesses have testified on the strength of some unauthenticated documents of mysterious origin or have simply expressed their opinions, making accusing speeches.

The prosecution has no other material against Brodsky.

The court must disregard the following:

1. Material relating to the special case heard in 1961, in connection with which there was a decision to close the case against Brodsky.

If either then or later Brodsky had committed an anti-Soviet crime or written anti-Soviet poetry, this would have been investigated by the state security organization.

Brodsky was indeed acquainted with Shakhmatov and Umansky, and was under their influence. But fortunately he freed himself from this influence a long time ago. Nevertheless the public prosecutor read out notes made in those years, giving them completely out of context and thus naturally arousing the anger of the public against Brodsky.

The public prosecutor gave the impression that Brodsky still holds to his former views, which is completely untrue. Many young people who belonged to Umansky's set were brought back to normal life by the influence of reasonable and mature people. The same thing has happened with Brodsky over the past two years. He has begun to work hard and to good effect. But now he has been arrested.

2. The question of the quality of Brodsky's poetry.

We do not yet know which of the poems in the dossier are actually by Brodsky, since his statement shows that a number of them are not his.

In order to judge whether these poems are decadent, pessimistic, or lyrical, we need an authoritative critical opinion; this question cannot be solved by the court or the two opposing parties.

Our task is to determine whether Brodsky is a parasite, living like a layabout on unearned income.

Brodsky is a poet-translator who has contributed his labour to the translation of poets from the fraternal republics, the people's democracies, in their struggle for peace. He is not a drunkard, an amoral person, or a profiteer. He is accused of receiving low fees and consequently of not working. (Counsel gives a description of the specific nature of literary work and the system of payment. She speaks of the great amount of work demanded by translation, the need to learn foreign languages and study the work of the poet to be translated. And the fact that not all work that is submitted is accepted and paid for.)

The systems of advance payment. The sums mentioned in the dossier are incorrect. According to Brodsky they should be greater. Need to check this. Insignificant sums. What did Brodsky live on? Brodsky lived with his parents who supported him while he was becoming a poet.

He had no sources of unearned income. He lived poorly, so as to be able to do the work he loved.

Conclusions: Brodsky's guilt is not proved. Brodsky is not a parasite and administrative sanctions should not be applied to him.

The importance of the decree of 4.11.1961 is very great. It is a weapon in the campaign to purge the city of genuine parasites and spongers. Unjustified application will discredit the decree.

The resolution of the Plenum of the Supreme Soviet dated 10.3.1963 obliges the court to look critically at the material before it, not to allow the condemnation of anyone who works, and to observe the rights of the accused to study their dossier and present proofs of their innocence.

Brodsky was unjustifiably detained on 13 February 1964 and deprived of the chance to present proofs of his innocence.

However, the evidence presented to the court is sufficient to show that Brodsky is not a parasite.

The court adjourns to confer. An intermission is declared.

The court returns and the judge reads out the sentence:

Brodsky systematically fails to fulfil the obligations of a Soviet man to produce material wealth and guarantee his own livelihood, as is evident from his frequent changes of work. He was warned by the KGB in 1961 and by the militia in 1962. He promised to take a regular job, but did not draw the correct conclusions and continued without work, writing his decadent poems and reading them out at evening gatherings. The report from the Committee for Work with Young Writers shows that Brodsky is not a poet. He has been condemned by the readers of the newspaper *Vecherny Leningrad*. Consequently the court applies the decree of 4.5.1961: to send Brodsky to a remote part of the country for five years' compulsory labour.

Volunteer militiaman (as they pass the defending counsel): Well then, comrade defendant, you lost, didn't you?

Recorded by Frida Vigdorova

Appendix 11

Letter to the Executive of the Leningrad Writers' Organization and the Executive of the Writers' Union of the RSFSR

On 25 April the Secretariat of the Leningrad Writers' Organization together with a number of persons who are not members of the Secretariat took the decision to expel me from the Writers' Union; ten days later this decision was confirmed by the Secretariat of the Writers' Union of the RSFSR. Two months later I was informed of this decision.

Neither before nor after the meeting of the Secretariat did a single member of the Union deign to talk with me. Not one of them would see me and explain what had happened. Not one of them asked me if I admitted the charges against me or, to use the language of the courts, if I pleaded guilty.

The meeting of 25 April took place in my absence—I was ill, as I informed the Secretariat in good time, asking it to defer the meeting for a few days. For some reason the Secretariat was in a great hurry; it obviously could not wait to carry out the ritual of my civic execution. It was in such a hurry that it even neglected such an unimportant matter as the absence of the accused. Criminal courts do not indulge themselves in such caprices, even when they are dealing with murderers or arsonists. The union of creative artists to which I have belonged for close on twenty years and within which I have engaged in unceasing and active work that has taken up a great deal of time and energy, this union has acted in an incredibly arbitrary manner, allowing its Secretariat to expel a longstanding member of the union in his absence, while he was ill, without listening to his defence—or rather without even confronting him with the charges against him.

I consider the action of the Secretariat on 25 April 1974 to be illegal. I strongly demand that my case be examined at a meeting of the Executive. I insist that the decision of the Secretariat was taken on the basis of unconfirmed, unproved, and unprovable charges. My literary and civic fate has been ruined on the strength of two or three sentences from private letters, which I do not in general regard as a proper subject for public scrutiny. No one has the right to organize a public hearing concerning not the actions of a man, but his way of thinking, and all the more so when this way of thinking has been arbitrarily reconstructed from a few sentences not meant for the public eye. All the other charges which were heaped up against me (but never put to me personally) are pure fabrications, which can be refuted without the slightest difficulty.

I repeat: I demand in the strongest possible terms that my case be discussed by the Executive. I regard the decision of the Secretariat, taken in my absence and without even a preliminary conversation with me, as illegal.

4 July, Leningrad.   E. G. Etkind, Professor, Doctor of Philology.